Microsoft® Office 2010
Plain & Simple

Katherine Murray

PUBLISHED BY
Microsoft Press
A Division of Microsoft Corporation
One Microsoft Way
Redmond, Washington 98052-6399

Library of Congress Control Number: 2010928517

ISBN: 978-0-7356-2697-3

9 10 11 12 13 14 15 16 17 QGT 7 6 5 4 3 2

Printed and bound in the United States of America.

Distributed in Canada by H.B. Fenn and Company Ltd.

A CIP catalogue record for this book is available from the British Library.

Microsoft Press books are available through booksellers and distributors worldwide. For further information about international editions, contact your local Microsoft Corporation office or contact Microsoft Press International directly at fax (425) 936-7329. Visit our Web site at www.microsoft.com/mspress. Send comments to mspinput@microsoft.com.

Microsoft, Microsoft Press, Access, ActiveX, Excel, Hotmail, InfoPath, Internet Explorer, OneNote, OpenType, Outlook, PivotChart, PivotTable, PowerPoint, SharePoint, SkyDrive, SmartArt, Windows, Windows Live, and Windows Vista are either registered trademarks or trademarks of Microsoft Corporation in the United States and/or other countries. Other product and company names mentioned herein may be the trademarks of their respective owners.

The example companies, organizations, products, domain names, e-mail addresses, logos, people, places, and events depicted herein are fictitious. No association with any real company, organization, product, domain name, e-mail address, logo, person, place, or event is intended or should be inferred.

This book expresses the author's views and opinions. The information contained in this book is provided without any express, statutory, or implied warranties. Neither the authors, Microsoft Corporation, nor its resellers, or distributors will be held liable for any damages caused or alleged to be caused either directly or indirectly by this book.

Acquisitions Editor: Juliana Aldous
Developmental Editor: Devon Musgrave
Project Editor: Carol Vu
Editorial Production: MPS Limited, A Macmillan Company

Technical Reviewer: Roger LeBlanc
Cover: Girvin
Copy Editor: Roger LeBlanc
Proofreader: Mary Rosewood
Indexer: Seth Maislin

Body Part No. X16-95443

[2012-08-03]

Contents

1 About This Book   1

2 Working in Office 2010   9

What do you think of this book? We want to hear from you!

Microsoft is interested in hearing your feedback so we can continually improve our books and learning resources for you. To participate in a brief online survey, please visit:

www.microsoft.com/learning/booksurvey/

Common Tasks in Office

Viewing and Editing Text in Word

Formatting in Word   81

Working with Special Content in Word 121

Working in Excel 145

Analyzing and Presenting Data in Excel 173

Creating a PowerPoint Presentation 207

Presenting a PowerPoint Slide Show 237

Working with Messages in Outlook   261

Organizing with Outlook   283

Creating a Publication in Publisher305

Customizing and Securing Office

What do you think of this book? We want to hear from you!

Microsoft is interested in hearing your feedback so we can continually improve our books and learning resources for you. To participate in a brief online survey, please visit:

www.microsoft.com/learning/booksurvey/

Acknowledgments

Every book has its own personality and style, and each project needs the talents and energies of many people in order to produce the beautiful, easy-to-read book you now hold in your hands. Writing this book has been a blast, in large part thanks to the following folks:

- Marianne Moon and Jerry Joyce, for developing a great, fun-to-write series that truly meets readers' needs

- Juliana Aldous, my acquisitions editor at the start of this project, who thought of me for the writing of this book

- Claudette Moore, my agent at Moore Literary Agency, for working out all the details and keeping things moving in her always kind and supportive way

- Carol Vu, project editor, for overseeing every detail of this project, keeping chapters flowing (through multiple passes), and always responding quickly to questions and comments

- Roger LeBlanc, for a great-as-usual copy edit, catching phrases that might make readers stumble and making sure the graphics are as clear as possible, and

- The composition team for their careful work in laying out this book in a way that helps readers understand and complete Office tasks easily

1

About This Book

This book is for those who believe computers are tools you use to accomplish what you need so that you can get on with the fun part of life. If you want to get the most from your computer and your software with the least amount of time and effort—and who doesn't?—you'll find *Microsoft Office 2010 Plain & Simple* to be a straightforward, easy-to-read guide. With the premise that your computer should work for you, not you for it, this book's purpose is to help you learn what you need to know about Microsoft Office 2010 quickly and efficiently so that you can be as creative, collaborative, and flexible as possible—and then get away from the computer and live your life.

No Computerspeak!

Let's face it—when there's a task you don't know how to do but you need to get it done in a hurry, or when you're stuck in the middle of a task and can't figure out what to do next, there's nothing more frustrating than having to read page after page of technical background material. And if a program includes a huge number of fun features that can help your work look better than ever, you don't want to spend a week learning how to tap into that. You want the information you need—with clear pictures showing just the right steps—and you want it now!

That's what this book is about. It's written in plain English, with no technical jargon and no computerspeak. No single task in the book takes more than two pages. Simply look up the task in the index or the table of contents, turn to the page, and there's the information you need, laid out in an illustrated step-by-step format. You don't get bogged down by the whys and wherefores: just follow the steps and find what you need to complete your task—and look good doing it—with a minimum amount of hassle. Occasionally, you might want to turn to another page if the procedure you're working on is accompanied by a *See Also* paragraph. There's a lot of overlap among tasks, and by using the *See Also* suggestions you can read related information without suffering through blocks of repeated text. You'll find useful *Tips* here and there, discover features that are new in this version of Office, and bump into a *Try This* or a *Caution* once in a while. By and large, however, you'll find text that remains true to the heart and soul of the book, which means that the information you need should be available to you at a glance and it should be *plain and simple!*

Useful Tasks . . .

Whether you use the programs in Microsoft Office for work, school, personal correspondence, or some of each, you'll find this book packed with procedures for everything you might want to do, from the simplest tasks to some of the more esoteric ones.

. . . And the Easiest Way to Do Them

Another thing I've tried to do in this book is to find and document the easiest way to accomplish a task. The Office programs often provide multiple methods for achieving a single result—and that can be daunting or delightful, depending on

the way you like to work. If you tend to stick with one favorite and familiar approach, the methods described in this book are the way to go. If you like trying out alternative techniques, go ahead! The ribbon interface in Microsoft Office 2010 gives you just the tools you need when you need them—pointing you to the fastest way to complete a procedure—but there is much in Office 2010 to explore. Feel free to invent your own ways of doing things or follow what I've provided here. Whatever helps you work most efficiently and effectively is the best path to choose.

A Quick Overview

This book is written with a few assumptions in mind. First, I'm assuming that Office 2010 is already installed on your computer. If it isn't, Microsoft Windows makes installation so simple that you won't need help anyway. I'm also assuming that you're interested in the most popular Office 2010 programs: Word 2010, Excel 2010, PowerPoint 2010, Outlook 2010, OneNote 2010, Access 2010, and Publisher 2010. Some of the other programs available either as part of the various Office 2010 versions or as standalone programs—such as Microsoft InfoPath, SharePoint Workspace 2010, and Microsoft Project 2010—are complex enough that you'll want to find specialized books devoted to that program.

Next, you don't have to read this book in any particular order. It's designed so that you can jump in, get the information you need, and then close the book and keep it near your computer until the next time you need it. You'll find that the

> **Tip**
>
> **Find out more about available books on various Microsoft Office 2010 programs by visiting the Microsoft Press page at *http://microsoftpress. oreilly.com*.**

book is organized into some sections that deal with the individual programs in Office 2010, and some that show you how to use the programs together. If you're new to Office 2010 or if you're stymied by the ribbon, you should first read sections 2 and 3, "Working in Office 2010" and "Common Tasks in Office 2010," for an introduction to the ways in which the programs look and work alike. Try out the step-by-step procedures that are common to most of the programs: working with the ribbon, using Backstage view, finding your way with tools and toolbars, changing views, working with pictures and diagrams, doing some research, and getting help if you need it. Learn how to work with the Office Web Apps for some of your favorite applications. Regardless of which program you're working in, you'll find that the tasks you want to accomplish are always arranged in the text in two levels. The overall type of task you're looking for is under a main heading such as "Inserting a Picture" or "Formatting a Worksheet." Then, under each of those headings, the smaller tasks within each main task are arranged in a loose progression from the simplest to the more complex.

Now that you know the overall approach, you may be wondering what's covered in this book. Sections 2 and 3 cover the basic tasks—and a few slightly more complex ones—that are common to all the Office 2010 programs.

Sections 4, 5, and 6 are dedicated to Microsoft Word 2010, and they'll take you step by step through the basics to some of the more complex tasks. If you're new to Word, section 4 is where you'll learn how to do all of the following:

- Create and share your documents

- Edit your text

- Move through the document using the Navigation pane

- Use Word's find-and-replace feature to take care of document-wide changes

- Correct your spelling and grammar

- Use the translation tools

- Add page numbers to your documents

- Use the Track Changes feature to mark changes in your documents

- Read and accept or reject the changes made to a document you've sent out to be reviewed

- Co-author a document in real time with others on your team

In section 5, you'll learn all about formatting your documents, including how to format text, lists, and tables; apply styles; align paragraphs; create a layout and divide a long document into sections or chapters; work with running heads; and wrap text around a graphic.

Section 6 gives you specific techniques for special tasks in Word 2010, whether you want to create and design a sophisticated cover page; add sidebars, math equations, pull quotes, and watermarks to liven up a document; or put together a huge mail-merge project to send by e-mail or printed letter. If your work involves technical or scholarly documents, you'll learn how to number headings and lines, create footnotes or endnotes, insert citations, and create a table of contents. This section also shows you how to create a Word 2010 form so that you can use your Word document to collect the information you need from others.

Sections 7 and 8 are all about Microsoft Excel 2010. Section 7 introduces you to the program and covers the basics to get you started: the column/row/cell composition of the worksheets and workbooks; entering, editing, and replacing data; formatting numbers and cells; adding and deleting columns and rows; formatting and organizing your worksheets; and setting up and printing your worksheets. In section 8, which is about analyzing and presenting your data, you'll discover some of Excel's more complex features. First you add *sparklines* to showcase your data in ways others can understand easily. You'll learn about *cell addresses* and *functions*, and you'll create a *PivotTable* along with slicers that will help you examine the relationships among your data. We'll discuss filtering the data to display only the items you want to work with, using the *AutoFill* feature to create a series of calculations, sorting your data, and more. And, if you'll be presenting your data at a meeting or in a report, I'll show you how to turn your boring old worksheets into snazzy, professional-looking charts that hold your audience's interest and make the results of the data immediately understandable to everyone.

Sections 9 and 10 are about Microsoft PowerPoint 2010, the immensely popular presentation program. Section 9 introduces you to the basics of the program—including the views, tabs, buttons, working area, and so on—and then takes you through the process of creating your presentation. You'll choose from professional themes and layouts to get started and learn how to add tables, SmartArt graphics, WordArt, and multimedia—video and sound—to your slides. One of the exciting new features in PowerPoint 2010 is the ability to edit video within the program—section 9 shows you how to do that, and add video styles as well. Section 10 takes you to the next level: the presentation of your slide show. You might have seen (or even given) a slide show that turned out to be a complete disaster. Everything went wrong, and both the presenter and the audience were mightily embarrassed. That won't happen again—PowerPoint 2010 and Windows 7 provide easy-to-use tools to ensure that your show will run smoothly. In this section, you'll learn how to create and print speaker notes and hand-outs; rehearse and time your show to fit into a specific time slot; run the show from a projector or from dual monitors; and, if your work involves traveling, take your presentation on the road.

Sections 11 and 12 cover Microsoft Outlook 2010, Office's e-mail program. Section 11 walks you through the basics: learning about the Outlook window; creating and sending e-mail messages; using Conversation View; reading the e-mail messages you receive; replying to those messages and/or forwarding them to someone else; attaching a file to a message you're sending; and opening the *attachments* you receive. Learn to use Quick Steps to automate the Outlook tasks you perform often and set up and manage the accounts and RSS subscriptions you want to receive regularly. And keep up to date with friends, family, and colleagues by using the Outlook Social Connector to access e-mail threads and status updates your contacts post. Section 12 takes a look at Outlook's other useful features, including the Calendar and the Contacts folder. You can use the Calendar to schedule your business or personal appointments on an hourly, daily, weekly, or monthly basis; and, if you're using Outlook with Microsoft Exchange Server, you can schedule meetings and even reserve a meeting room. If you share calendars with others, you can manage your schedules using the Shared Calendar view. This section also shows you how to use your Contacts folder to manage your contact information, with as much or as little detail as you want to include—telephone numbers, home or work addresses, and so on. You can also create customized electronic business cards that you can exchange via e-mail with your business partners.

Section 13 walks you through the creation of various marketing publications in Microsoft Publisher 2010. Publisher is a page-layout program with a creative spark that enables you to easily create newsletters, reports, business cards, brochures, award certificates, banners, menus, résumés, and more, using a wide variety of professionally designed templates. You select the type of publication you want to create, choose a design, and then insert your own text, pictures, and other items. If you have the time and you're feeling creative, you can, of course, modify any of the existing designs or create your own and save them for reuse. Now Publisher 2010 includes support for high-quality typographic features and makes it easier than ever for you to finalize your files and work with a commercial printer.

Section 14 is about the newest addition to Microsoft Office—OneNote 2010. Microsoft OneNote was available in previous versions as a standalone application, but now it is a part of all Microsoft Office 2010 editions. Use OneNote to gather notes from Word 2010, PowerPoint 2010, and Outlook 2010. Capture notes easily with ink, voice, text, and more. Clip notes from Web pages, find notes by author, share your notebooks, and much more. This section shows you how to integrate OneNote 2010 into your Office 2010 daily tasks.

Section 15 concentrates on Microsoft Access 2010—a relational database program. If you need to understand and work with a database program, this is a good place to start. In addition to basic information about databases, tables, and forms, you'll discover how Access 2010 makes designing and managing a database easier than ever with prebuilt templates, Application Parts, Office themes, Quick Start fields, navigation forms, and calculated fields. What's more, you can add data visualizations to your reports to showcase your data in ways others can understand easily.

Section 16 is about customizing and securing Office. Now you can customize just about anything in all the Office 2010 programs—the ribbon, the Quick Access toolbar, the window, the status bar, your user information, the spelling and grammar checkers, and more. We'll also talk about an extremely important topic: your computer's security. We'll discuss all the precautions you can and should take to protect your files and guard against the bad stuff we all know is out there in cyberspace. I'll show you how to add or remove Office components and how to run some easy-to-use automatic diagnostics if you encounter any problems with your Office programs and your computer.

What's New in Office 2010?

As you may know, the previous version of Office, Office 2007, brought significant change to the traditional look and feel of the Microsoft Office applications by introducing the ribbon. Instead of requiring you to wind your way through countless menus and dialog boxes, the ribbon offers you the most common tools in a set of tabs at the top of the window and displays additional tools only as they are needed based on the tasks you are performing at the moment. This means that the screen is less cluttered and the tools are easier to find and use than ever before.

Office 2010 builds on this improvement in the design of the ribbon by extending it to all Office 2010 applications. (Previously, the ribbon was available only in some applications.) You'll also find that you can customize the ribbon to fit the way you work, which includes hiding it completely if you like.

In addition to this continuing design enhancement, the new features in Office 2010 and the program's improved ease of use speak directly to the changing ways people are working today. For example, now Office 2010 is available in both 32-bit and 64-bit versions, so that users with 64-bit processing can take full advantage of all that processing power, and security has been increased and simplified for users so that much of the safeguarding happens before you even open your files. A new Protected View also restricts the level of editing available on files you download from the Web or receive from unfamiliar sources.

Another big story throughout Office 2010 is the addition of the new Backstage view. Backstage view brings together all the tools you need to open, save, print, and work with the files you create in your Office 2010 applications. You can print and preview in a single window, recover unsaved documents, check file accessibility, save in a variety of formats, and much more—all from Backstage view.

Overall the key features throughout Office 2010 build on one of three design themes:

- **Bringing your ideas to life**   New picture editing tools, expanded text effects, high-quality typographical support, new themes and templates, and a whole set of data visualizations and conditional formatting features enable you to showcase your data—no matter what kind of file you're creating—more attractively and effectively than ever. Video editing and styles, the Animation Painter, and new broadcast capabilities in PowerPoint 2010 bring more life to your presentations. And improved inking capabilities throughout all the applications make it easier for you to gather and highlight content in the manner you are most comfortable collecting it.

- **Working together more effectively**   Now teams can share Office 2010 documents seamlessly with Microsoft SharePoint Workspace 2010 sites and co-author documents and presentations using SharePoint Server 2010 or Windows Live. A number of sharing features make it possible for you to work collaboratively and update files naturally whether you're working at home or school, in a small or large office. Streamlined communications features show you the online presence of others working on your file and enable you to contact them easily by clicking an option on their contact card.

- **Work anywhere, anytime**   Now Office Web Apps are available for Microsoft Word 2010, PowerPoint 2010, OneNote 2010, and Excel 2010 that enable you to post and share files from any location you have Web access. You can also create a Web database in Access 2010 that enables you to collect and manage data easily on the Web.

The appearance of Office 2010 is extremely dynamic, so be aware that the look of the ribbon will change depending on the screen resolution you're using. That is, with a high resolution, you'll see many more individual items on the ribbon than you will if you're using a low resolution. With a low resolution, you'll find that items are contained under a button, and only when you click the button are the items then displayed. To see this effect, resize the width of a window in Word, Excel, PowerPoint, or in an Outlook message, and note that items are hidden when you decrease the size of the window and that they appear when you increase the size of the window. The programs in Office 2010 were designed using a screen resolution of 1024 by 768 pixels, so this is the resolution we've used in the graphics you'll see throughout this book.

Tip

Office Mobile 2010 brings the Office 2010 interface and applications to your smartphone as well. Office Mobile 2010 is sold separately from Microsoft Office 2010. You can use Office Mobile 2010 with Windows Mobile 6.5 and Windows Phone 7 smartphones. You can download Office Mobile 2010 directly through Marketplace on your device.

A Few Assumptions

This book is based on a few educated guesses about what you, the reader, would like to learn about Office 2010. Perhaps your computer is solely for personal use—e-mail, the Internet, and so on. Or you might run a small business or work for a giant corporation. Considering these varied possibilities, this book assumes that you are familiar with computer basics—the keyboard and your little friend the mouse, for example—and that you're connected to the Internet, company intranet, or both. Also assumed is that if you're working on a corporate network, that you're familiar with the specialized and customized tools, such as a Microsoft SharePoint site or a file-management system, that are being used on the network. You'll also see from the examples in the book that familiarity with the basics of Windows 7 or Windows Vista is assumed. Whichever version of Windows you're using, you may find two other Microsoft Press books helpful: *Windows 7 Plain & Simple* and *Microsoft Windows Vista Plain & Simple*.

A Final Word (or Two)

This book has three basic goals:

- To help you complete the tasks you most want to accomplish in Office 2010.

- To show you new Office 2010 features and techniques that will make your work easier (or more fun).

- And, finally, if the book achieves those first two goals, reaching the third should be a piece of cake: To help you *enjoy* using Office 2010. Or, if having *fun* with software feels like a bit of a stretch, perhaps at least you'll get your work done faster so that you can turn your attention to things you really enjoy.

I hope you'll have as much fun using *Microsoft Office 2010 Plain & Simple* as I had writing it. The best way to learn is by *doing,* so let's get you started using this book.

2

Working in Office 2010

In this section of the book, we'll discuss the various programs in Microsoft Office 2010—their similarities and differences, and the ways they work separately and together. Depending on which version of Office you're running, you might have some or all of the programs installed on your computer. All the Office programs have elements in common—namely, the ribbon and Backstage view. The ribbon brings you all the tools you need by displaying them in tabs and tab groups across the top of the application window. You can customize the ribbon in Office 2010 to create your own tabs and tab groups. And Backstage view enables you to easily create, open, print, save, and share files by pulling together all the file management tools in one easy-to-use window.

This chapter focuses on these two common features available throughout the Office 2010 applications, and it introduces you to the various tools and procedures you'll use to navigate the programs using both the mouse and the keyboard. Along the way, you'll learn how to use the dialog boxes you discover, work with shortcut menus you display by right-clicking an element, use keyboard shortcuts to speed up your work, use Paste with Live Preview to paste copied information just the way you want it to appear, and use various Help features to learn more about tools and tasks in Office 2010.

What's What in Office 2010?

There are a number of versions of Microsoft Office 2010 available for users with differing needs. If you work with Office 2010 in a large corporate setting, you may be using Office Professional Plus 2010, which includes a larger number of Office applications than, say, Office Home and Business 2010. Here's a quick rundown. Find your version in this list so that you know which programs are likely to be available in your copy of Office 2010:

- Office Professional Plus 2010 brings together all the applications, with an emphasis on connectivity and mobility. In this version, you'll find Word, Excel, Outlook, PowerPoint, Publisher, Access, OneNote, InfoPath, SharePoint Workspace, and Communicator.

- Office Professional 2010 focuses on functionality by including the more popular programs, including Word, Excel, Outlook, PowerPoint, Publisher, Access, and OneNote.

- Office Home and Business 2010 offers the reliable standard applications to home and small business users who need power and dependability but aren't likely to need data management or connectivity features. The programs in this version include Word, Excel, Outlook, PowerPoint, and OneNote.

The following list introduces you to the most common programs in Microsoft Office 2010 and gives you a brief description of each program's purpose. Depending on which version of Office 2010 you have and whether you purchased any additional Office programs, you might have some or all of these programs installed on your computer.

Microsoft Office 2010 Programs

Microsoft Access 2010 is a relational database program for storing, retrieving, and analyzing data.

Microsoft Excel 2010 is a worksheet program for organizing, analyzing, and graphing data.

Microsoft OneNote 2010 is an electronic note-taking program for gathering, sharing, and organizing handwritten, typed, copied, drawn, or recorded notes.

Microsoft Outlook 2010 is an e-mail program and a great way to manage your contacts, tasks, and schedules.

Microsoft PowerPoint 2010 is a program for developing and sharing professional presentations.

Microsoft Publisher 2010 is a desktop publishing program for intricate placement of text and graphics on the printed page or on the Web.

Microsoft SharePoint 2010 is a program that enables you to create a shared workspace where you and team members can share files, create document libraries, discuss projects, and more.

Microsoft InfoPath 2010 (Designer and Filler) is a set of two programs that make it easy to design effective forms and enter the data you want to collect.

Microsoft Word 2010 is a powerful word processing program for doing everything from writing a letter to writing a novel to creating mass mailings.

Microsoft Office Tools are programs you can use in conjunction with the main Office programs:

- **Microsoft Clip Organizer** provides easy access to Clip Art and similar content.

- **Microsoft Office 2010 Language Preferences** control the languages identified and used in your programs.

- **Microsoft Office Upload Center** enables you to upload files to Web servers using the Microsoft Office Upload Center tool.

- **Microsoft Office Picture Manager** organizes, edits, and creates quick access to your pictures.

Using the Ribbon

All Office 2010 programs now use the ribbon to bring you the tools you need to create, work with, save, and share your files. The ribbon is organized in a similar way in all programs, organizing tools on tabs that reflect common tasks you want to complete in each application. For example, in Word, the tabs are Home, Insert, Page Layout, References, Mailings, Review, View, and Add-Ins.

Within each tab, *tab groups* contain tools related to a specific aspect of that task. The Insert tab in Word, for example, includes tab groups for Pages, Tables, Illustrations, Links, Header & Footer, Text, and Symbols. When you want to add a picture to your Word document, you click the Insert tab and then click Picture in the Illustrations group to complete the task.

Explore the Ribbon

1. Open any Office 2010 program.

2. Click a tab on the ribbon.

3. Click a button to execute a command.

4. Click a down arrow to open a gallery or a list, or click a dialog box launcher to open a dialog box.

5. Point to an item in a gallery to see its effect on the content of your document.

6. Click an object in the program window.

7. Click the contextual tab that appears.

8. Click the tool you would like to use to work with the selected object.

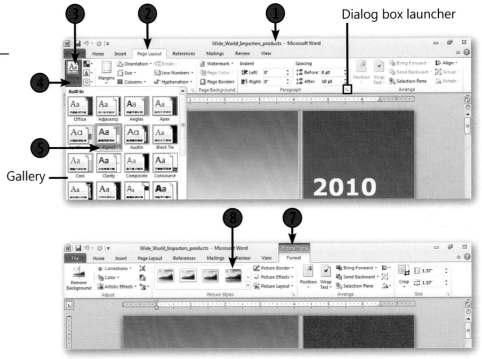

Dialog box launcher

Gallery

Tip

The ribbon is composed of tabs, groups, and tools. When the ribbon is minimized, you see only the tabs. You can display the full ribbon by clicking a tab or pressing Ctrl+F1.

See Also

Read "Customizing the Ribbon" on pages 392–393 if you'd like to learn how to create your own tabs and tab groups so that you can customize the ribbon for your Office 2010 programs.

Set the Ribbon Display

1. When you begin using Office 2010, the ribbon is displayed by default. Hide the ribbon by clicking the Minimize The Ribbon.

2. Display the ribbon by clicking a tab. The ribbon appears until you click a tool or click in your document.

3. To redisplay the ribbon, click Maximize The Ribbon.

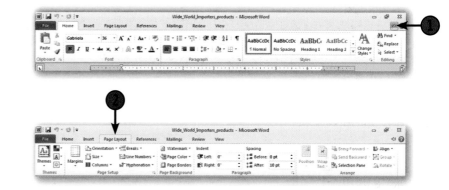

Try This!

With the ribbon in its displayed state, double-click the active tab to minimize the ribbon, and then click any tab to display the ribbon temporarily. Click in your file to minimize the ribbon again. Double-click the active tab to have the ribbon always displayed. Press Ctrl+F1 to hide the ribbon, and press Ctrl+F1 again to have the ribbon always displayed.

Using Galleries and Lists

Each tab in an Office 2010 program offers you a different set of tools related to a specific task. The File tab, which contains Backstage view, and the Home tab, offering the most common tools, appears in all Office 2010 programs.

Within each tab you'll find tab groups, displaying tools you can click to execute a command or display a gallery. The different lists and galleries offer you ready-made styles and options you can apply to the content in your document.

Explore the Galleries

1 In any Office 2010 program, locate a tab group that shows examples of styles or options you can select. You can also click an object in the file to display a contextual tab for that item.

2 Click the More button in the lower right corner of the display.

3 Point to the various choices in the gallery. The changes are previewed in your file. Click the option you want to apply.

Continue exploring the different tabs and galleries in this and other Office programs.

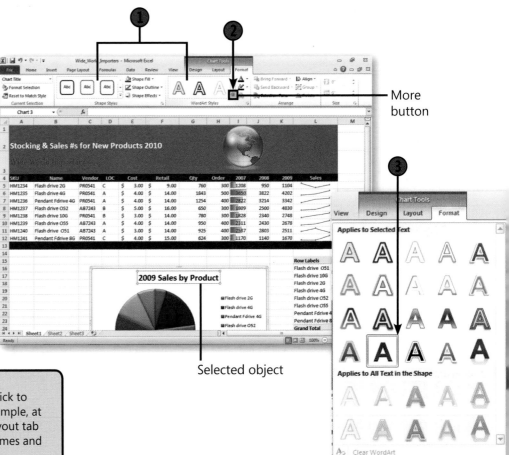

More button

Selected object

Tip

Some galleries also include commands you can click to continue your work with a specific object. For example, at the bottom of the Themes gallery in the Page Layout tab of Word and Excel, you'll find the Browse For Themes and Save Current Theme commands.

Display Lists and Choose Commands

1 To display a list of commands on a tab, click any tool showing a down arrow.

2 On the displayed list, click a command with a right-pointing arrow to display additional choices for that command.

3 Click a command with an ellipsis (...) to open a related dialog box.

To close a list without executing a command, click outside the list.

Use the Tools

1 Point to a tool on the toolbar, and wait for a ScreenTip, showing the tool button's name, to appear.

2 Some tools have two parts: the tool button and a down arrow. The two parts of the tool are highlighted independently. To apply the setting shown on the button, click the tool. To display a list of choices for that tool, click the down arrow.

3 If a tool button looks "pressed," click it again if you want to turn off that feature.

See Also

Read "Customizing the Quick Access Toolbar" on pages 394–395 for information about modifying the Quick Access toolbar in your favorite Office 2010 applications.

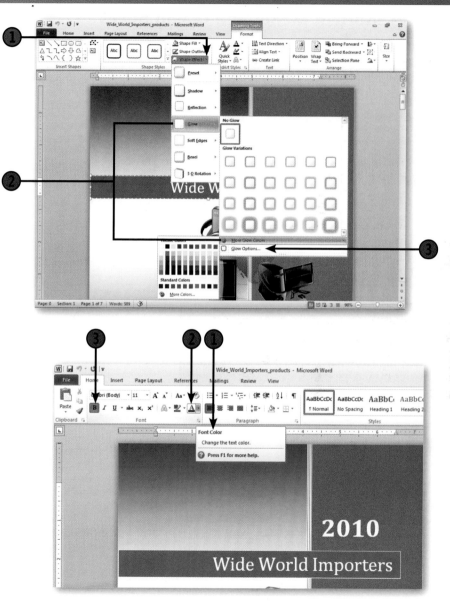

Using Shortcut Menus and Dialog Boxes

Word 2010 also offers many shortcut menus and dialog boxes that provide additional ways to choose the tools and settings you need. You can right-click an object in your file to display a shortcut menu showing choices related to that object, and you can click dialog box launchers to display dialog boxes of options related to the task you want to complete.

Use the Shortcut Menus

1 Right-click any content or location in your program where you want to execute an action.

2 Choose the action you want from the shortcut menu that appears.

Tip ✓

Items that are gray on menus or toolbars are items that aren't available at the moment. For example, if you haven't selected anything, the Cut and Copy commands are gray because there's nothing selected to cut or copy.

Tip ✓

You can use a shortcut key to choose a tool in a shortcut menu by typing the underlined letter in the tool you want to select.

Working with Dialog Boxes

1 Click any command that shows an ellipses (...) or

2 Click a dialog box launcher in a tab group on the ribbon.

3 Choose the settings you want to apply to the item.

4 Click OK to save your changes.

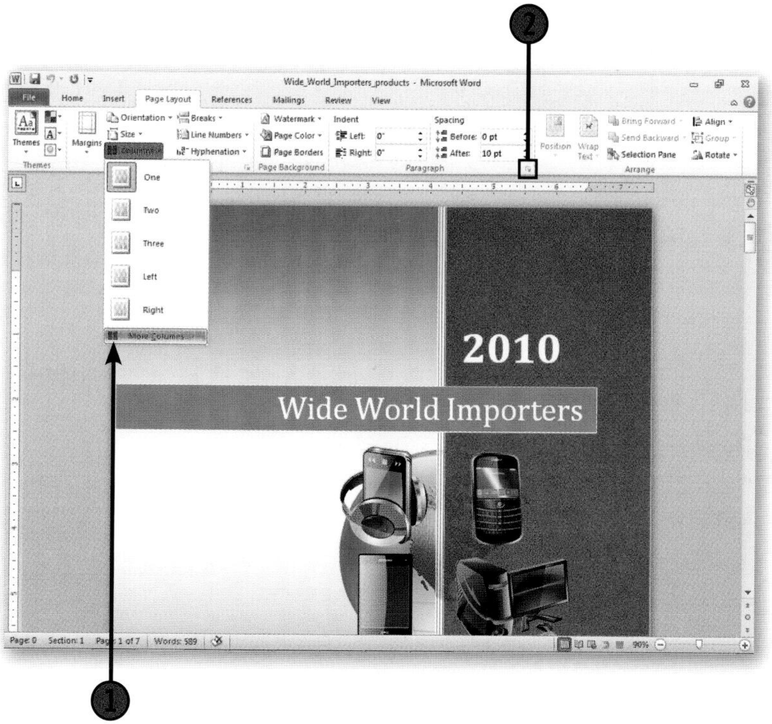

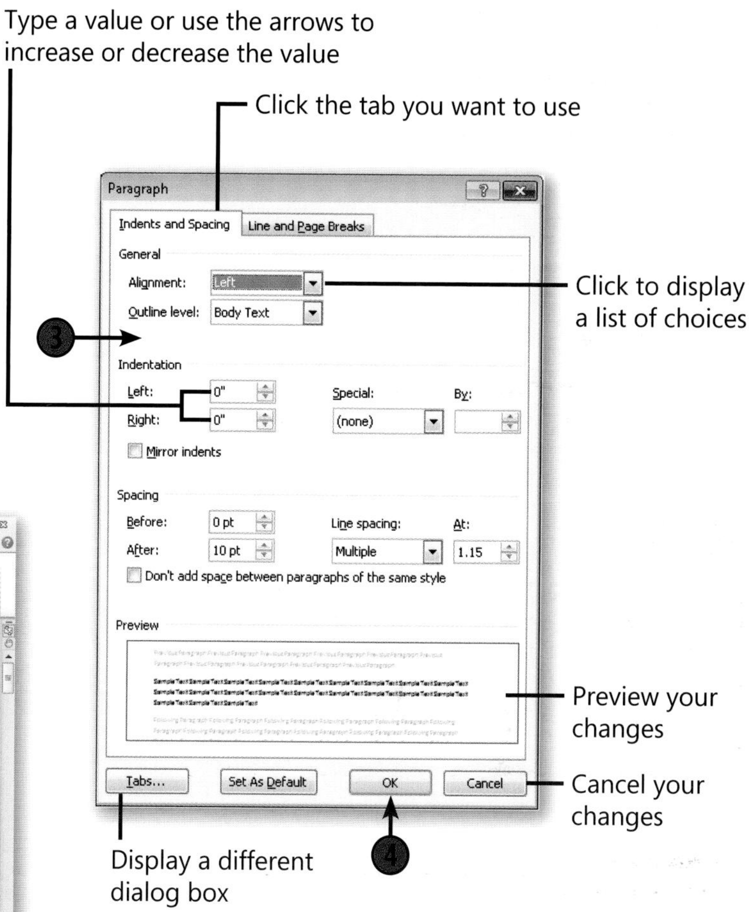

Type a value or use the arrows to increase or decrease the value

Click the tab you want to use

Click to display a list of choices

Preview your changes

Cancel your changes

Display a different dialog box

Using Only the Keyboard

If you prefer to keep your hands on the keyboard instead of using the mouse, you can do almost everything using Office and program-specific keyboard shortcuts. By activating the command tabs and the ribbon, you can use the displayed keys to navigate and to execute commands and activities. There are also many keyboard shortcuts you can use to execute some of the most common commands and activities.

Browse the Ribbon with Your Keyboard

1 Press and release the Alt key to display the KeyTips for access to the tabs and the ribbon.

2 Type the letter for the tab you want. You can also type the number for any item on the Quick Access toolbar or to open the Office menu.

3 Type the letter or the keyboard shortcut to access the item you want on the ribbon. If a gallery or a drop-down menu appears, use the arrow keys to select the item you want, and then press Enter.

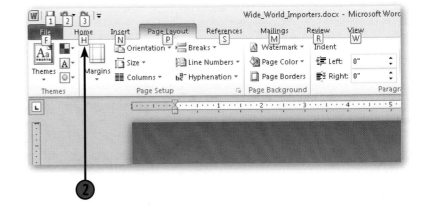

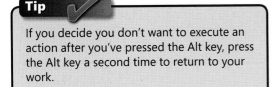

Tip

If you decide you don't want to execute an action after you've pressed the Alt key, press the Alt key a second time to return to your work.

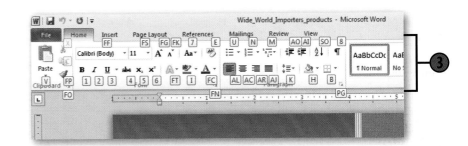

Use Keyboard Shortcuts

1. Use the keyboard shortcuts shown in the table at the right to execute the action you want. Not all shortcuts are appropriate for all programs all the time.

2. If you want to switch from mouse methods to keyboard methods, point to the button or other item you want to work with, and note the keyboard shortcut in the ScreenTip. Then use that keyboard shortcut.

3. If you don't see the keyboard shortcut you want in the table or in a ScreenTip, search Help for "keyboard shortcuts."

See Also

Read "Getting Help" on pages 24–25 for information about using Office 2010's Help system.

Common Keyboard Shortcuts

Action	Keyboard Shortcut
Copy and delete (cut) selected content	Ctrl+X
Copy selected content	Ctrl+C
Paste content	Ctrl+V
Hide or minimize ribbon	Ctrl+F1
Apply/remove bold formatting	Ctrl+B
Apply/remove italic formatting	Ctrl+I
Apply/remove underline formatting	Ctrl+U
Align paragraph left	Ctrl+L
Align paragraph center	Ctrl+E
Align paragraph right	Ctrl+R
Add/remove space before paragraph	Ctrl+0 (zero)
Apply double line spacing	Ctrl+2
Apply single line spacing	Ctrl+1
Apply Normal style	Ctrl+Shift+N
Change case	Shift+F3
Undo last action	Ctrl+Z
Redo last action	Ctrl+Y
Open shortcut menu	Shift+F10
Check spelling	F7
Save document	Ctrl+S
Save As	F12
Print (show Print dialog box)	Ctrl+P
Open Help	F1

Moving and Copying Content

Office programs, and most other programs, use a tool called the *Clipboard* as a temporary holding area for content that you want to move or copy to another part of your document, to another document in the same program, or to a document in another program. You simply park your text on the Clipboard and then, when you're ready, you retrieve it and "paste" it into its new location. One of the challenges with the Clipboard is that the format of information you copy and paste can be unreliable—one time you get the right font and color for a heading, for example, but the next time you don't necessarily get the result you wanted.

Now Office 2010 includes the Paste with Live Preview feature, which enables you to control how the information you copy is pasted into your file. Depending on the type of information you've copied—text, numbers, pictures, or objects—you are given a series of choices for the way the information is pasted. And what's more, you can preview your choice before you selected it. Nice.

Cut or Copy Information

1 Select the text you want to cut or copy.

2 Do either of the following:

Click the Cut button (or press Ctrl+X) to delete the selected text and store it on the Clipboard.

Click the Copy button (or press Ctrl+C) to keep the selected text where it is and place a copy on the Clipboard.

See Also

Read "Customizing Your Editing" on page 398 for information about modifying the default settings for the way items are cut and pasted in your document.

Tip

You can use the Office Clipboard to store items other than text, including pictures, tables, objects, and even data from Excel 2010 worksheets or Access 2010 data tables.

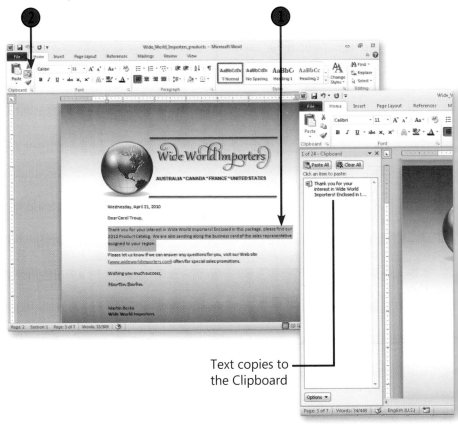

Text copies to the Clipboard

Paste Information Using Paste with Live Preview

1. Click in your document where you want to insert the information.

2. In the Clipboard group of the Home tab, click the Paste button.

3. Hover the cursor over each paste option to see how the information will look at the selected position. Click the option you want to apply.

4. You can change the format of the pasted information by clicking the Paste Options button and choosing the option you want to use.

Copy and Paste Multiple Items

1. Display the Clipboard by clicking the dialog box launcher in the Clipboard group on the Home tab.

2. Click the item to be inserted. Click Paste.

3. Click Clear All to empty the Clipboard.

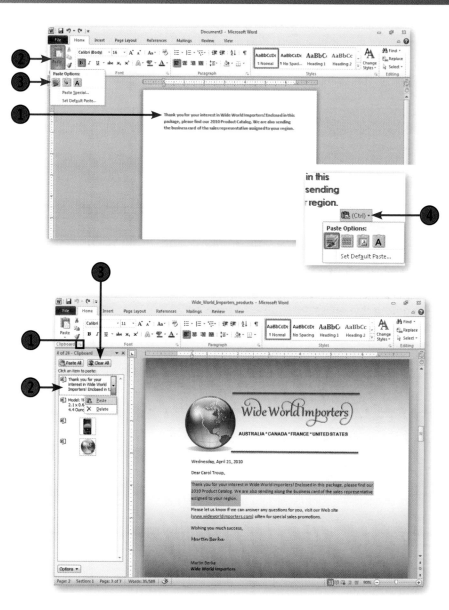

Working with Backstage View

All the tools you need to create, save, share, and choose options for your Office 2010 files are now available in Backstage view. This convenient view presents the various commands as tabs so that you can easily find the task you want to complete and choose the options you need associated with it.

When you first click the File tab, Backstage view appears and the Info tab is displayed. This tab displays the file's properties and authors, and gives you access to the commands you need to set permissions, prepare to save the file, and work with file versions. Other tabs in Backstage view—such as Recent, New, Print, and Save & Send—give you access to existing and new files and help you print and share the files you create. Additionally, you set program options and get Help in Backstage view.

Finding File and Program Information

1. Click File to display Backstage view.

2. Review the file's properties.

3. Choose the tools you want to work with in the center of the Backstage view window.

Tip

To close Backstage view and return to your file, click the File tab a second time.

Try This!

Click Manage Versions in the Info tab of Backstage view and choose Recover Draft Versions. A dialog box opens showing unsaved versions of your file so that you can open and save the content. In this way, you can recover information that you might have accidentally forgotten to save.

Recently views files

Common file tasks

Printing a File

 In Backstage view, click Print.

2 Set print options in the center of the Print window.

3 Preview the file by clicking the arrows near the page number at the bottom of the document preview to move through the document.

4 Drag the Zoom slider to change the size of the document display.

5 Click Print to print the file.

Tip

You can print a document directly to a OneNote 2010 notebook by clicking the Printer setting arrow and choosing Send To OneNote 2010. When the Selection Location In OneNote dialog box appears, choose the notebook and section where you want to insert the document and click OK.

Tip

The tools available in Print Settings vary from application to application.

Tip

In Word, you can click the Print All Pages arrow (the first item under Settings), and choose the pages you want to print. If you want to print on both sides of the page but your printer doesn't support dual-sided printing automatically, you can do it manually by clicking Print All Pages and choosing Only Print Odd Pages. Click Print to print the pages, and then remove them from the printer, make sure they are in sequential order, and then put them back in your printer to print the even pages. Click Print All Pages again, and this time click Only Print Even Pages and click Print.

Getting Help

Nothing can replace this book, of course, but Office 2010 does provide you with other resources to help solve problems you might encounter. We're using Word Help here to illustrate the ways you can get help in all your Office programs.

Browse for Help

① In your program, press the F1 key to display the Help window for that program.

② Click a category that reflects what you want to learn.

③ Find what you want to do, and then click the link that seems relevant to your question.

④ If the font size is too small or too large, click the Change Font Size button, and choose a font size from the menu.

⑤ To print the topic, click the Print button.

⑥ To return to either the list or the articles, click the Back button. To return to the list of categories, click the Back button again.

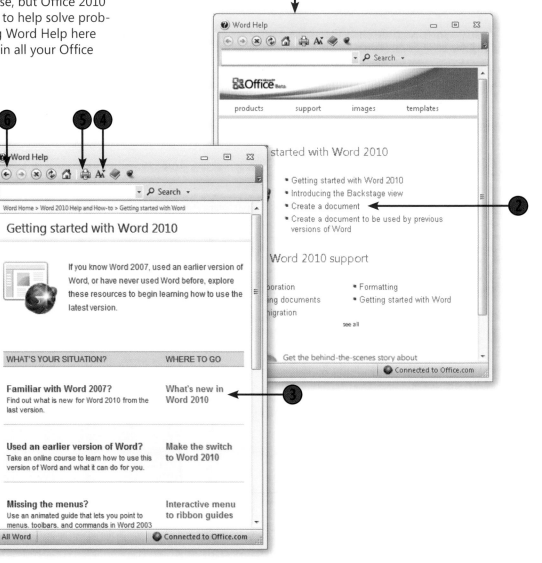

Search for Help

1 Type your Search text.

2 If you want to specify which Help resources you want, click the Search down arrow, and then click the resource.

3 Click Search.

4 Click a search result that seems relevant.

5 If there's more than one page of results, click the Next button at the top and bottom of the search results to see any additional pages.

6 Close the window when you've finished.

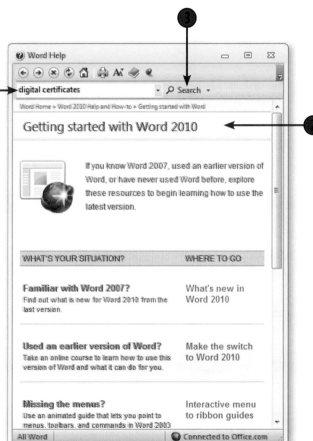

Saving Your Work

While you're working on your document, you'll want to save it frequently to make sure that it's preserved for posterity—or at least until you've completed it, printed it, or shared it with others for review. After you've named and saved the file, the Save As dialog box won't appear for subsequent saves.

Save the File

1. In Word, Excel, PowerPoint, and Publisher, you can click the Save button on the Quick Access toolbar. In OneNote, your information is saved for you automatically. And in Access, the file is saved automatically when you create it, although you can click the Save button to save individual items, such as a new table.

2. Type a name for the file in the File Name box if you don't want the name that the program proposes. File names can be as long as 250 characters and can include spaces, but you can't use the \ / * ? < > and | characters.

3. If you'll always want to save the file to your default location, click Hide Folders.

4. If you don't want to save the file in the suggested format, select the format you want.

5. Click Save.

Tip
In some applications, like Word 2010, you will also see the Save Thumbnail check box. Click this box if you want to see a preview of the file in a folder window.

Tip
After you save the file, continue to work on it as needed, saving your work frequently by clicking the Save button or pressing the keyboard shortcut Ctrl+S.

Office's File Formats

Beginning with Office 2007, Microsoft Word, Excel, Power-Point, and Access saved files in a different format that was more efficient and flexible than the format used in previous versions. Some people you trade files with may be using different versions that produce files in different formats than the program you are using in Office 2010. Fortunately, you can save your Office 2010 files in earlier formats if this is a problem for you, or you can get a file converter (available from Microsoft Downloads) that enables your friends and colleagues to view and work with Office 2010 files.

If you decide not to use the latest formats available in the various Office 2010 applications, however, be aware that you won't be able to use some of the programs' very cool new features. For example, features such as video styles in PowerPoint or text effects in Word will not be available to you. Review the following descriptions of the formats used in Word, Excel, and PowerPoint to see which formats work best for you. To see the list of all available formats, choose Save As from the Office menu, and, in the Save As dialog box, scroll through the Save As Type list. To see a description of the Access file format choices, see "Open an Existing Database File" on page 367.

- **Document, Workbook, or Presentation**   This is a format that was new with Office 2007 that enables all of the programs' new features. Files in this format can't be opened in earlier versions of their respective programs unless you've downloaded and installed a special translating filter program. The new format has the standard file extension with an added "x" (for example, .docx, .xlsx, .pptx).

- **Macro-Enabled Document, Workbook, or Presentation**   This is the same format as the Document, Workbook, or Presentation format, except that it contains macros.

- **XML Document or Presentation**   This is a plain Text file that includes all the text and the XML coding. This format is used primarily in a corporate setting where transforms are created to extract and/or reformat information that will be stored for reuse.

- **Word, Excel, or PowerPoint Template**   This new form of template, first available in Office 2007, also enables the new features of the program.

- **Word, Excel, or PowerPoint Macro-Enabled Template**   This is the same format as the Template format, except that it can contain macros.

Other File Formats for Office Programs

- **Word, Excel, or PowerPoint 97–2003 format**   This is the binary file format used in previous versions of these programs. Although it provides compatibility with earlier versions, saving in this format disables some of the advanced features of the 2007 programs.

- **Word, Excel, or PowerPoint 97–2003 Template**   This is the binary file format for templates used in previous versions of Word.

- **Single File Web Page**   This format creates a Web page and stores all the graphics in the same file.

- **Web Page**   This format creates a standard HTML-format Web page whose graphics are stored in a separate folder.

- **Rich Text Format**   This is a binary file that contains the text and formatting information but little else. It provides compatibility with many programs.

- **Plain Text**   This text file contains only the text of the document and no formatting.

3

Common Tasks in Office

In this section of the book, we'll cover some of the step-by-step procedures that are common among most of the programs in Office 2010. Each program, of course, has its differences, but you'll find a great amount in common among the various applications. The ribbon and Backstage view make it easy for you to find your way to the tools and options you need no matter which program you are using. And many features work in similar ways—for example, the steps are basically the same in all the applications when you're adding, editing, and enhancing photos and drawings. After you've placed your pictures, you can edit them, crop them, add special effects, and so on. You can put text inside an assortment of shapes to create pull quotes, advertising blurbs, and other interesting effects; and, using the alchemy of WordArt, you can transmute words into wonderfully colorful three-dimensional art.

You can have your Office 2010 program insert the date and/or time that you created your document or presentation; you can display your topics visually using Office 2010's SmartArt; you can translate words and phrases on the fly with the Mini Translator tool; and you can use Office's built-in research feature to look up definitions of words or get information about just about anything simply by clicking a word or a name.

Working with Old Documents

When you open a file that was created in a version of Microsoft Office Word, Excel, PowerPoint, or Access prior to 2007, Office 2010 opens the file in Compatibility mode. This means that some of the new features of your program won't be available. To use these features, you need to convert the file to the program's 2010 format.

Convert the Document

1. With your Office 97–2003 format file open, click File to display Backstage view.

2. Click Convert.

(continued on next page)

Caution

When you upgrade the file format of the document, the file won't be usable by people who have earlier versions of the program unless they've installed the Office Compatibility pack, which enables them to read and save this type of file. In Microsoft Access 2010, databases saved in the 2010 format can't be opened or accessed from previous versions of Access.

Convert the Document *(continued)*

3 A dialog box appears asking you whether you want to convert the file. If you want Office 2010 to convert files automatically in the future, select the Do Not Ask Me Again About Converting Documents check box.

4 Click OK. The original file won't be over-written because its file extension is different from that of the updated file.

5 Work on the file, using all the features of your program.

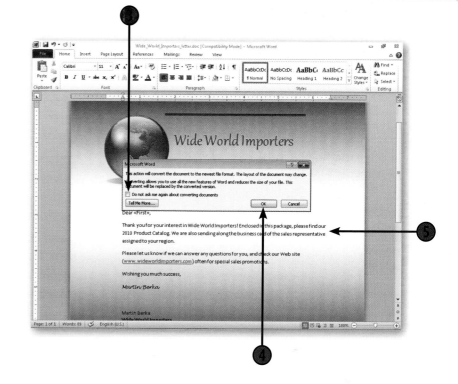

Microsoft Word Compatibility Checker

The following features in this document are not supported by earlier versions of Word. These features may be lost or degraded when you save this document in an earlier file format. Click Continue to save the document. To keep all of your features, click Cancel, and then save the file in one of the new file formats.

Summary	Occurrences
Content controls will be converted to static content.	5
Help	
Charts will be converted into a single object that can't be edited in earlier versions of Word.	1
Help	
Shapes and textboxes will be converted to effects available in this format.	11
Effects on text will be removed.	58

☑ Check compatibility when saving documents

Continue   Cancel

Tip ✓

If you need to send an upgraded file to someone who has an earlier version of the Office program but doesn't have the Office Compatibility pack, point to the arrow at the right of the Save As command on the Office menu, and choose the Office program's 97–2003 Format from the gallery that appears. Then save the file normally. As a result, you might lose some advanced features in your file, but at least the other person will be able to read it.

Inserting Pictures

In Word, Excel, PowerPoint, Publisher, OneNote, Access, and Outlook, you can add different types of picture files to a single document—photographs and drawings, for example—provided the pictures are in one of the file formats that are recognized by Office 2010. Once you've added the picture file, you can add picture styles, apply artistic effects, and edit and enhance the picture.

Insert a Picture

1. Click in your document where you want to insert the picture.

2. On the Insert tab, click the Picture button to display the Insert Picture dialog box.

3. Navigate to the folder that contains the picture you want, and select the picture file from the list.

4. Do either of the following:

   • Click Insert to place the picture in your document.

   • Click the down arrow at the right of the Insert button, and choose to link to the file only or to insert and link to the file.

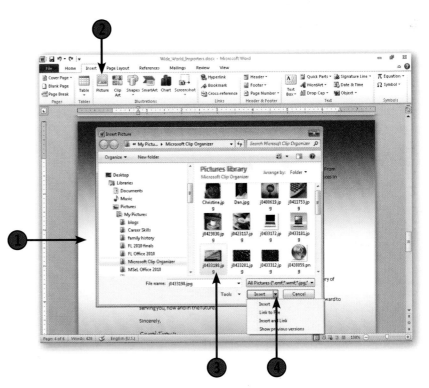

Tip

If you link to the picture, the image in your document will be updated if the picture is updated. Linking without inserting the entire file can substantially reduce the file's size.

Display a Specific File Type

● In the Insert Picture dialog box, choose the folder with the files you want to view.

● Click the File Type arrow and choose the format you want from the list.

● Double-click the picture you want to add to your document.

Picture Format Name	File Format
Windows Enhanced Metafile	.emf
Windows Metafile	.wmf
JPEG File Interchange Format	.jpg, .jpeg, .jfif, .jpe
Portable Network Graphics	.png
Windows Bitmap	.bmp, .dib, .rle
Graphics Interchange Format	.gif, .gfa
Compressed Windows Enhanced Metafile	.emz
Compressed Windows Metafile	.wmz
Compressed Macintosh PICT	.pcz
Tag Image File Format	.tif, .tiff
WordPerfect Graphics	.wpg
Computer Graphics Metafile	.cgm
Encapsulated PostScript	.eps
Macintosh PICT	.pct, .pict

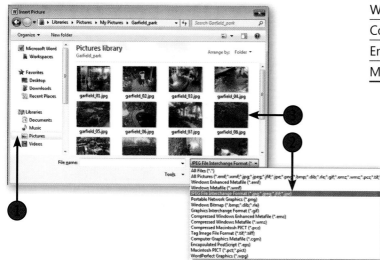

See Also

Read "Editing a Picture" on page 36 for information about editing your picture files using Microsoft Office 2010, and "Adding Clip Art" on page 40 for information about including your pictures in the ClipArt collections.

Changing the Size of a Picture

You can change the size of the pictures you add in Office 2010 so that they fit perfectly in the amount of space you have available in your file. You might also want to crop your photo to focus attention on the most important elements. In Office 2010, cropping your photos and increasing or decreasing picture size are both simple tasks.

Crop It

① Click to select the picture if it isn't already selected and to activate the Picture Tools Format tab.

② On the Picture Tools Format tab, click the Crop tool in the Size group. If the list appears, click Crop.

③ Place the cropping mouse cursor over a Cropping handle.

(continued on next page)

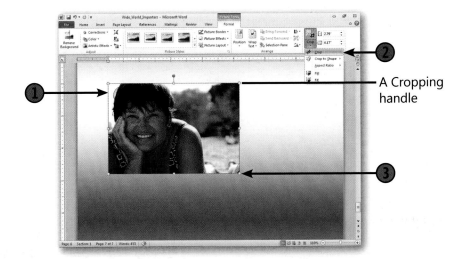

A Cropping handle

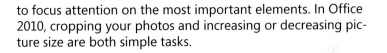
Try This!

Now in Office 2010 you can crop a photo to a shape to add special touches to your files. Add a photo to your page by clicking Insert, Picture, and choosing the photo you want to add. Click Insert to paste the photo at the cursor position. Now click the photo and click the Picture Tools Format tab. In the Size group, click the Crop arrow, and point to Crop To Shape. Click the shape you want to apply to the photo and watch what happens on your page! The photo is cropped to the shape you selected. You won't want to use this often in your publications and worksheets, but once in a while it's a fun feature.

Crop It *(continued)*

4 Drag the handle to crop the picture to include only the elements you want to show. Notice that a gray screen shows you the area of the picture that will be discarded.

5 Click the Crop button again to crop the photo and turn off cropping.

Tip

If you want to crop your photo to a specific shape, you can set the aspect ratio before you crop. To do this, click the Picture Tools Format tab and click the Crop arrow in the Size group. Point to Aspect Ratio, and click the ratio you want to apply to the image.

Size It

1 Click the picture if it isn't already selected.

2 Drag a sizing handle on the picture to modify the size of the picture.

Tip

When you drag a sizing handle, your picture can sometimes become distorted. To make sure the picture keeps its current shape, press and hold the Shift key while you resize the image.

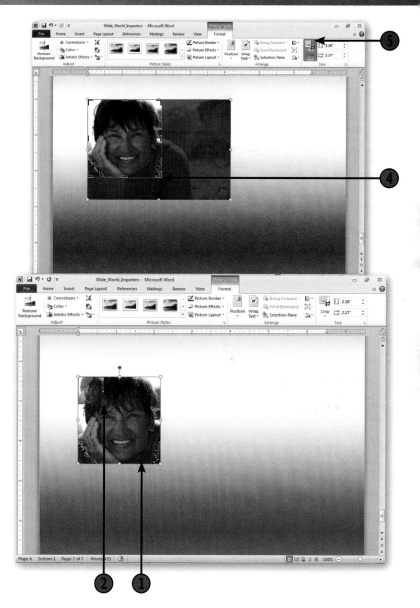

Editing a Picture

After you've placed a picture in your document, workbook, presentation, notes page, data record, or mail message, you can edit the picture by adjusting its color, brightness, and sharpness. You can also enhance the photo by applying special filters called Artistic Effects. These features enable you to improve your pictures and make them look just the way you want.

Apply Artistic Effects

1 Click the picture to select it.

2 Click the Picture Tools Format tab.

3 In the Adjust group, click the Artistic Effects arrow.

4 Point to various effects to preview them on the photo, and click the one you want to apply.

Tip

You can change specific characteristics—such as the transparency level or the number of shades used—of the Artistic Effects you select by clicking Artistic Effects Options at the bottom of the Artistic Effects gallery.

Change Contrast and Color

1 Click to select the picture if it isn't already selected, and click the Picture Tools Format tab if it isn't already displayed.

2 Click the Corrections tool to sharpen or soften the image or change the brightness and contrast. Select your choice.

(continued on next page)

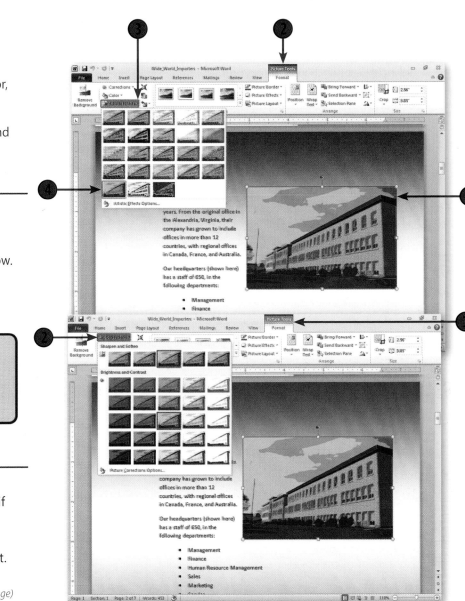

Change Contrast and Color   *(continued)*

③ Click the Color tool to change the color saturation and tone or to recolor the picture. Click the one you want to apply.

You can choose the thumbnail in the gallery that reflects the setting you'd like to apply to your picture or click Picture Corrections Options at the bottom of the gallery to display the Format Picture dialog box. In the Format Picture dialog box, you can change the characteristics of the picture effect you want to apply.

Rotate It

① Click to select the picture if necessary, and click the Picture Tools Format tab.

② Drag the Rotation handle to rotate the picture.

When you edit a picture, you're editing only the copy of it that you've inserted into your document. If you want to change the original picture file, you need to edit it in a separate program—for example, in the Windows Live Photo Gallery that comes with Windows 7.

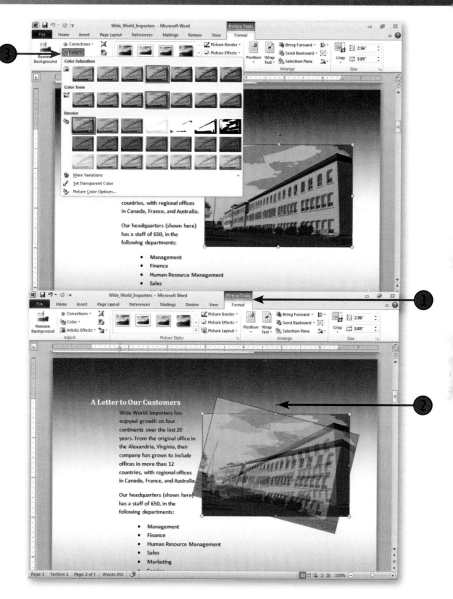

Enhancing Your Pictures

Word includes a number of features that make it simple to take ho-hum photos, drawings, or diagrams and make them look great. You can apply picture styles—preset formats that spruce up your images—or enhance the images with special picture effects."

Add Picture Styles and Effects

1. With the picture selected, point to the different styles in the Picture Styles section of the ribbon to see how your picture looks when you apply that style, and then click the one you want.

2. Click the Picture Border button, and move your mouse through the gallery to see the effects of a different picture-border color, weight, or pattern. Click any effects you want to add.

3. Click Picture Effects to add or change the 3-D rotation, shadow, reflection, glow, or soft edges.

4. If, after all that hard work, you don't like the result, click the Reset Picture button to reset the entire picture to the way it looked when you first inserted it.

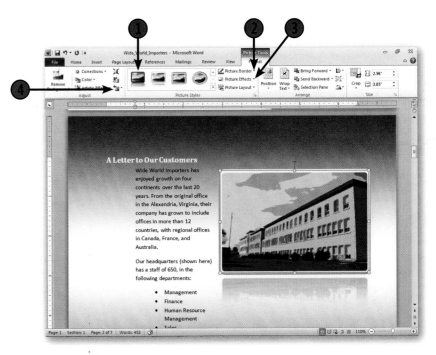

Tip

If you want to set precise values for brightness, contrast, shadow, or 3-D settings, including rotation, click the dialog box launcher in the Picture Styles group. This displays the Format Shape dialog box. To rotate a picture 90 or 180 degrees, click the Rotate button in the Arrange section of the ribbon.

Caution

The Reset Picture button resets all the changes you've made, including any cropping or sizing. If you want to undo only one or two changes, use the Undo button on the Quick Access toolbar.

Making Your Pictures Pop

One of the secrets to creating a truly compelling image is to help people looking at the photo focus on the part you most want them to see. Word 2010 includes a great tool that removes the picture background for you so that you can ensure readers are seeing the most important part of your picture."

Remove the Picture Background

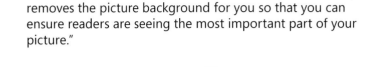

① Click the picture you want to change.

② Click the Picture Tools Format tab.

③ In the Adjust group, click Remove Background.

④ Click Mark Areas To Keep, Mark Areas To Remove, or Delete Mark as needed to adjust the purple masking. (This is the background area that will be removed.)

⑤ When the picture is marked the way you want it, click Keep Changes.

⑥ To reset the picture and return the background, click Discard All Changes.

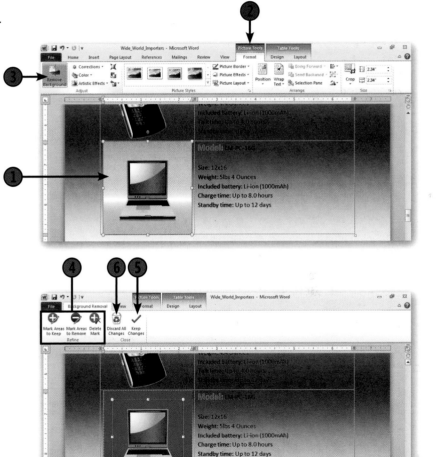

Tip

Using the Remove Background command takes a little practice, but it enables you to create some professional effects and fun pictures for the documents and publications you create.

Adding Clip Art

When you're looking for just the right piece of clip art to illustrate a story, an article, or a presentation, you can hunt through different categories or conduct a search using keywords. Microsoft Clip Art gives you all kinds of art to choose from—cartoon clip art, photographs, videos, and audio clips.

Find and Insert Clip Art

1. Click in your document where you want to add the clip art.

2. On the Insert tab, in the Illustrations group, click the Clip Art tool.

3. In the Clip Art pane, type a keyword or keywords to describe the type of picture you want.

4. In the Results list, click the clip-art collection you want to see. To select only certain categories, expand the list under the collection, and select the check box for each category you want to display.

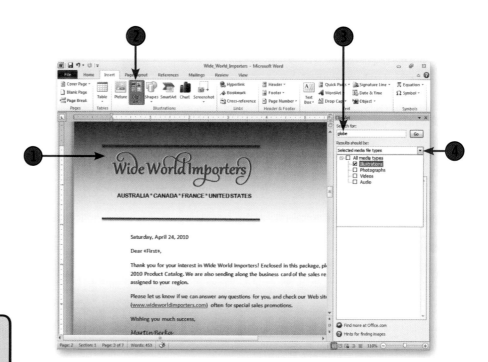

(continued on next page)

> **Tip** ✓
>
> You can save pictures, drawings, and other graphic elements to your ClipArt collections so that you can use them again later. Click the Windows Start button and type **Clip Organizer** in the search box. Click Microsoft Clip Organizer and use the tool to set your own categories and add your own picture and media files. The files you add will be available through the ClipArt pane in your Office 2010 programs.

Find and Insert Clip Art (continued)

⑤ Click Go.

⑥ In the Results list, click the clip art you want to add to the page.

⑦ When the clip art is on the page, you can click it and resize or rotate it so it fits the space in your document.

⑧ Use the tools in the Picture Tools contextual tab to further fine-tune the art.

Try This!

After you add clip art to your document, you can change the way information wraps around the art by clicking the Wrap Text tool in the Arrange group of the Picture Tools Format tab. In the list that appears, click the way you want information to wrap around the art. (The small icons on the left show you how each selection works.)

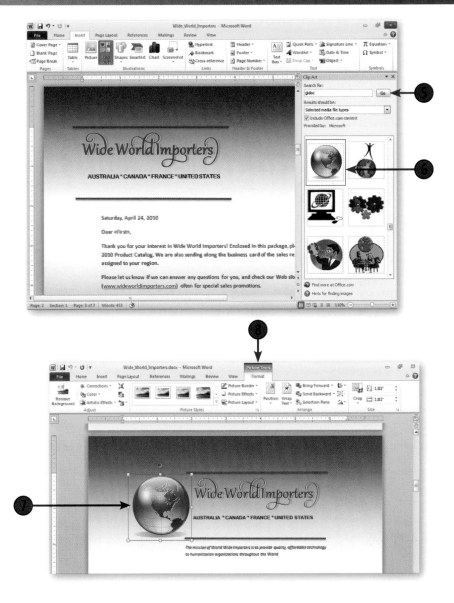

Inserting Screenshots

For some of the projects you create, you may want to capture images of your computer screen. This might be important, for example, when you are creating training materials. You can easily add screenshots directly in your Office 2010 files using the Insert Screenshot tool.

Add a Screenshot

1 Click in the document where you want the screenshot to appear.

2 Click the Insert tab, and click Screenshot.

3 In the gallery of screen images that appears, click the screen you want to add.

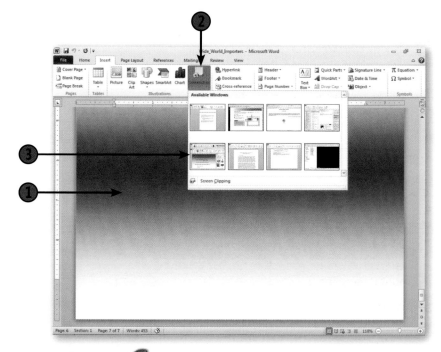

Tip

You can also grab just a portion of a screen by using the Screen Clipping command at the bottom of the Screenshot gallery. Click the Insert tab, click Screenshot, and click Screen Clipping. Click and drag to select the portion of the screen you want to insert in your file. When you release the mouse button, the clipping is inserted at the cursor position.

Tip

After you add the screenshot to your document, you can click it and apply special formatting touches like a shadow, frame, artistic effects, or other style by choosing the tools you want to use in the Picture Tools Format tab.

Tip

If you want to save a screenshot to a file so that you can insert it as a picture in other documents, right-click the image and click Save Picture As in the shortcut menu. Choose the folder where you want to save the file, enter a file name, and click the Save As Type arrow to choose the format in which you want to save the file. Then click Save to save the file so that you can use it again later.

Adding Shapes

Shapes are drawing objects that you can manipulate in many ways to create unusual and eye-catching effects. You can also use shapes as containers for text, which allows you to create callouts, pull quotes, advertising blurbs, and so on, producing all sorts of interestingly shaped special effects. Shapes are available in Word, Excel, PowerPoint, OneNote, Publisher, and Outlook.

Draw a Shape

1. Click in your document where you want to insert the shape. On the Insert tab, click Shapes, and click the shape you want in the gallery that appears.

2. Hold down the left mouse button, and drag out the shape.

3. Adjust the shape by dragging it to where you want it and using the handles to resize or rotate the shape.

4. Use the Bring Forward or Send Backward tool to adjust the layering if necessary.

5. Use the tools on the Drawing Tools Format tab to customize the appearance of the shape.

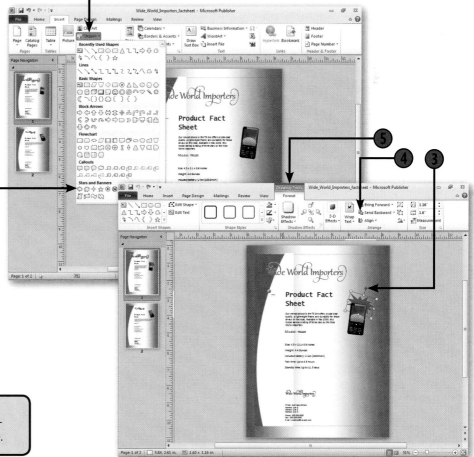

> **See Also**
>
> Read "Formatting a Shape" on page 44 for information on modifying the appearance of a shape.

Formatting a Shape

Once you add a shape to your file, you can format it to add extra impact. You might want to change the color of the fill or outline of the shape, add a 3-D effect, apply a shadow or style, or add text to the shape.

Format the Shape

- Click to select the shape if it isn't already selected.

- Point to different shape styles, and click the style you want.

- Display the Shape styles gallery and choose a look for the shape.

- Use the Shadow or 3-D Effects gallery to add any special effects you want.

- If you want to add text to the shape, click the Edit Text button to insert a text box, and then enter your text. Note, however, that all the Callouts shapes automatically contain a text box.

- To add special effects—such as a fill pattern, a fill transparency, or arrow styles—adjust the properties of the text box; or, for other advanced customizations, click the More button to open the Shape Styles gallery, and click Advanced Tools to display the Format AutoShape dialog box.

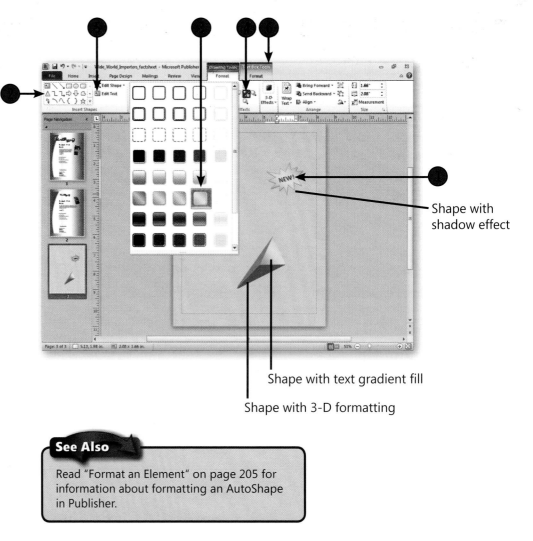

Shape with shadow effect

Shape with text gradient fill

Shape with 3-D formatting

See Also

Read "Format an Element" on page 205 for information about formatting an AutoShape in Publisher.

Inserting the Date and Time

If you want to indicate the date and/or time that you created your document or presentation, or if you want the current date and/or time shown, you can have Word, PowerPoint, Publisher, or the Outlook Editor insert either or both for you.

Insert the Date and/or Time

1. Click in the document where you want the date and/or time to appear.

2. On the Insert tab, click the Date & Time button to Display the Date And Time dialog box.

3. Select the format you want and the information to be included.

4. Specify the language you want to use if it isn't your default language. If the selected language supports more than one type of calendar, select the calendar you want to use.

5. Select the Update Automatically check box to have the date and/or time updated each time you open, save, or print the document. Clear the check box if you want the original date and/or time to be displayed.

6. Click OK.

Tip

The date and/or time are often placed in a document as part of the running head. Use the header and/or footer features that are unique to each program to insert the date and/or time in the running head.

Tip

The Date And Time dialog box is slightly different in different programs. For example, the Calendar list isn't available in Word or Outlook unless a language with more than one calendar appears. Also, for no apparent reason, the location of the Update Automatically check box is moved around in the different programs.

Creating Stylized Text

Office 2010 enables you to create special effects with text by using WordArt. You can use vibrant colors, 3-D effects, unusual shadows, and outline effects—all designed to give your text an artistic look and make it stand out on your page.

Although the way you work with WordArt is a bit different in some of the Office programs, the main method and the results are similar. The steps in the following procedure show you how to create WordArt in Word and in Outlook.

Create a WordArt Object

1. On the Insert tab, click the WordArt button to display the WordArt gallery.

2. Click the WordArt style you want.

3. Type your text. You can also transform existing text into WordArt, by selecting the text before you click the WordArt button.

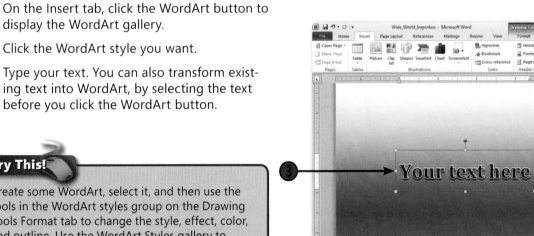

Try This!

Create some WordArt, select it, and then use the tools in the WordArt styles group on the Drawing Tools Format tab to change the style, effect, color, and outline. Use the WordArt Styles gallery to apply a three-dimensional effect.

See Also

Read "Formatting a Chart" on pages 204–205 for information about using WordArt in Excel and PowerPoint.

Fine-Tune the Result

1 Click to select the WordArt if it isn't already selected, and use the Sizing handles to change the size of the WordArt.

2 Click Text Effects in the WordArt Styles group of the Drawing Tools Format tab to display the gallery of choices.

3 Preview the different text effects by pointing to the different choices. Click the effect you want to apply to the text.

Tip ✓

To change the colors of dual-colored or multicolored WordArt, on the Drawing Tools Format tab, click the Shape Fill button, point to Gradient on the drop-down menu, click More Gradients, and modify the colors on the Gradient tab of the Fill Effects dialog box.

Inserting a SmartArt Diagram

SmartArt is a sophisticated diagramming tool included in Word, Excel, PowerPoint, and Outlook that enables you to show your ideas visually. Whether you want to compare product lines, show a production process, or highlight your organizational chart, SmartArt gives you an easy way to show relationships and processes professionally.

Create a Diagram

1. On the Insert tab, click the SmartArt button to display the Choose A SmartArt Graphic dialog box.

2. Select the type of diagram you want.

3. Click a diagram type, and review the information about that diagram.

4. Click OK to create the diagram type you want.

5. Click the first item and type the text you want to add.

6. Click in the next item, and type the text. Continue entering text, doing any of the following:

   • Press the Tab key to make the entry a subentry of the previous item (or click Demote), or Press Shift+Tab to elevate the entry one level (or click Promote).

   • Press Enter to finish the current item and insert a new line for text.

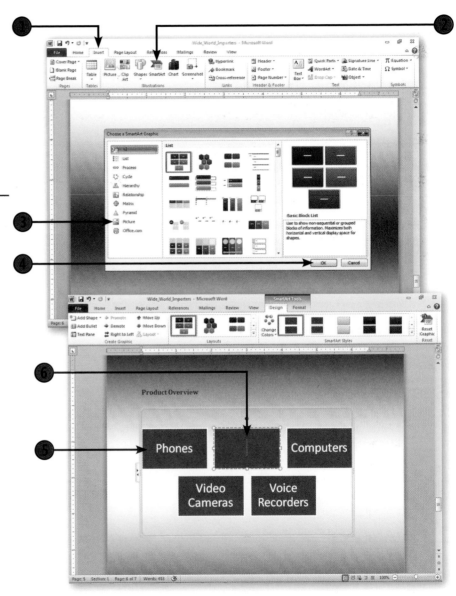

Modify the Diagram

- On the SmartArt Tools Design tab, click Change Colors in the Smart-Art Styles group and choose the color scheme you want to assign to the diagram.

- Point to the different Quick Styles, and click the one you want.

- Click Add Shape to add another object to the diagram.

- Click a new layout if you want to change the design.

- Click the frame of the diagram, and drag a corner or side of the frame to change the diagram's size.

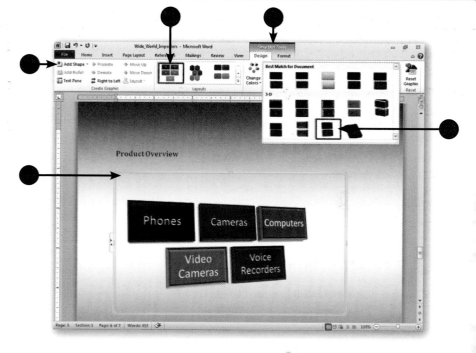

Tip ✓

If you prefer to use the Text Pane to add and edit the text for your SmartArt diagram, click Text Pane in the Create Graphic group of the SmartArt Tools Design tab. When the Text Pane is displayed, you can click in the text entries to type new text or edit existing text.

Tip ✓

You must use the new file formats to create SmartArt graphics. When you save a document that contains SmartArt in the 97–2003 file format, the SmartArt is converted into a picture that you can't modify.

Translating Your Text

Today it's not unusual to be working with colleagues or chatting with friends from other countries. Office 2010 now includes improved language tools that help you translate text on the fly. The Mini Translator pops up over your document to provide quick translations within easy reach. And you can now set your language of preference so that correct usage—complete with pronunciation—is only a click away.

Choose a Translation Language

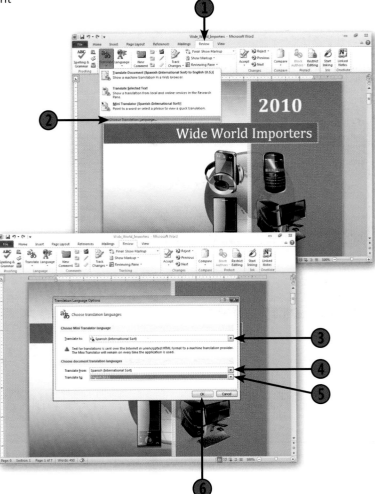

1. On the Review tab, click Translate in the Language group.

2. Click Choose Translation Language.

3. In the Translation Language Options dialog box, click the arrow in the Choose Mini Translator Language and click the language you want to translate to.

4. Click the Translate From arrow and click the language you want to translate from.

5. Click the Translate To arrow and choose the language you want to translate documents and sections to.

6. Click OK.

Tip

You can also install new languages and even install keyboard configurations that enable you to type and proofread your documents with other language character sets. Click Language and choose Language Preferences to install additional languages for your Office 2010 programs.

Use the Mini Translator

1. On the Review tab, click Translate in the Language group and click Mini Translator.

2. Select the text in your document you'd like to translate.

3. Hover the mouse pointer over the text and the Mini Translator appears.

4. Click the Expand icon to open the Translation page of the Research task pane so that you can find out more about the translation.

5. Click the Copy icon to copy the translated text for pasting in another location.

6. Click the Play icon to hear the translation pronounced.

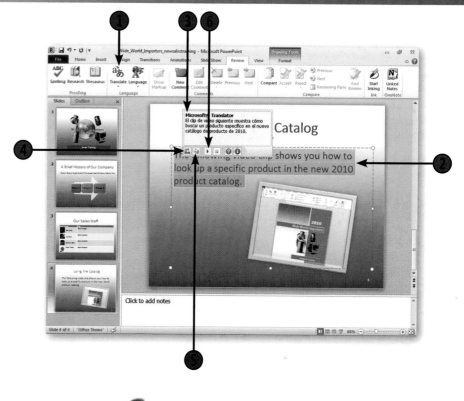

Tip

If you plan to use the Play feature so that you can hear the translation pronounced, be sure to have the volume on your computer turned on and set to an adequate level.

Tip

Click Update Services (the tool farthest to the right in the tools row of the Mini Translator) to display a list of services used in translation. You can click Update to choose different services or update the services being used.

Researching a Subject

Wouldn't it be great to look up the definition of a word directly from your computer? Or to get information about something simply by clicking a word or a name? Well, you can do this in Word, Excel, PowerPoint, Publisher, OneNote, and Outlook, by using the built-in research feature.

Do Some Research

- Click a word (or select a group of words) that you want information about.

- On the Review tab, click the Research button.

- Select the resource or the types of resources you want to use.

- Click Go.

- Review the results.

- Click any links to more information in the Results pane that look relevant.

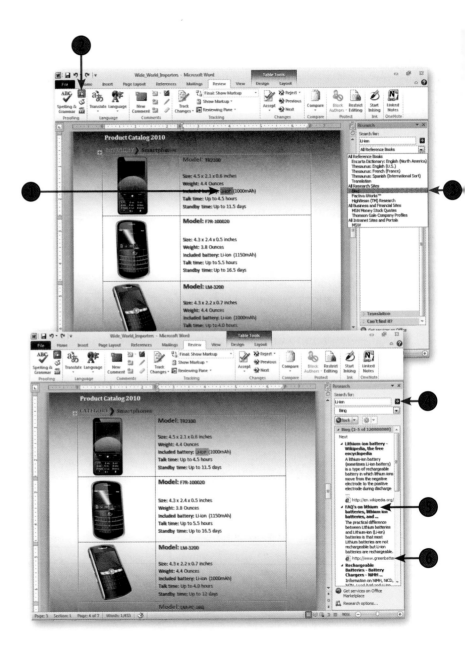

Tip

To quickly open the Research pane, hold down the Alt key and click the word you want to look up.

Caution

Some research services charge to view the full content of their results. If there's a charge, you'll see an icon indicating the amount next to the search result.

4

Viewing and Editing Text in Word

Microsoft Word 2010 makes it easier than ever for you to create professional-looking documents—complete with pictures, fancy layouts, and more—without a lot of effort. Whether you are a new or experienced Word user, you will catch on quickly to the way the tools are arranged to help you find what you need. And the many templates, themes, and quick styles give you a head-start on creating documents that you want to have a put-together look.

This section introduces you to the Word 2010 window and covers the basic skills you'll use every day: creating different kinds of documents using Word's templates; editing, copying, and moving text; adding page numbers; correcting your spelling and grammar; and using Word's co-authoring and Track Changes features to edit documents in real time and keep track of document revisions. If you're not familiar with Word, step through the first few tasks and see just how easily you can produce great-looking documents. If you're already comfortable with Word, find your way quickly to the exciting new features Word 2010 offers.

Turn the page for a short visual tour of Word's new interface. Then jump right in! If you get stuck in some way, you'll find the answers to most of your questions in other sections of this book, or in Word's Help system.

What's Where in Word 2010?

The Word 2010 window offers layout that's easy to use and understand and that you can customize to fit your needs. The pictures on these two pages show some common features you'll see when you're working in Word. I've identified many of the screen elements for you, but it's a good idea to explore Word's interface while you're looking at these two pages. For example, click each of the tabs on the ribbon and familiarize yourself with what's on them. If you're not sure what the tools

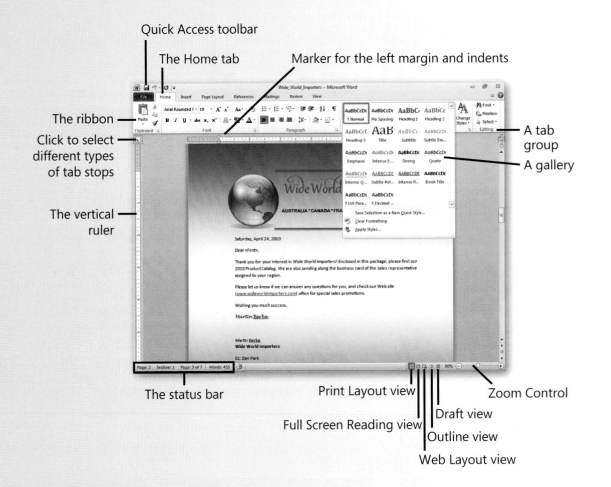

Quick Access toolbar

The Home tab

Marker for the left margin and indents

The ribbon

Click to select different types of tab stops

A tab group

A gallery

The vertical ruler

The status bar

Print Layout view

Zoom Control

Full Screen Reading view

Draft view

Outline view

Web Layout view

do, point to one of them to display a *ToolTip* that tells you the tool's name and gives you a pretty good idea of that particular tool's function.

The following picture shows more of the Word 2010 interface. As you experiment with it, you'll find that Word has different tabs for different tasks, tools that appear exactly when you need them for the job you're doing right that minute, and many more features that you'll discover as you work in Word.

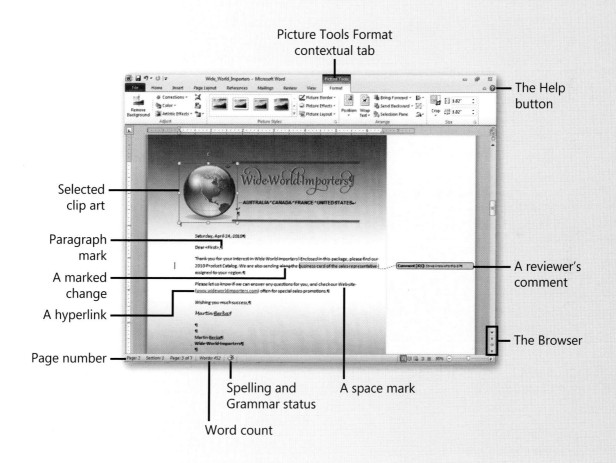

Picture Tools Format contextual tab

Selected clip art

Paragraph mark

A marked change

A hyperlink

Page number

Spelling and Grammar status

Word count

A space mark

The Help button

A reviewer's comment

The Browser

Creating a New Document

You can start Word several different ways, but the tried-and-true method is to choose Microsoft Word 2010 from the Windows Start menu. When Word starts, it automatically opens a new blank document for you. If you've been experimenting and Word is already running, you can open a new blank document with a few mouse-clicks.

Start Word and Enter Some Text

1 If Word is already running and you've entered some text, click File to display Backstage view and choose New. Double-click Blank Document to create a new blank document. If Word isn't running, start it by clicking the Windows Start button and choosing Microsoft Word 2010.

(continued on next page)

Tip

When would you want to use paragraph marks? If having the right number of spaces between words and sentences is important, or if you want to see what kinds of formatting codes are being used "behind the scenes" in your document, click the Show/Hide tool in the Paragraph group (it resembles a paragraph mark) to display paragraph marks.

Tip

To better see the formatting marks, as well as your text, use the Zoom Control at the bottom of the window to increase the magnification, as shown here.

Start Word and Enter Some Text *(continued)*

- If you want to show paragraph marks and other formatting marks such as spaces and tabs, click the Show/Hide tool in the Paragraph group of the Home tab. Click the button again if you want to hide the marks.

- Type your text. When you reach the end of a line, continue typing. Word automatically moves, or *wraps*, your words to the next line.

- Press Enter to start a new paragraph.

- Click Save on the Quick Access Toolbar, enter a name for the file, and click Save. To quickly save the document while you're working, press Ctrl+S.

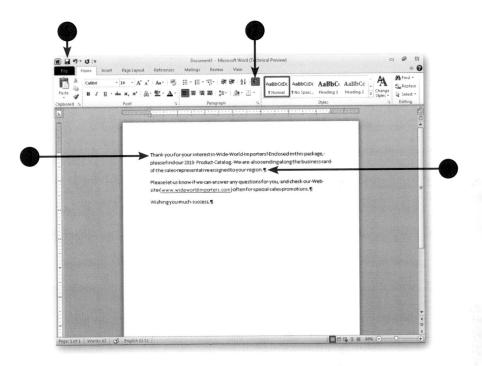

Tip

Just want a few paragraphs to play with? Type "=rand()" to have Word enter some random text for you to use. If you'd rather see Latin text, use "=lorem()" instead.

Composing Different Types of Documents

Word 2010 offers dozens of templates you can use to quickly create all kinds of documents and gives you access to Office Online, where you can download even more. When you start a new document based on a template, the document already contains its own design elements, such as tables, borders, columns, and more. The template's predefined styles are set to ensure that all your paragraphs look good together. All templates are completely customizable, which means that you can easily change them to suit your own needs. The templates you'll find online also come from a variety of sources, so you might discover substantial differences both in design and in function as you experiment and modify the templates you find.

Start the Document

1 Click File to display Backstage view, and choose New. The New window displays a set of template categories available from Office.com.

2 Click the category of the templates you want to view by performing one of the following actions:

- Click Recent Templates to see the templates that you've used recently, and double-click the one you want to use.

- Click Sample Templates to view templates Word 2010 offers as samples, including examples of letters, reports, resumes, and more. Double-click one to open a new file based on the template.

(continued on next page)

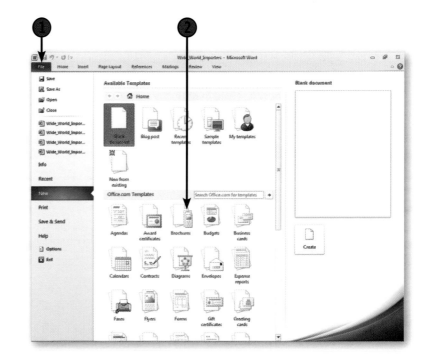

Start the Document *(continued)*

- Click My Templates to display the New dialog box and your custom templates. Double-click a template to create a document.

- In the Office.com area, click a folder to open it and display the templates in that category that are available for download, and double-click the one you want to use.

- Click New From Existing to display the Open dialog box so that you can open an existing document as a template.

3 In the Template category, click the template you want to view.

4 Click Download to open the new document. If you previously clicked Sample Templates to choose a category, click Create.

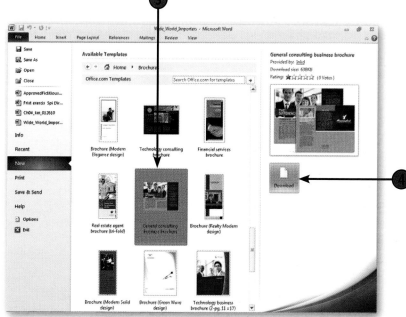

Tip

The new document you create is based on the template you selected; it is not actually the template file itself. In the new document, replace any placeholder text with your own text, and add any other elements you want your document to include.

Word's Views

Word 2010 gives you several ways to view your document as you work on it. Most Word users develop a preference for one view or another, but each view offers a different perspective to help you accomplish the task at hand. To change the view, you can click the View tab and choose the view you want from the Document Views group or click any of the five view buttons on the far right side of the status bar at the bottom of the Word 2010 window.

Print Layout View

Print Layout view is the standard working view for print documents, and this is the view you see by default when you begin working in Word. Print Layout view shows you how your document will look when it's printed—the page and line breaks, the placement of pictures, the way text wraps around pictures or other items, the arrangement of columns, the distance of the text from the edge of the page, and so on.

Full Screen Reading View

Full Screen Reading view makes it easy to read and comment on documents on your screen. This view gives you the maximum space on-screen so that you can scan the text easily by hiding some of the window elements—for example, the tabs, the ribbon, and the status bar are hidden from view.

Web Layout View

Web Layout view enables you to see how your documents will look if they are posted online as Web pages. All the elements of your page are displayed, but the font size, line length, and page length are adjusted to fit the window, just as they are on many Web pages.

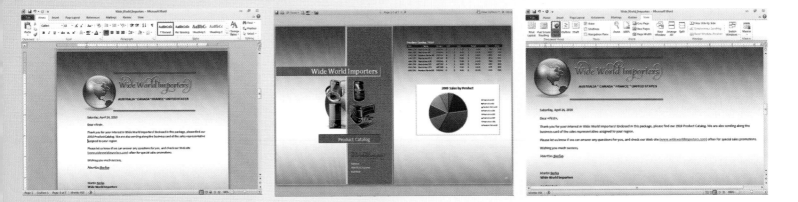

Outline View

Outline view shows your document as an outline, with the paragraph formatting defining the levels of the outline. By default, Word's standard heading styles have corresponding outline levels—Heading 1 is level one, Heading 2 is level two, and so on—and other paragraph styles, such as Normal, are treated as regular text. You can use Outline view to organize your topics before you start writing, or you can use it to reorganize an existing document.

Draft View

Draft view is designed to make it as easy as possible for you to enter and edit text. In earlier versions of Word (pre-2007), Draft view was called Normal view, and the idea was to provide a long continuous flow of text so that you could simply focus on the content and add all the bells and whistles—including headers and footers—later.

Print Preview

Print preview is designed to show you just how your document will look when you print it. Now available as part of the print process in Backstage view, print preview gives you a close-up view, one page at a time, or two or more pages at once. Use print preview to make sure your document's layout is exactly the way you want before you go ahead and print it. Unlike Word's other views, you switch to this view by clicking File on the ribbon and clicking Print. You can then preview, set print options, and print the document, all from the same view.

Reading a Document

To help you cut down on the amount of paper that piles up in the so-called "paperless office," Word's new Full Screen Reading view is designed to make it simple and pleasant to read documents without printing them. If you like it, that's great—you'll save some trees, as well as some clutter.

Read

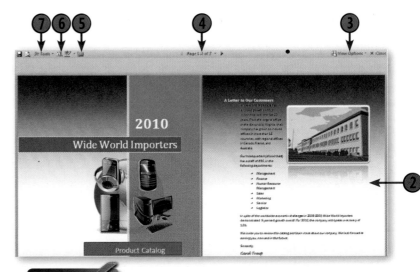

1. If you're not already in Full Screen Reading view, click the Full Screen Reading button on the status bar to display your document for easy reading.

2. Move the mouse to the left or right edge of the screen until the cursor turns into a little hand, or press Page Up or Page Down to move to the previous or next page or pair of pages.

3. Click the View Options button, and specify how you want to view the page or pages, whether you want to do some typing in the document, and whether you want tracked changes and comments to be shown.

4. Click the Page button to go to a specific page, location, or heading, or to display the Document Map or the Thumbnails pane.

5. Click Insert Comment if you want to add a comment to the document you're reading.

6. Click Mini Translator to translate text you select in the document.

7. Click Tools to display additional choices for the ways you can work with the file in Full Screen Reading view.

8. When you've finished, press the Esc key or click the Close button to exit Full Screen Reading view.

Tip Word 2010 is set to display any Word attachments in your e-mail in Full Screen Reading view. If you prefer not to use this view, you can turn it off from the Document Views gallery.

Tip The Ink Comment choice will appear in your Tools menu in Full Screen Reading view only if you have a Tablet PC or a drawing tablet installed that enables you to use ink features in Word 2010.

Try This! Add a comment to a document you're viewing in Full Screen Reading view by clicking the View tab and clicking Full Screen Reading in the Document Views group. Click to position the cursor in the document and then click Insert Comment. A comment box appears on the page, anchored to the cursor position. Type your comment and then click outside the comment to add it to the document.

Editing Text

Whether you're creating a newsletter for your neighborhood association, a financial report, or your master's thesis, it's likely that you're going to need to go back into your document and do some editing. Word 2010 makes editing as easy as possible and gives you a variety of ways to do it. To edit existing content, you simply select it and make your changes, or if you prefer, you can type over the existing text to replace it.

Select and Modify Text

1. Click at the beginning of the text you want to delete.

2. Drag the mouse over all the text to select it, and then release the mouse button.

3. Press the Delete key. The selected text is deleted.

4. Select some text that you want to replace with new typing.

5. Type the new text. The selected text is automatically deleted and replaced by the new typing.

6. Click Save.

Thank you for your interest in Wide World Importers! Enclosed in this package, please find our 2010 Product Catalog. We are also sending along the business card of the sales representative assigned to your region. Different representatives are available in each of five regions.

Please let us know if we can answer any questions for you, and be sure to check our Web site (www.wideworldimporters.com) often for special sales promotions.

Thank you for your interest in Wide World Importers! Enclosed in this package, please find our 2010 Product Catalog. We are also sending along the business card of the sales representative assigned to your region.

Please let us know if we can answer any questions for you, and be sure to check our Web site (www.wideworldimporters.com) often for special sales promotions.

Thank you for your interest in Wide World Importers! Enclosed in this package, please find our 2010 Product Catalog. We are also sending along the business card of the sales representative assigned to your region.

Please let us know if we can answer any questions for you, and be sure to check our Web site (www.wideworldimporters.com) often for special sales promotions.

Thank you for your interest in Wide World Importers! Enclosed in this package, please find our 2010 Product Catalog. We are also sending along the business card of the sales representative assigned to your region.

Please let us know if we can answer any questions for you, visit our Web site (www.wideworldimporters.com) often for special sales promotions.

Tip

If you prefer to type over text without selecting it, use Overtype mode. To turn it on, click the File tab to display Backstage view and click Options. On the Advanced tab, select the Use The Insert Key To Control Overtype Mode option. Click OK, and then press the Insert key to turn on Overtype mode; press Insert again to turn off overtyping.

Tip

If you accidentally delete some text, immediately click the Undo button on the Quick Access Toolbar to restore the deleted text.

Discovering the Many Ways to Work with Text

Word offers you a variety of ways to do most things. You might, for example, be able to use a tool, a menu item, a keyboard shortcut, a task pane, or a mouse-click to accomplish the same result. Why are there so many choices? Well, one reason is that we all work differently. Given several choices, we usually do some experimenting, find the way that works best for us and that we're most comfortable with, and then stick with it. Another reason is that certain methods work best in certain situations.

Text-Selection Methods

To select	Use this method
Characters in a word	Drag the mouse over the characters.
A word	Double-click the word.
Several words	Drag the mouse over the words.
A sentence	Hold down the Ctrl key and click anywhere in the sentence.
A line of text	Move the pointer to the far left of the window, and click when you see a right-pointing arrow.
A paragraph	Move the pointer to the far left of the window, and double-click when you see a right-pointing arrow.
A long passage	Click at the beginning of the passage, and then hold down the Shift key and click at the end of the passage.
Noncontiguous blocks of text	Drag the mouse to select the first block. Hold down the Ctrl key and drag the mouse to select the second block.
A vertical block of text	Click at the top-left corner of the text block. Hold down the Alt key and drag the mouse over the text block.
The entire document	Press Ctrl+A.

Copying and Moving Methods

To do this	Use this method after you've selected the text
Move a short distance	Drag the selection to the new location.
Copy a short distance	Hold down the Ctrl key, drag the selection to the new location, and release the Ctrl key.
Move a long distance or to a different document or program	Click the Cut tool, click at the new location, and click the Paste tool and choose the Paste Option, or right-click at the new location and click the Paste Option you want to apply. Alternately, you can press Ctrl+X, click at the new location, and press Ctrl+V.
Copy a long distance or to a different document or program	Click the Copy tool, click at the new location, click Paste, and choose the Paste Option you want to apply. Or press Ctrl+C, click at the new location, and press Ctrl+V.
Copy several items and insert all of them in one place	Click the Copy tool, select the next item, click Copy tool again, and repeat to copy up to 24 items. Or hold down the Ctrl key, select multiple items, and then click Copy. Click at the new location, open the Office Clipboard, and then click the Paste All button.
Move a long or short distance	Press F2, click at the new location, and press Enter.
Copy a long or short distance	Press Shift+F2, click at the new location, and press Enter.

Tip ✓

When you use the F2 key or the Shift+F2 key combination, the selected material is stored in Word's short-term memory, where it's remembered only until you paste it into another location or execute any other Word activity.

Navigating Your Document

Word 2010 includes a great new feature called the Navigation Pane that enables you to search for and find just the content you're looking for in your document. The Navigation Pane makes it simple for you to search through your document by clicking headings, choosing pages, or entering words or phrases in a search box.

Using the Navigation Pane

① Click the View tab.

② Display the Navigation Pane by selecting the Navigation Pane check box in the Show group.

③ By default, the pane shows a list of headings in your document. Click the heading of the section you want to display.

④ Click the Pages tab. The pane shows thumbnail images of all the pages in your document. Scroll through the list, and click the page you want to see.

(continued on next page)

Tip

To limit the search to a specific part of a document, select that part of the document before you open the Find And Replace dialog box.

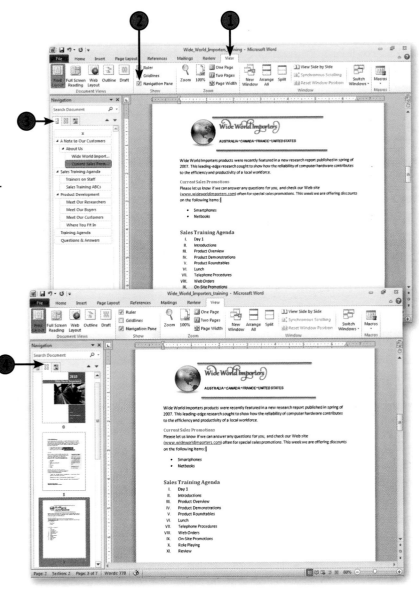

Using the Navigation Pane   (continued)

5 Click the Search Results tab. Type a word or phrase in the search box, and Word 2010 shows all occurrences of that text in the document. Click the text at the point in the document you want to display.

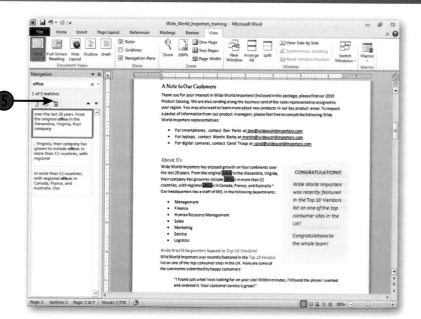

Search and Find Objects

Click the magnifying glass tool in the Search Document box to display a list of additional choices, as described in the following table.

Additional Search Choices

Choose	To Do This
Options	Displays the Find Options dialog box so that you can enter your preferences for the search operation
Find	Displays the Find tab of the Find And Replace dialog box so that you can enter Find choices
Replace	Displays the Replace tab of the Find And Replace dialog box so that you can enter what you want to find and replace
Go To	Displays the Go To tab of the Find And Replace dialog box so that you can move directly to a page or object you specify
Graphics	Moves to the next graphic in your document
Tables	Moves to the next table in your document
Equations	Finds the next equation in your document
Footnotes	Moves to the next footnote
Comments	Displays the next comment in your document

Replacing Text

When you need to replace a word or phrase with a different word or phrase in several places in your document, you can let Word do it for you automatically. It's a great way to use Word's speed and power to make quick work of those tedious document-wide changes.

Replace Text

- Display the Navigation Pane.
- Click the Search Document arrow to display the options list.
- Click Replace.

(continued on next page)

See Also

Read "Navigating Your Document" on pages 66–67 for information about broadening or narrowing a search.

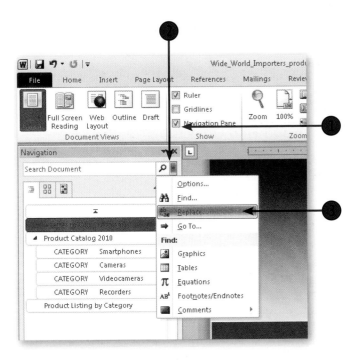

Replace Text *(continued)*

④ In the Find And Replace dialog box, type the text you want to find in the Find What text box.

⑤ Click More to display all the search options. After you click it, the dialog box displays more options and the button changes to Less.

⑥ To narrow the search, click Format and specify the formatting of the text you're searching for.

⑦ To replace nontext items, click Special and specify any element that's associated with the text.

⑧ Type the replacement text. Click the Format button to specify any formatting the replacement text should have. Use the Special button to specify a nontext element.

⑨ Click one of the following:

- Replace, to replace the found text and find the next instance of the search text

- Replace All, to replace all instances of the search text with the replacement text

- Find Next, to find the next instance of the search text without replacing it

⑩ Click Close when you've finished.

Tip

If you used the Replace All button and the results aren't quite what you expected, click the Undo button on the Quick Access toolbar. You can then try the replacement again—this time with more specific search parameters.

Correcting Your Spelling and Grammar

Today there is so much competition for the documents we read (or not) that it's important to make sure your documents are the best they can be. Word 2010 includes features that help you ensure that your spelling is correct, your words are used correctly, and your grammar would make even your sixth-grade English teacher smile. Word 2010 points out potential spelling, usage, or grammar problems by displaying helpful little green squiggles under a word or phrase. When you see a squiggle, click it; then you can choose what you want to do to correct the mistake—if it really is a mistake.

Correct a Spelling Error

① Right-click a red squiggle to see one or more suggestions for correcting the error.

② Click the suggestion you want to use.

③ If you believe that what you have isn't an error but is something that Word doesn't recognize, click Ignore to have Word ignore this one instance, click Ignore All to have Word ignore the word throughout this document, or click Add To Dictionary to have Word ignore the word throughout all your documents.

Correct a Contextual Spelling Error

① Right-click a blue squiggle to see one or more suggestions for fixing improper word usage.

② Click the suggestion you want, or choose to ignore this error or this word throughout the document.

> **Tip**
>
> If Word didn't offer any suggestions when you right-clicked a squiggle, return to your document and try to correct the error yourself. If the squiggle remains, right-click it, and then see whether there are any suggestions.

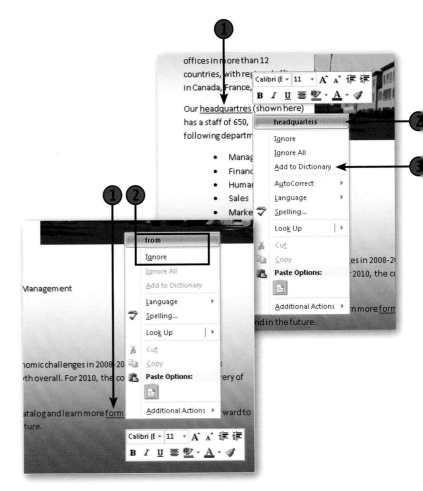

Correct the Grammar

 Right-click a green squiggle.

2 If the shortcut menu suggests alternative phrasing, click to use the alternative. If only a description of the problem is shown, click in the document and edit the text as suggested.

3 If you're sure your grammar is correct, click Ignore Once.

4 If you want to know why the text was marked, click About This Sentence for an explanation of the grammar rules involved.

Automatically Correct Your Misspellings

1 Right-click one of your own common misspellings, point to AutoCorrect on the shortcut menu, and choose the correct spelling from the list of suggestions.

2 Check your document, and observe that the correct spelling has replaced your misspelling.

3 Continue composing your document. Note that if the same misspelling occurs again, Word corrects it for you.

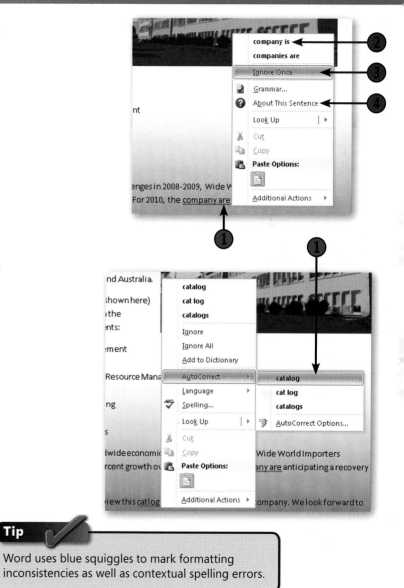

See Also

Read "Customizing the Spelling and Grammar Checkers" on page 400 for information about modifying the way Word checks your spelling and grammar, and "Customizing Your Spelling Dictionaries" on page 401 for information about using and editing custom dictionaries.

Tip

Word uses blue squiggles to mark formatting inconsistencies as well as contextual spelling errors.

Correcting Text Automatically

Are there some words that you always seem to misspell no matter how hard you try to remember the right spelling? To back you up, Word provides a useful feature called AutoCorrect that you can use to correct common misspellings of certain words. You can also customize the AutoCorrect feature to include your own common typing errors and misspellings, and you can make AutoCorrect work even harder for you by defining special AutoCorrect entries.

Add Entries

1. Click the File tab to display Backstage view.

2. Click Options.

(continued on next page)

Tip

To modify the way the AutoCorrect feature works, open the AutoCorrect dialog box, and clear or select check boxes to specify what you want AutoCorrect to do.

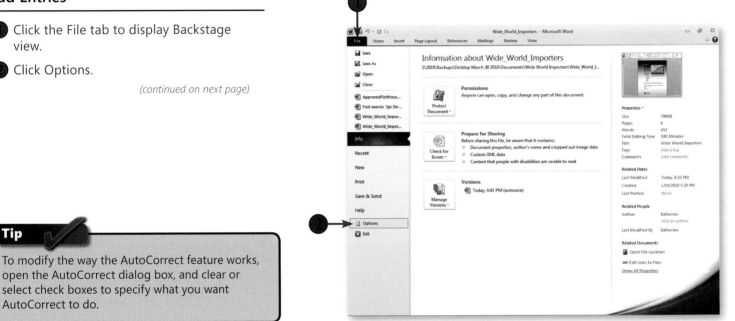

Add Entries *(continued)*

● Click the Proofing tab.

● Click the AutoCorrect Options button.

● On the AutoCorrect tab of the AutoCorrect dialog box, with the Replace Text As You Type check box selected, enter into the Replace text box the abbreviated or misspelled text that you often type. In the With text box, type the text that you want to replace the incorrect or abbreviated text you typed.

● Click Add.

● Add any other entries you want. When you've finished, click OK, and then click OK again to close the Word Options dialog box.

● In your Word document, type the text you entered in the Replace box, type a space, and make sure your corrected entry has been inserted.

Adding Page Numbers

We all know what a time-consuming hassle it is to try to put the unnumbered pages of a long document back in the right order after they've gone flying all over the place. Don't let this happen to you! Add page numbers easily to Word documents that are more than a few pages long.

Insert Page Numbers

1. On the Insert tab, click the Page Number tool in the Header & Footer group. On the list, point to the location where you want the page number to appear.

2. Click the page-numbering design you want in the gallery that appears.

3. If you want to change the numbering format or the way the pages are numbered in a multisection document, click Page Number again, and choose Format Page Numbers from the displayed choices.

(continued on next page)

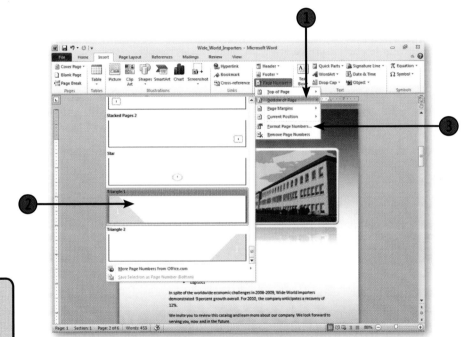

Tip

You can also add page numbers when you're working with a header or footer in Word. Click in the header or footer area, and the Header & Footer Tools Design tab becomes avaliable. Click Page Number in the Header & Footer group on the left end of the ribbon, and follow the steps on these two pages to add the page number as you want it to appear.

Insert Page Numbers   *(continued)*

4 In the Page Number Format dialog box, select the numbering format you want.

5 If you have more than one section in your document, specify whether you want the page numbering to be continuous or to restart at the beginning of each section.

6 Click OK.

7 If you don't like the way the page number looks or where it's positioned, click Page Number, choose Remove Page Numbers, and then choose a different numbering format.

See Also

Read "Change the Header and Footer" on page 115 for information about changing the appearance of all items in running headers and footers.

Co-Authoring in Word 2010

Now in Word 2010, you can share your documents and review and edit content at the same time others are working in the file. Once you save the file to your Microsoft SharePoint Workspace 2010 or your Windows Live SkyDrive account, users who have the permissions they need to access the file will be able to open, edit, and save the file, as well as leave notes for you or contact you directly while you're working on the file. While you're editing together, you can contact your co-authors through e-mail, instant messaging, and more, enabling you to ask and answer questions in real time while you work.

Co-Authoring a Document

1. Open the document you want to share using Windows Live SkyDrive or SharePoint Workspace where the file is stored.

2. When a co-author logs in to the file, Word 2010 notifies you.

3. Review edits made by your co-author.

4. Edit and save the document normally. Your changes will be visible to your co-authors as well.

> **Tip** ✓
>
> If you are using Office 2010 Professional Plus, SharePoint Workspace 2010 is included as part of your Office version. Other users can use Windows Live Sky-Drive (available at *www.skydrive.live.com*) to create an account for file sharing and co-authoring in Word 2010.

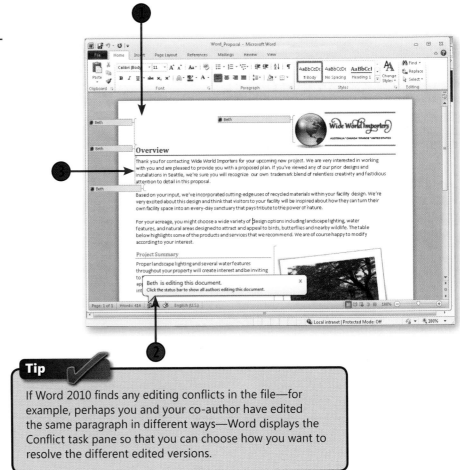

> **Tip** ✓
>
> If Word 2010 finds any editing conflicts in the file—for example, perhaps you and your co-author have edited the same paragraph in different ways—Word displays the Conflict task pane so that you can choose how you want to resolve the different edited versions.

Connecting with a Co-Author

① Click the status bar to display the list of authors currently working on the document.

② Review the presence indicator to make sure the co-author you want to contact is available.

③ Click the co-author's name to display the contact card.

④ Click the tool representing the type of contact you want to make.

⑤ Type your information, and press Enter or click Send.

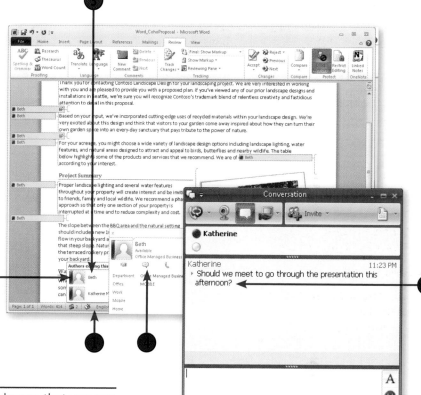

Ways to Contact a Co-Author

Tool	Name	Description
	E-mail	Opens a blank message window so that you can send your co-author an e-mail message.
	Instant Message	If your co-author's status is set to Available, you can start an instant message conversation.
	Voice Call	You can click to choose the phone number for your co-author and dial the number.
	Contact Options	You can choose other ways of contacting your co-author, which might include having a video call, setting up a meeting, visiting a shared site, or controlling contact options.

Tip ✓

The options available to you in your instant messaging program depend on the communications services you are running. Microsoft Communicator 2010 enables you to make voice calls, video calls, and more. Not all instant messaging clients support all communications features, however.

Marking and Reviewing Changes in a Document

When you have a document that needs to be reviewed or changed and you want to mark the changes you or others make, you can use the Track Changes feature in Word 2010. When this feature is turned on, additions, deletions, moves, and even formatting changes are marked so that you can see them easily. You can also add comments that appear in the margins of the document. When you're reviewing the edited document, you can accept or reject any change or comment, view the changes made by individual reviewers, and even view the document as it was before the changes were made. You can also view the document as it would look if you accepted all the changes.

Review a Document

 Open the document to be reviewed.

 On the Review tab, in the Tracking group, click Track Changes.

③ Click Final Showing Markup so that you can see your changes.

④ Click Reviewing to display changes in a pane on the left side or at the bottom of the window.

⑤ Edit the content as usual.

⑥ To insert a comment, click New Comment in the Comments group and type your comment.

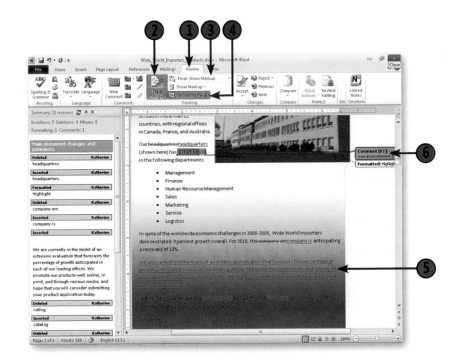

Review Changes

1 Open a document that has been reviewed and edited. If it's marked as Read-Only, save it using a different name.

2 On the Review tab, click the Track Changes button, if it's selected, to turn off marking changes.

3 Switch to Final Showing Markup view if it isn't already selected.

4 Click Show Markup, and specify the types of changes you want to be displayed. If you don't want to see the markup from every reviewer, specify which reviewers' changes you do want to see.

5 Choose to accept, reject, or locate each change in the document. To accept all the changes, click the down arrow on the Accept button and choose Accept All Changes In Document from the drop-down menu. To reject all changes, click the down arrow on the Reject button, and choose Reject All Changes In Document.

6 When you've finished, switch the view to Final, review the document for any errors, and then save and close it.

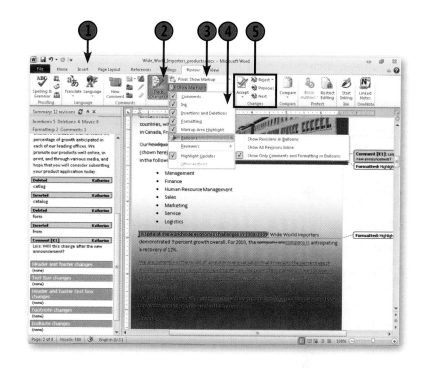

Tip

Note that paragraphs you've moved are indicated by a double underline, and that their original location is indicated by a double strikethrough.

Tip

To compare two versions of the same document and mark the changes, click the Compare button on the Review tab, and choose Compare from the drop-down menu. To combine separate files that contain marked changes by different reviewers, click the Compare button, and choose Combine from the drop-down menu.

Comparing Documents Side by Side

When you want to look at two documents at the same time to compare their content, Word will place the documents in adjacent windows. This is helpful when you want to check two versions of a document and compare terminology, format, or overall design. If you like, you can have Word 2010 scroll through both documents at the same time, or you can manually choose how to navigate through the documents.

View the Documents

1. Open the two documents you want to view and compare.

2. In one document, click the View tab.

3. Click the View Side By Side tool.

4. If a dialog box appears and asks you which documents you want to view, double-click the other document you want to view, and click OK.

5. If you don't want the documents to scroll together, in the Window group of the View tab, click the View Side By Side tool again to expand the window section (if it's collapsed) and the Synchronous Scrolling button to turn off the scrolling. Click Synchronous Scrolling again to resume the coordinated scrolling.

6. Scroll through the documents. When you've finished, click the View Side By Side tool to turn off that view.

> **Tip**
>
> If the two windows don't start at the same part of the document when you scroll through them, turn off Synchronous Scrolling, scroll through one window until it displays the same top line as the other window, and then turn Synchronous Scrolling back on.

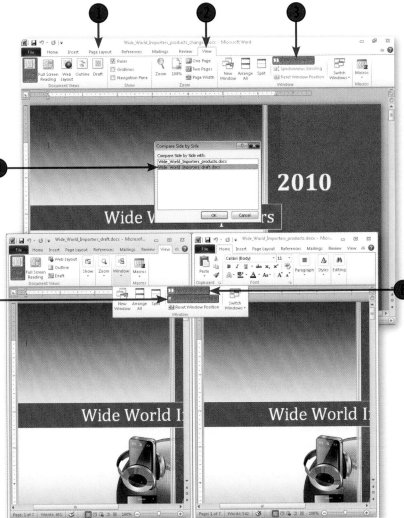

5

Formatting in Word

You don't have to look far to realize that documents today are prettier than they used to be. Today, we are used to seeing colorful documents with attractive layouts, color, photos, and more. We aren't particularly wowed by sophisticated designs today—chances are that someone created that complicated, multipage document on a desktop PC. Even if spending an afternoon formatting in Microsoft Word 2010 isn't your idea of a good time, you can easily create professional-looking, inviting letters, reports, memos, and newsletters by using many features Word offers to make the process as easy as possible. You'll find themes, styles, high-quality typography font support, colors, borders, shading, decorative lines, and other design elements that Word 2010 provides to help you create, design, and maintain consistency throughout the documents you produce at work, at school, or at play.

We'll cover a lot of topics in this section, including creating, formatting, and working with lists and tables; applying fonts and special typographic features; laying out your pages; and using automatic hyphenation to improve the overall look of the layout. We'll also look at setting up a long document, such as a book or report that you intend to have bound, dividing it into chapters or sections, and adding running heads; flowing text into columns like those in a newspaper or magazine; and wrapping text around a graphic for a polished, professional look.

Controlling the Look: Themes, Styles, and Fonts

Word 2010 offers you a comprehensive set of powerful tools that make it simple for you to create professional-looking documents you can access easily and share with others all over the globe. Word's tools help you build great pages with a minimum of hassle by simplifying the design process and providing templates that help keep you from going overboard with design possibilities. Here are the tools you'll use to create effective and consistent designs:

- **Themes** Word 2010 themes are the master controllers of your page design. When you choose a theme for a document, with a single click you can set the fonts used for headlines and text; the color scheme for the entire document; and the effects for shapes, lines, charts, and more. The beauty of themes is that they coordinate many different elements of your design, and that means you can choose an entirely different look by selecting a different theme. When you choose a new theme, all elements—text, shapes, colors—that are connected to the theme change to reflect your new choice. You can change the whole theme or choose to change only individual elements—the default fonts, for example, or the color scheme or shading effects. Word comes with many built-in themes, but you can also design and save your own themes. See "Choosing a Theme for Your Document" on the facing page for information about choosing and changing themes.

- **Paragraph Styles** Paragraph styles in Word 2010 enable you to create a style to define how you want your paragraphs to look. You can make choices for the line spacing, indents, tab spacing, borders, shading, and more.

- **Character Styles** Character styles control the look of individual text characters—for example, boldfaced, italicized, or underlined emphasis; strikethrough, superscript, color, and shadow effects; and spacing between characters. If you specify the font as something other than the theme's default font, the character style can also define the font and font size. Otherwise, the font is determined by the chosen theme.

- **Linked Styles** Linked styles include settings that control both paragraph and character formatting—for example, in a single style you can define the paragraph layout, including the alignment and line spacing, as well as the appearance of the characters for the entire paragraph, including font, font size, emphasis, and effects. See the tip on page 84 for information about creating your own styles.

- **Table Styles** Table styles define the appearance of your tables—for example, the shading of rows or columns and the thickness of the gridlines. See "Formatting a Table" on page 102 for information about using table styles.

- **List Styles** You can set up list styles to determine the way you want bulleted and numbered lists to look. For example, you might want to choose the kind of bullet that is used and control how far the paragraph is indented. See "Formatting a List" on page 97 for information about using list styles.

- **Direct Formatting** You can use direct formatting to create customized words, paragraphs, or blocks of text. For example, you can apply bold formatting to a couple of words for emphasis, or select a quotation and add italics to it. For best results, use styles regularly to keep your formatting choices consistent, but you can use direct formatting to change the look of items you won't be repeating in your document. If you use direct formatting and later want to use the same formatting again, you can either use that formatting to create a new style or copy the formatting and apply it elsewhere by using the Format Painter tool. See "Copying Your Formatting" on page 95 for information about using the Format Painter tool.

Choosing a Theme for Your Document

Use themes to orchestrate the look of your entire document—from the headings to the fonts to the colors to the shadows. Once you choose a theme, your choices for fonts, colors, and styles are coordinated with that theme so that you get a professional look no matter what kind of formatting you apply.

Choose a Theme

1. On the Page Layout tab, click the Themes button to display the Themes gallery.

2. Do any of the following:

   - Point to a theme to preview that theme in your document.

   - Click the theme you want to use.

   - Click More Themes on Microsoft Office Online to find more themes online, and select the theme you want.

   - Click Browse For Themes to display the Choose Theme Or Themed Document dialog box. Select a theme or a document that contains the theme you want, and click Open.

   - Click Reset To Theme From Template to revert to the original theme for the document.

3. Use the tools on the Home, Insert, and Page Layout tabs as you normally would, selecting from the theme fonts, colors, and spacing options you want to apply to your text.

Tip

If you don't see a preview of the changes when you point to different themes, click File to display Backstage view and choose Options. In the General tab, make sure a check mark appears in the Enable Live Preview check box. If the box is blank, click the check box to add the check mark. Click OK.

Formatting Text with Styles

Even short informal notes deserve a little formatting. You might choose a new font for the boring, old Times Roman. Maybe you'll use a different color. Or perhaps you'll go all out for your document and apply font, color, spacing, and alignment options as you create a new format. Word makes it easy for you to quickly add formatting to selected text or set all the formatting for the paragraphs to give your documents a consistent and professional look. You can apply formatting whenever you want—before you type, while you're typing, or after you've typed all your text.

Apply a Quick Paragraph Style

1. Click in the paragraph that you want to format or select multiple paragraphs to which you want to apply the same formatting.

2. On the Home tab, point to a style to preview it. Click the style if you want to use it.

Apply Character Formatting Styles

1. Select the text you want to format.

2. On the Home tab, point to any style that isn't a paragraph style—that is, one that doesn't have a small paragraph mark (¶) at the left of its name—to preview it. Click the style if you want to use it.

Tip

To create a custom style, format your text or paragraph the way you want it, and then select the text you just formatted. On the Home tab, click the More button in the lower right corner of the Styles gallery, and click Save Selection As A New Quick Style. In the Create New Style From Formatting dialog box that appears, type a descriptive name for the style, and click OK. Presto! You've created your own style.

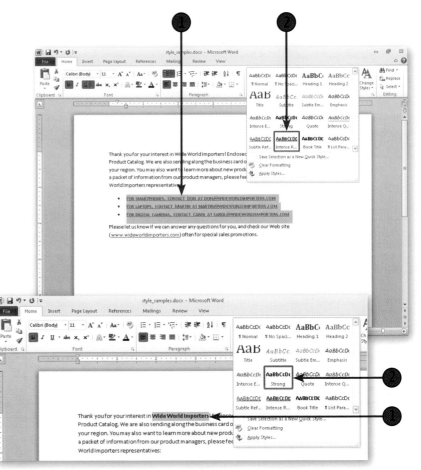

Choosing Styles from the Styles Window

The styles you see in the Styles gallery in the Home tab are likely only a portion of the total number of styles available with your document. You can display the whole list of styles available to you—and choose from the displayed list of Quick Styles—by working with the Styles pane.

View Your Styles

1. On the Home tab, click the Show The Styles Window button at the bottom-right corner of the Styles group.

2. Select the Show Preview check box at the bottom of the Styles list if it isn't already selected.

3. Click in a paragraph, or select the text, paragraphs, or table cells to which you want to apply the same formatting.

4. In the Styles list, click the style you want to apply.

5. If the style you want isn't listed, click Options, and, in the Style Pane Options dialog box, under Select Styles To Show, click All Styles, click OK, and then click the style you want.

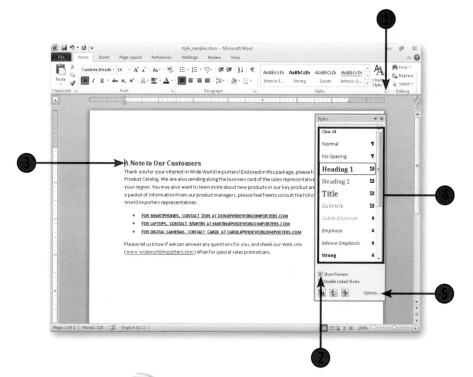

Try This!

To find styles quickly, open the Quick Styles gallery, and click Apply Styles to display the Apply Styles window. Click in a paragraph, or select the text you want to format. Click the Apply Styles window, and start typing the name of the style you want. Press Enter when the name of the style you want is displayed.

Changing Character Fonts

The font you choose for your document greatly influences the overall tone and effect of the design you create. An open font may communicate a relaxed, easy-to-read style. A small, dark font may appear more intense or business-like. Word 2010 enables you to choose fonts easily—and change them as you like—throughout your document. What's more, you can take advantage of high-end typographic features available with some OpenType fonts, which gives you an even greater number of ways to display and fine-tune the fonts in your document.

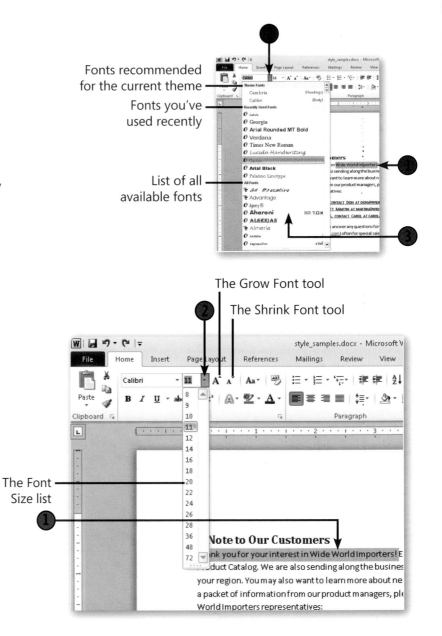

Fonts recommended for the current theme

Fonts you've used recently

List of all available fonts

The Grow Font tool

The Shrink Font tool

The Font Size list

Change the Font

1. Select the text whose font you want to change.

2. On the Home tab, click the Font list down arrow.

3. Click the font you want to use.

Change the Font Size

1. Select the text whose font size you want to change.

2. On the Home tab, do any of the following:

   - Click the Font Size down arrow, and select a font size from the drop-down list that appears.

   - Click the Font Size list, and type the font size you want.

   - Click the Grow Font button or the Shrink Font button to increase or decrease the font size.

Applying Stylistic Sets

1 Open the document in which you want to use the stylistic sets.

2 Select the text you want to change.

3 Click the dialog launcher in the lower right corner of the Font group.

4 In the Font dialog box, click the Advanced tab.

5 Click the Ligatures arrow and choose Standard Only.

6 Click the Stylistic Sets arrow and choose a set. Notice that the Preview window shows the changes the stylistic set will make for your selected text.

7 Click OK to save your changes.

Tip

Not all fonts can support OpenType features in Word 2010. Gabriola is one font you can use to experiment with different stylistic sets and number styles.

Setting Paragraph Alignment

The way you align the paragraphs in your document influences the way the reader's eye is drawn down the page. A centered paragraph communicates something that stands out, like a heading, an introductory paragraph, or a special product announcement. A right-aligned paragraph is usually a special element, offering a caption or a note. Left-aligned text is a typical alignment for print and Web documents. You can experiment with the various alignments to achieve just the right look for the way you'll be using that particular paragraph. With Word 2010, you can adjust the alignment of an individual paragraph, several paragraphs, or all your paragraphs with a single setting.

Set the Alignment

1. Click in a paragraph, or select all the paragraphs whose alignment you want to set.

2. On the Home tab, click any of the following:

   - The Align Text Left button, to align the paragraph with the left margin or left indent, creating a ragged right edge

   - The Center button, to center each line of the paragraph, creating both a ragged left edge and a ragged right edge

   - The Align Text Right button, to align the paragraph with the right margin or right indent, creating a ragged left edge

   - The Justify button, to align the paragraph with both the left margin or left indent and the right margin or right indent by adding any necessary space between words

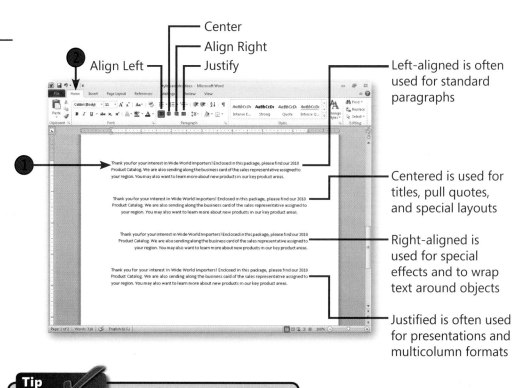

Center

Align Right

Align Left — Justify

Left-aligned is often used for standard paragraphs

Centered is used for titles, pull quotes, and special layouts

Right-aligned is used for special effects and to wrap text around objects

Justified is often used for presentations and multicolumn formats

Tip

Consider using a style instead of direct formatting to ensure consistency in your document if you're going to use this formatting more than once.

Adjusting Paragraph Line Spacing

The spacing of the lines of text in your paragraph help control the readability of your text. This spacing is known as *leading* (pronounced "ledding"), and it is something you can change in Word 2010. Too little space makes the lines of text looked squashed together and difficult to read; too much space also creates a sense of tension for the reader, who has to make the visual jump from line to line in your document. Creating just the right spacing for your paragraphs helps readers read at their ease and also draws the reader's eye from one line to the next.

Set the Line Spacing Within a Paragraph

1. Click in a paragraph, or select all the paragraphs in which you want to change the line spacing.

2. In the Paragraph group of the Home tab, click the Line And Paragraph Spacing tool.

3. Select the line spacing you want.

4. Click to set your own spacing preference.

5. On the Indents And Spacing tab of the Paragraph dialog box, select the spacing you want from the Line Spacing drop-down list:

   - Exactly creates a specified space between lines regardless of the font size used.

   - At Least creates a minimum space between lines, which can increase if you use large font sizes.

   - Multiple specifies how many lines of space you want between the lines of text.

6. Use the arrows or type a value. For the Exactly and At Least settings, this is a distance measurement, usually in points; for Multiple, this is the number of lines of space. Click OK.

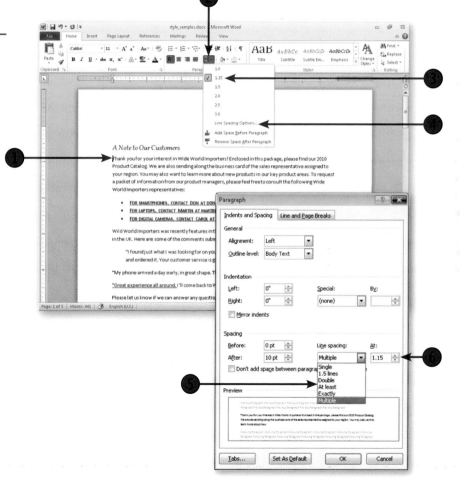

Setting Spacing Between Paragraphs

The amount of space you set between paragraphs in your document can make a big difference in the readability and overall look of your text. You can use one of Word 2010's preset spacing settings or customize the settings to fit your own document design.

Set the Line Spacing Between Paragraphs

1 Click in a paragraph, or select all the paragraphs where you want to set the spacing.

2 In the Paragraph group of the Home tab, click the Line And Paragraph Spacing tool.

3 Click Add Space Before Paragraph or Add Space After Paragraph.

4 If you want to customize the spacing, click Line Spacing Options to display the Paragraph dialog box.

(continued on next page)

Tip ✔

After you get the spacing just the way you want it, you can save the new settings by creating a style you can apply to other text you want to format in this same way. Select the text with the format you want to save, right-click your selection, and point to Style. Click Save Selection as a New Quick Style, type a name for the new style, and click OK. Now you'll be able to select your new format in the Styles gallery in the Home tab.

Set the Line Spacing Between Paragraphs *(continued)*

5 In the Before and After boxes, use the arrows or type a value for the space before (above) the first line of the paragraph and for the space after (below) the last line of the paragraph.

6 Select the check box in the Spacing area if you don't want to include space between paragraphs of the same style.

7 Click OK.

8 If you want to remove the space before or after the selected paragraph or paragraphs, click the Line And Paragraph Spacing tool again, and choose Remove Space Before Paragraph or Remove Space After Paragraph from the menu.

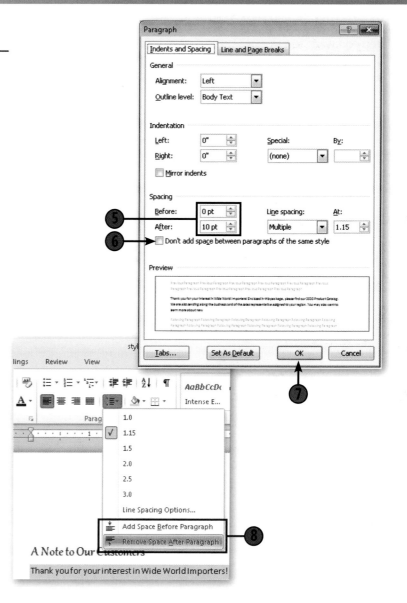

Caution

Note that the distance between two paragraphs is the sum of the space below the first paragraph and the space above the second paragraph. Keep this in mind so that you don't end up with a bigger space between paragraphs than the space you intended.

Tip

Some commonly used keyboard shortcuts are for line spacing and "space-before" spacing. Press Ctrl+1 for single spacing, Ctrl+5 for 1.5-line spacing, Ctrl+2 for double spacing, and Ctrl+0 (zero) for 1 line before the paragraph. Ctrl+0 is a toggle, so you can use it to change a paragraph from 1 line before to no lines before.

Indenting a Paragraph

When you want to call extra attention to a paragraph, you can use an indent to do that. An *indent* is the amount of space a paragraph or a first line is set off from the left margin, right margin, or both. You might want to indent the entire paragraph (moving it inward from the left and right margins), indent the paragraph to either the left or right side, or indent only the first line of the paragraph. You can also create a hanging indent to format bulleted items in a list.

Indent the Paragraph

● Click in a paragraph, or select all the paragraphs for which you want to set a first-line indent.

● On the Home tab, click the dialog launcher in the Paragraph group to display the Paragraph dialog box.

● Click in the Left box, and use the arrows or type a value for the distance you want the text indented from the left margin.

● Click in the Right box, and set the distance for the right indent from the right margin.

● Select the Mirror Indents check box if you want the left and right indents to switch depending on whether they're on odd-numbered or even-numbered pages. This option is designed for two-sided documents, so you'll notice that the Left label changes to Inside and the Right label changes to Outside.

● Click in the Special box, and select either of the following:

  • First Line, to indent the first line

  • Hanging, to indent all lines in the paragraph except the first line

● Click in the By box, and use the arrows or type a value to specify the size of the indent.

● Click OK.

Tip

Using the ruler, you can easily set the indents by dragging the Left Indent, First Line Indent, and Right Indent markers. You can also create a left indent in a paragraph by clicking the Home tab and then clicking the Increase Indent tool. When you set indents using the Paragraph dialog box, however, you can specify precise values for all the indents.

Formatting with Tabs

When you need to line up text at a certain point in your document, you can use a tab to do the trick. Setting a tab stop on the ruler causes the cursor to stop at that point when you press Tab in your document. You can set tab stops at any point on the horizontal ruler you want them to appear; what's more, you can choose to create left, center, right, or decimal tabs to line up the text differently, according to your needs. By default, Word 2010 includes tab stops every half inch along the width of the horizontal ruler. You can set new tabs by clicking on the ruler to add a tab or use the Tabs dialog box to do the trick.

Set Your Tabs

1. If the ruler isn't already displayed, click the View Ruler button at the top of the vertical scroll bar to display the ruler.

2. Click in a paragraph, or select all the paragraphs in which you want to set the tabs.

3. Click to select the type of tab you want. Each click selects a different type of tab or other ruler marker.

4. Click in the ruler where you want the tabs. If necessary, drag a tab stop to a new location to adjust it. Drag a tab stop off the ruler to delete that tab stop.

5. If you want to modify a tab stop or set a tab leader—a dotted, dashed, or solid line—double-click any tab stop on the ruler to display the Tabs dialog box.

6. Make the changes you want.

7. Click Set.

8. Make any changes you want to other tabs, and then click OK.

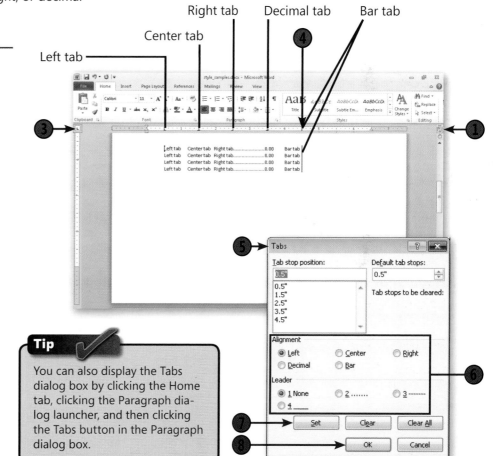

Tip

You can also display the Tabs dialog box by clicking the Home tab, clicking the Paragraph dialog launcher, and then clicking the Tabs button in the Paragraph dialog box.

Adding Emphasis and Special Formatting

In addition to the paragraph and character styles you'll apply to your text, in some situations you will want to add special formatting settings—like italics or bold—to selected text. Italics might show the reader that you're referring to the name of a book, for example; bold could draw attention to a particular element; strikethrough might show content that has been deleted, and so on. Word 2010 offers several special formatting options you can apply to your text.

Format the Text

1. Select the text you want to format.

2. On the Home tab, use any combination of the formatting buttons to add the formatting you want. Click a button a second time to remove that formatting.

3. If there isn't a button for the formatting you want, click the Font dialog launcher to display the Font dialog box.

4. Do any of the following:

   - Select a font color.

   - Select the type of underline, and the underline color you want.

   - Select any effect or combination of effects. Note, however, that there are some effects that can't be combined with others.

5. Click OK.

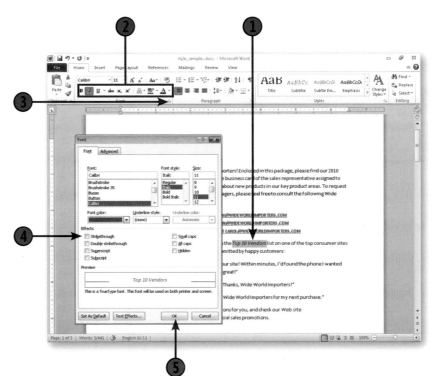

See Also

Read "Formatting Text with Styles" on page 84 for information about using Quick Styles to add emphasis.

Tip

If you're not sure what a formatting button does, point to it, and wait for the ScreenTip to appear. In addition to describing the button's function, ScreenTip shows you which keyboard shortcut you can use instead of clicking the button with the mouse.

Copying Your Formatting

You can select and copy formatting settings you like and then apply them to other text in your document by using the Format Painter tool. This feature enables you to apply a format consistently throughout your document without repeatedly choosing the formatting settings you want to use. You can use the Format Painter to apply the format one time or multiple times in the current document.

Copy the Formatting

① If paragraph marks aren't displayed in your text, click the Home tab, and then click the Show/Hide ¶ button.

② Select the text whose formatting you want to copy. If you want to copy paragraph formatting, make sure your selection includes the paragraph mark at the end of the paragraph.

③ On the Home tab, click the Format Painter button.

④ Drag the Format Painter over the selected text to apply the formatting, and then release the button.

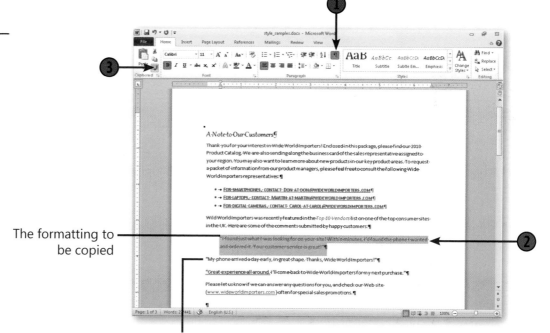

The formatting to be copied

Drag over text to apply the formatting

Tip ✓

To copy formatting to several locations, double-click the Format Painter button after you've selected your text. You can then copy the formatting to as many places as you want. When you've finished, press the Esc key or click the Format Painter button again.

Caution !

You can't copy multiple types of formatting at one time. For example, in a selection where the first word is formatted in bold and the next word is in italics, only the bold formatting will be applied when you use the Format Painter.

Tip ✓

To copy only paragraph formatting, select only the paragraph mark before you click the Format Painter button.

Creating a Bulleted or Numbered List

Bullets and numbered lists give you a great way to present information in clear, concise ways. Not only does Word 2010 add numbers or bullets automatically to your list, adding consistent spacing between the number or bullet and the text, but it keeps track of the order of items in your list so that if you move an entry, Word renumbers things to keep items in the correct order. You can also have the numbering skip paragraphs and you can even split a list by restarting a series at 1.

Create the List

1. Start typing the first line of your list. Make sure you're using the paragraph style you want for the list.

2. In the Paragraph group of the Home tab, click the Numbering button for a numbered list or the Bullets button for a bulleted list.

3. After completing the first line, press Enter to start the second list item.

4. When you've completed the list, press Enter twice to turn off the list formatting.

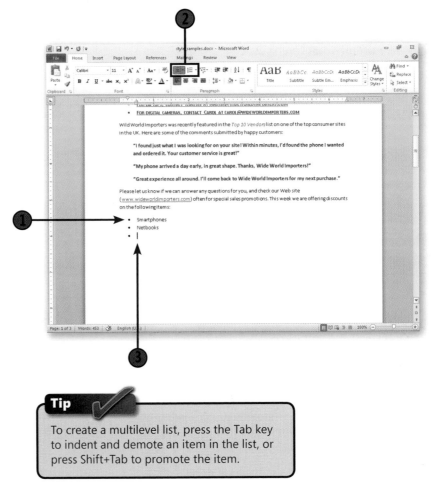

Tip ✓

In some circumstances, you may need to insert unnumbered paragraphs between the items in a numbered list. To restart numbering in the list after the unnumbered paragraph, right-click the first item in the continued list, and click either Restart Numbering or Continue Numbering.

Tip ✓

To create a multilevel list, press the Tab key to indent and demote an item in the list, or press Shift+Tab to promote the item.

Formatting a List

Using regular bullets or numbers may be fine for a fairly straightforward document, but what if you want to get a little fancy? You can use Word 2010's other numbering or bullet features—for example, applying the outline-numbering scheme—to make your lists a little more distinctive.

Change the Format

● Select your list.

● On the Home tab, click the down arrow at the right of either the Bullets, Numbering, or Multilevel List button to display the gallery for that button.

● Move the mouse pointer over the different bulleted or numbering schemes, and preview the way your list will look with each scheme.

● Click the bulleted or numbering scheme you want.

When you point to an item in the gallery...

...you see a live preview of the numbering scheme in your text

Tip

You can apply character styles to an existing list to customize its appearance. However, applying other styles might remove the bullets or the numbering. For example, if you apply the Strong character style to a list, the bullets or numbers will remain; if you apply the Normal paragraph style, the bullets or numbers will be removed.

See Also

Read "Formatting Text with Styles" on page 84 for information about applying different styles, and "Adding Emphasis and Special Formatting" on page 94 for information about applying special formatting.

Creating a Table from Scratch

If you tend to think of tables merely as containers for numbers, think again. Tables give you a great way to organize almost any kind of information, whether that includes text, numbers, pictures, equations, or shapes. There are many ways to create a table, but the easiest and most versatile way involves creating an empty, unformatted table that includes the number of rows and columns you want. You then can easily add content, format, and modify the table as you want it to appear.

Create the Table

1. Click in your document to position the cursor where you want the table to begin.

2. On the Insert tab, click the Table button. Move the mouse pointer to select the number of rows and columns you want in your table, and then click to insert the table.

3. Click in the first cell, and type your content.

4. Press Tab to move to the next cell, and add your content. (Press Enter only to start a new paragraph inside a table cell.) Continue pressing Tab and entering content to complete your table.

5. If you've reached the end of your table but you still need to enter more items, press Tab, and Word adds a new row.

Tip

To move to the previous cell, press Shift+Tab. To insert a tab inside a cell, press Ctrl+Tab.

See Also

Read "Creating a Table from Text" on page 100 for information about converting existing text in paragraphs into text in a table.

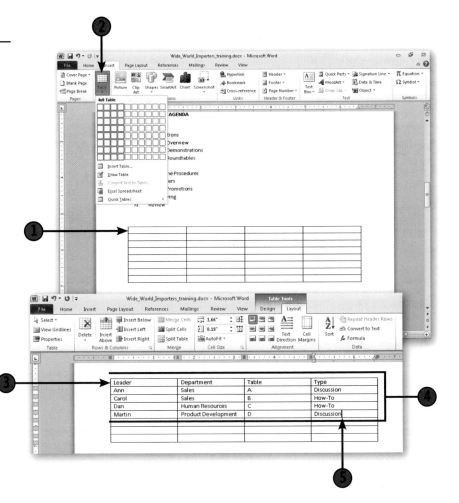

Using a Predesigned Table

Word 2010 includes many predesigned tables you can use to display your information. These tables are called Quick Tables, and you'll find them in the Tables gallery available in the Insert tab. You can choose from among calendar and traditional table styles. In the same way that you use templates for creating specialized types of documents, you can use a Quick Table to create a specialized type of table, complete with formatting and related material—a title or a caption, for example.

Choose a Table

1. Click in your document where you want the table to appear.

2. On the Insert tab, click the Table button, point to Quick Tables, and click the type of table you want.

3. Drag the mouse over the content of the table, and press the Delete key to remove the sample text.

4. Click in the top-left cell, and type your information. Use the Tab key to move through the cells, and type the rest of your content.

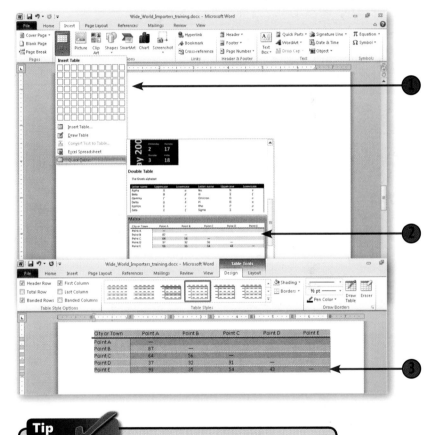

Tip

Once you've formatted the table the way you want it to appear, you can save the modified table as a Quick Table by selecting it, clicking Table on the Insert tab, clicking Quick Tables, and choosing Save Selection To Quick Tables Gallery.

See Also

Read "Formatting a Table" on page 102 for information about formatting a table.

Tip

After you've created the table, you can modify its appearance by applying table styles or other formatting.

Creating a Table from Text

Perhaps when you began entering content in your document you started out pressing Tab to line up the text, but now you want to change the text to a table. One benefit of using a table instead of tabs is that your format is protected when you change margin settings, choose a different font, or modify the page layout.

Convert the Text

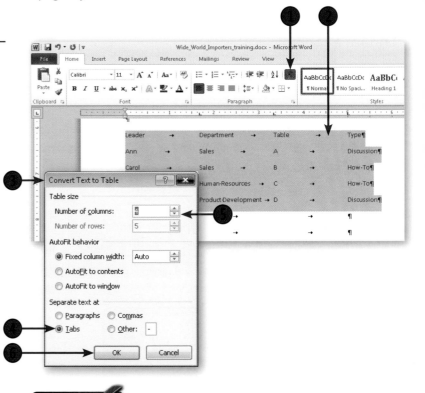

1. Click the Show/Hide tool in the Paragraph group of the Home tab to display spaces, tabs, and paragraph marks in your text. Examine the text to make sure that the information is correctly separated by tabs, commas, paragraphs, or other marks. Delete any extra tabs (more than one tab between columns, for example) even if this affects the current alignment.

2. Select all the text.

3. On the Insert tab, click the Table button, and click Convert Text To Table to display the Convert Text To Table dialog box.

4. Select the type of mark you've used to separate the columns of text.

5. Verify the number of columns you want. If there are more columns than you had in the text, repeat steps 1 through 4.

6. Click OK.

7. If you're not happy with the way the table looks, click the Undo button, and repeat steps 1 through 6.

Tip ✓

To convert text in a table to regular text, click in the table and, in the Data group of the Table Tools Layout tab, click Convert To Text.

Tip ✓

You can convert regular text to text in a table for many reasons other than just aligning columns. When the information is contained in a table, you can sort it, add or delete columns, and even do some math with it. To do some simple math in the table, click the Formula button on the Table Tools Layout tab.

Adding or Deleting Rows and Columns

Sometimes your tables grow larger than you expected them to, and you need to change the layout by adding rows and columns. You can easily add rows and columns anywhere in the table. Similarly, if you want to reduce the size of the table, you can remove the rows and columns you don't need.

Add a Row or Column to the Table

1. Click in the table next to where you want to add a row or column.

2. On the Table Tools Layout tab, choose what you want to add.

Try This!

Create a table with three columns and three rows. Click in the top-left cell. Drag the mouse to the right to select the first two cells. Click the Table Tools Layout tab, and then click Insert Left. With the new columns selected, click Insert Above. Note that the number of rows and columns that are inserted is based on the number of rows and columns in which cells were selected. Now try deleting rows and columns to revert to the size of the original table.

Delete a Row or Column from the Table

1. Click in a table cell that's in the row or column you want to delete.

2. On the Table Tools Layout tab, click Delete, and choose what you want to delete.

Caution

If you want to delete content from a row or column without deleting the row or column itself, make sure your selection doesn't extend above or below the table. If it does, you'll delete whatever part of the table is selected, as well as its content.

Tip

To delete the content of a row or column without deleting the row or column itself, select the row or column, and press the Delete key.

Tip

You can delete multiple rows or columns by selecting all elements you want to delete before you click Delete.

Formatting a Table

Once you get the basic data in the table, you may want to spruce it up a bit. A table gives you a great way to organize almost any kind of information, and you can use styles and formatting options to help readers understand what you want your data to convey. For example, you can use shading to delineate certain cell groupings, add borders to draw attention to particular cells, or use the formatting tools to vary the dimensions and alignment of the text and call attention to key elements in the table.

Format the Table

1 Click anywhere inside the table.

2 In the Table Styles group of the Table Tools Design tab, select a style for the table.

3 Select or clear the check boxes to turn the various formatting options on or off, as desired.

4 Select the cell or cells to which you want to add or from which you want to remove shading, click the Shading button, and select a color to add shading, or select No Color to remove shading.

5 Select the cell or cells to which you want to add or from which you want to remove borders, click the Borders button, and select the borders you want, or select No Borders to remove the borders.

6 Click the Layout tab, and use the tools to add or delete rows or columns, to set the dimensions of the rows and columns, and to set the text alignment, the text direction—that is, horizontal or vertical—and the margins.

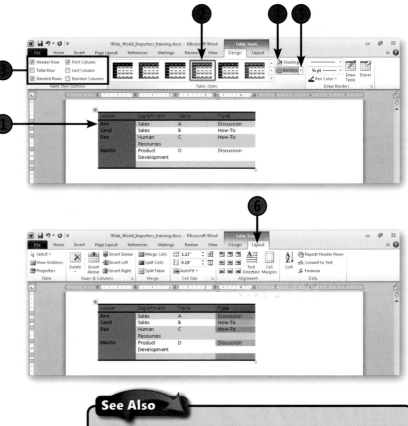

See Also

Read "Using a Predesigned Table" on page 99 for information about using a template to create a preformatted table that you can modify to fit your own document.

Improving the Layout with Hyphenation

When you left-align text in your document, the right margin remains uneven, which sometimes is referred to as having a *ragged right* edge. If you choose justified alignment for the text—which creates an even left and right margin for your content—Word might insert big white spaces between words, especially in columnar text. You can easily repair these common problems by having Word 2010 automatically hyphenate the document.

Set Automatic Hyphenation

1 On the Page Layout tab, click the Hyphenation tool, and choose Automatic from the list that appears.

2 If you don't like the way Word hyphenates, click the Hyphenation tool again, and choose Hyphenation Options from the gallery to display the Hyphenation dialog box.

3 Specify whether or not you want to allow hyphenation of capitalized words.

4 Specify the maximum distance between the end of the last word and the edge of the column.

5 Specify whether you want to limit the number of consecutive end-of-line hyphens. (In many books, including this one, a limit of two consecutive end-of-line hyphens is customary.)

6 Click OK.

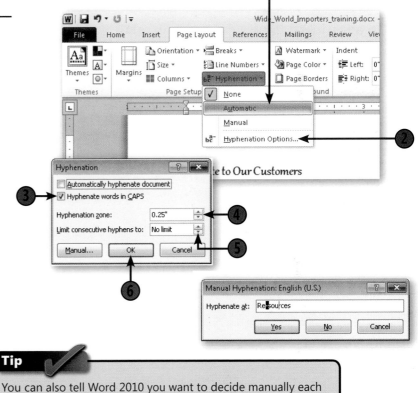

> **Tip** ✓
> If you want to use automatic hyphenation in a document but want a few specific paragraphs to remain unhyphenated, create and use a separate paragraph style (or use direct paragraph formatting) for those paragraphs. Make sure that you select the Don't Hyphenate check box on the Line And Page Breaks tab of the Paragraph dialog box.

> **Tip** ✓
> You can also tell Word 2010 you want to decide manually each time a hyphen is used by clicking the Manual button in the Hyphenation Options dialog box. At each hyphenated word in your document, Word will prompt you to decide whether you want to hyphenate the word or not.

Laying Out the Page

Not all documents you create will be printed—some you might post directly to your blog or share via e-mail with a friend or coworker. But when you create a document you plan to print, you need to tell Word how you want the page to be set up, indicating which paper size you're using, whether the page will be printed in landscape or portrait orientation, the size of the margins, and so on. If the document will be printed on both sides of the paper or is going to be bound, you can tell Word to accommodate those design elements as well. A good template will usually set up the specifics for you, but you might need to readjust the settings a bit to get everything exactly right.

Set Up a Standard Page

① On the Page Layout tab, click the Size button, and, in the gallery that appears, select the size of the paper you want. If that size isn't listed, click More Paper Sizes, and specify your paper size on the Paper tab of the Page Setup dialog box.

(continued on next page)

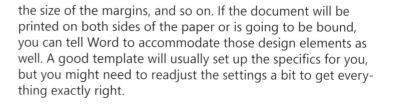
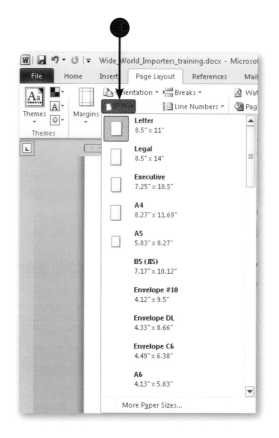

Set Up a Standard Page *(continued)*

● Click the Margins button, and select the margins you want. If that size isn't listed, click Custom Margins, and specify your margins on the Margins tab of the Page Setup dialog box.

● Click the Orientation button, and select the orientation you want for the page: Portrait (longer than wide) or Landscape (wider than long).

Tip

The *gutter* is the extra space you add to the margin where the document is to be bound so that the text won't be hidden by the binding.

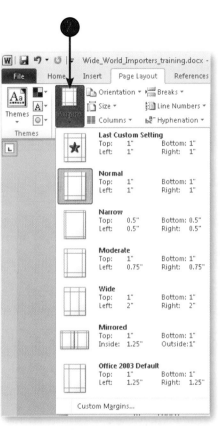

Creating Special Page Setups

Depending on the type of document you're creating, you may want to create margins that change according to whether you're viewing the front or back of the page. Likewise, preparing a document that will be bound means that you have a few additional margin issues to think about.

Set Up a Two-Sided Document

1. On the Page Layout tab, click the Margins button, and click Custom Margins to display the Page Setup dialog box.

2. On the Margins tab, click Mirror Margins in the Multiple Pages list.

3. Set the document's side margins using the Inside and Outside boxes. The Inside margin will be on the left side of odd-numbered (right-hand, or *recto*) pages and will be on the right side of even-numbered (left-hand, or *verso*) pages.

4. Click OK.

Tip

You can apply a gutter to any document layout. For a document that's set up for one-sided printing, you can specify the gutter location as the left side of the paper or the top of the paper. For a multiple-page layout, Word 2010 uses the default location of the gutter for the type of layout you choose. Use the preview to see the placement of the gutter.

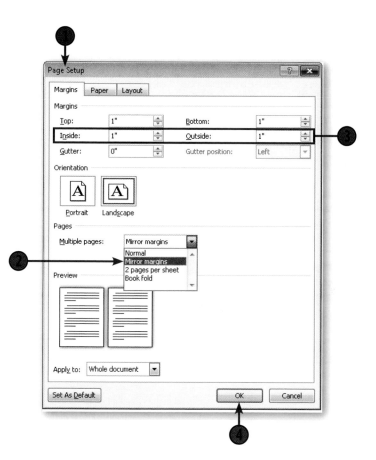

Set Up a Bound Document

1. Click the Page Layout dialog launcher to display the Page Setup dialog box.

2. On the Margins tab, specify a value for the gutter.

3. If the Multiple Pages list is set to Normal, specify whether the gutter (and therefore the binding) should be on the left side or at the top of the page. For other Multiple Pages settings, the gutter position is set automatically.

4. Click OK.

Tip

You can save your Page Setup settings to use as the default values for your document by clicking the Set As Default button in the lower left corner of the Page Setup dialog box.

Creating Headers and Footers

One characteristic of longer documents is that they are likely to need headers and footers that provide identifying information about the file. A header might include, for example, the name of the document (or a shortened version of the name), and a footer might include the author's name as well as the page and section numbers. Word 2010 enables you to add and work with headers and footers directly on your document page. You can create simple headers and footers by choosing the style you want from the gallery or customize the look to fit your own needs.

Create a Header and a Footer

- On the Insert tab, in the Header & Footer group, click the Header tool.

- Click the item in the gallery representing the Header style you'd like to add.

(continued on next page)

Tip

You aren't limited to the header and footer styles Word offers in the gallery; you can create your own by changing the font, color, and size; adding lines and pictures; and even inserting document properties like the title or creation date of the document.

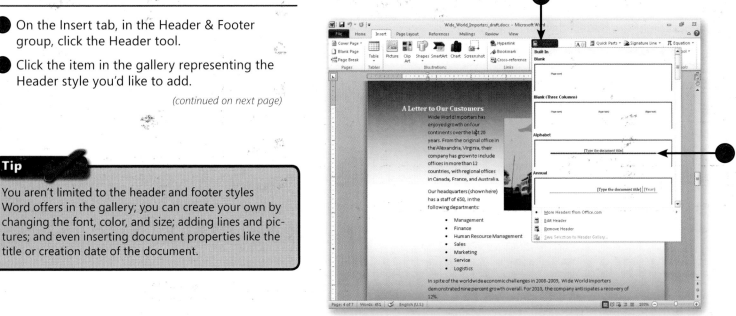

Create a Header and a Footer *(continued)*

3 If there are placeholders in the header, click the placeholder field or text, and select or type your information.

4 Click the Footer tool, select the gallery style you want to use, and enter the footer information.

5 Click the Close Header And Footer tool in the Header & Footer Tools Design tab to return to the main part of your document.

6 If you want to edit the contents of the header or footer, double-click it to activate the area, and make your changes.

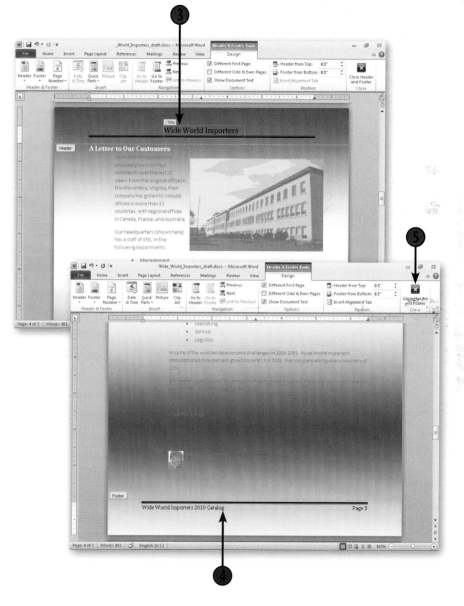

Changing Page Orientation Within a Document

Yes, it sounds complicated, but you can easily set up your document to include different orientations within a single file. Sometimes your document might call for regular text printed in portrait orientation, alongside a large table that prints in landscape orientation on a following page. By dividing the document into sections, you can set up each section with its own orientation.

Create a New Section

1 Click at the point in the document where you want to change the orientation.

2 Add a section by clicking the Breaks tool in the Page Setup group of the Page Layout tab and clicking Next Page. This adds a section break that begins a new section on the next page.

Tip ✓

You can add a number of different types of section breaks within Word when you need to control various elements like header and footer format, text flow, and content organization.

See Also

Read "Creating Sections" on pages 114–115 for information about creating new sections of different types within long documents.

Change the Page Orientation

 Select the part of the document whose page orientation you want to change.

② In the Page Setup group of the Page Layout tab, click Orientation.

③ Click the orientation you want.

④ Use the Zoom Control on the status bar to see your pages in detail, and verify that the layout is what you want.

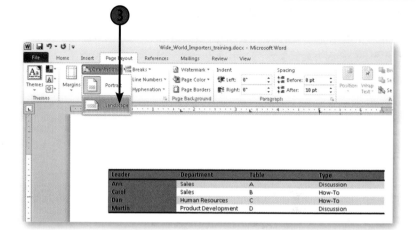

Tip

When you change the orientation of selected text, you're actually creating two new sections: one for the selected text and another for the text that follows the selection.

Caution

To return to the previous orientation, you need to create another section and choose the orientation you want to return to.

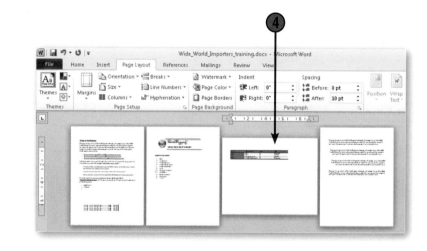

Flowing Text into Columns

Suppose that you're working on a newsletter and you decide that instead of having one long column of text you'd like to break the page up into multiple columns. You can do this easily in Word 2010. It's best to start with content you've already created, and then Word 2010 will reflow the text into the columns you choose.

Change the Number of Columns

① Set the page margins and orientation the way you want them to appear in your document.

② On the Home tab, click the Show/Hide ¶ tool if it isn't already turned on.

③ Select all the text that you want to flow into columns.

④ On the Page Layout tab, click the Columns tool, and click the number of columns you want to include. Word turns the text you selected into a separate section by inserting continuous section breaks before and after the selected text.

(continued on next page)

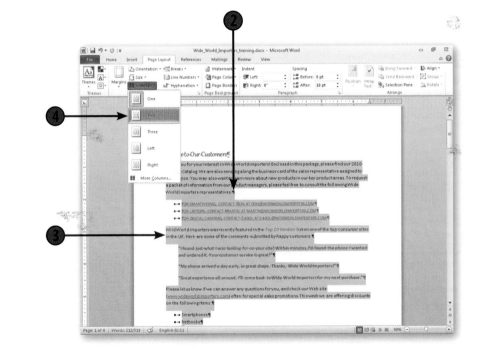

Change the Number of
Columns *(continued)*

- If you want to adjust the columns, click anywhere in the column section.

- Click the Columns tool again, and click More Columns in the Columns gallery to display the Columns dialog box.

- If you don't want even-width columns, clear the Equal Column Width check box, and then specify the width you want for each column.

- Select the Line Between check box if you want to display a vertical line centered between adjacent columns.

- Make sure the settings are applied only to the selected text, and then click OK.

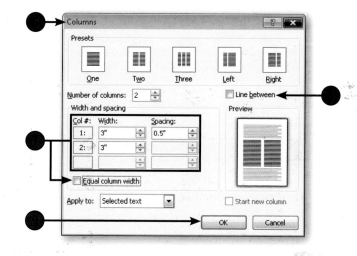

Tip

You can tell Word whether you want the columns to be applied to a specific section of text (for example, if you want to create a multicolumn list within a long document) or to be used throughout the document by choosing the setting you want in the Apply To field. If you want to create columns for just a portion of text, select the text first, display the Columns dialog box, enter your settings, and click the Apply To arrow. Choose Selected Text. You want the column changes to apply to the entire document, click Apply To and choose Whole Document; then click OK.

Creating Sections

If you are creating a long document, you will find it easier to work with and navigate if you create sections to help organize your content. Often in long documents you will use special features such as alternating headers or footers, page numbers, figure numbering, citations, and more. Getting these elements to behave correctly—showing the right numbering sequence, for example, or alternating on right and left pages as you'd like them to—requires that you add sections to help control the way Word works with the pages.

Start a New Section

① In the document you want to divide into different sections, place the insertion point at the beginning of the paragraph that starts a new section.

② In the Page Setup group of the Page Layout tab, click the Breaks tool, and click the Odd Page section-break option in the gallery. Word inserts the section break in front of the insertion point.

Tip ✓

In traditional print publications, a new section begins on an odd page, and if possible, sections or chapters end on an even page.

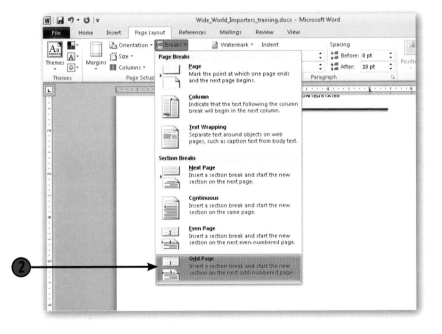

Change the Header and Footer

1. On the Insert tab, click the Header tool in the Header & Footer group, and click Edit Header in the gallery.

2. On the Header & Footer Tools Design tab, click the Link To Previous button to turn it off and to disconnect the header from the header in the previous section.

3. Replace the old header text, if any, with the text for your new running head.

4. Click the Go To Footer button to move to the footer, and repeat steps 2 and 3 for the footer. If the document is set for a different running head on the first page, or for different running heads on odd-numbered and even-numbered pages, repeat steps 2 and 3 for those running heads.

5. Click Close Header And Footer when you've finished.

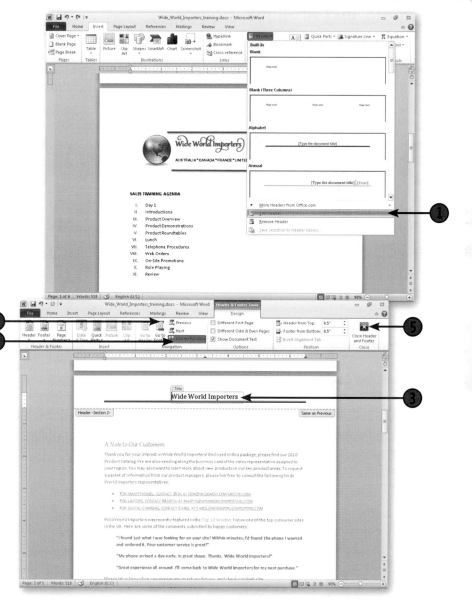

Wrapping Text Around a Graphic

Just a few years ago, making text flow around a picture in a document was a big deal. Today, Word 2010 can do it easily for you. Wrapping text around an item adds another level of polish to the professional look of your document. However, using one of the standard text-wrapping configurations doesn't always produce the desired effect. If this happens in your document, you can easily customize the way Word wraps the text.

Control Text Wrapping

① Click the object to select it. Drag the object to the place you want it to appear.

② On the appropriate Format tab for that item (for example, the Picture Tools Format tab or the Drawing Tools Format tab), click the Text Wrapping button, and specify the text-wrapping option you want.

(continued on next page)

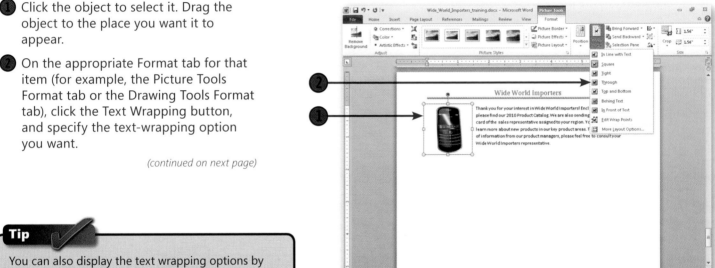

Tip

You can also display the text wrapping options by right-clicking a picture in your document and pointing to Wrap Text. Simply click the option you want to apply to the picture and the text is reflowed as you selected.

Control Text Wrapping *(continued)*

3 If the text wrapping still doesn't look the way you want, click the Text Wrapping button again, choose More Layout Options from the menu, and make your custom layout settings in the Layout dialog box. Click OK when you've finished.

You can also customize the way text wraps around your object by using the Edit Wrap Points option in the Wrap Text tool. Select the object and then click Edit Wrap Points and drag the boundary handle to change the shape of the object boundary. The text rewraps to conform to the changes you make.

Sorting Your Information

Earlier in this section, you learned how tables help you organize and display information. You can take the display of your information a step further and help your readers find what you hope they will find easily by sorting the information you display in tables and lists. Word 2010 can easily sort the tables and lists you create in alphabetical or numerical order so that your readers can easily make sense of the data you present.

Sort a Table

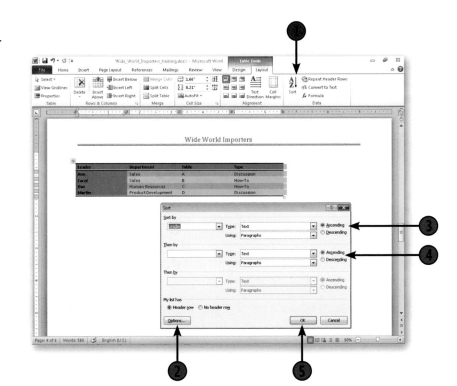

1. Click anywhere in the table, and choose the Sort tool in the Data group of the Table Tools Layout tab.

2. In the Sort dialog box, specify whether the table will contain a header row (a row that shows the column titles).

3. Specify the title of the column you want to use to sort the table, the type of content in the column, and whether you want the information to be sorted in ascending or descending order.

4. If you want to conduct a second-level or third-level sort, enter the criteria.

5. Click OK.

Tip

If your table includes a header row and you want Word 2010 to leave that row out of the sort, click the Header Row radio button in the Sort dialog box before you click OK to complete the sort.

Sort a List

 Select the entire list.

In the Paragraph group of the Home tab, click the Sort tool.

In the Sort Text dialog box, specify the type of information that's in the list, whether you want to sort by words or by paragraphs, and whether you want the information to be sorted in ascending or descending order.

Click OK.

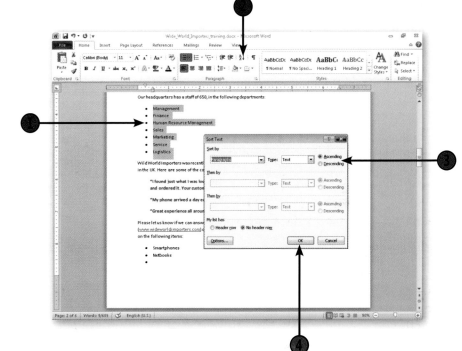

Reorganizing a Document

Earlier in this section, you learned about Navigation view, which enables you to view and work with your document by headings, pages, or search phrases. Outline view provides another powerful way for you to view the structure of your document and to rearrange the order of presentation of the topics. The outline structure assumes that you've used specific heading and body styles to organize your document into a hierarchy of topics and subtopics.

View a Document's Outline

1. Click the View tab and click Outline to display Outline view.

2. In the Outline Tools group, specify the lowest level of heading to be displayed.

3. Click to expand or collapse the content under the selected heading.

4. Click to change the outline level of the selected text by promoting it one level or demoting it one level, or to change body text to a heading or a heading to body text.

5. To move a section, click the plus sign to select the entire section, and drag the section up or down.

A plus sign indicates that there's some content under the heading.

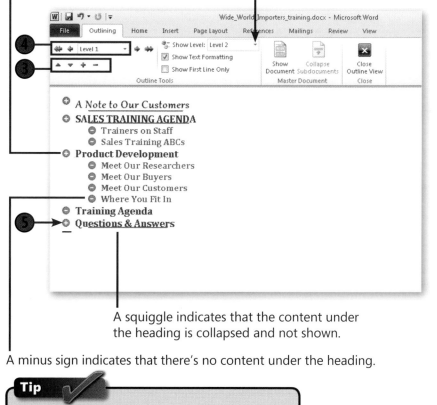

A squiggle indicates that the content under the heading is collapsed and not shown.

A minus sign indicates that there's no content under the heading.

Try This!

Drag a topic's plus or minus sign to the left to quickly promote the topic's outline level, to the right to demote it, or to the far right to turn it into body text. Changing the outline level also changes the style that's assigned to that paragraph.

Tip

To quickly expand or collapse a section, double-click the plus sign next to the heading.

6

Working with Special Content in Word

Sure, you may use Microsoft Word 2010 most often for letters, reports, newsletters, and flyers. But every once in a while, in addition to the normal, run-of-the-mill documents you create, you may need to do something special—like create a cover page for a report, add an equation to a proposal, include citations listing your references for some research you've done, or create a professional table of contents so readers can find their way through your document easily. Word 2010 includes a wide selection of predesigned cover pages that you can use as is or customize to better coordinate with your needs. Additionally, this section talks about inserting equations, using text boxes to create sidebars and pull quotes, and creating watermarks. If your document needs footnotes or endnotes, Word not only numbers them automatically but updates the numbers for you if you add or delete a note, and even figures out their exact placement on the page. We'll also discuss adding citations, creating a table of contents, and finalizing your document.

And then there's the mail merge feature—a great time-saver when you need to send the same information to a few individuals or to a large group of people. You provide a *main document* and a *data source,* and Word combines, or merges, the information into a new, personalized document or personalized e-mail messages.

Numbering Headings and Lines

When you are preparing a document that will be peer-reviewed (for example, an article for a professional journal) or distributed to a team of reviewers who will be asked to provide feedback, adding numbers to the headings and lines makes it easy for reviewers to comment on the relevant sections. You can add numbers to your Word 2010 headings by using the Multilevel List tool, and you can control line numbers of text using various tools in the Page Layout tab.

Number the Headings

1. Verify that you've applied the correct styles to all the headings.

2. Click in the first heading paragraph.

3. On the Home tab, click the Multilevel List button, and click one of the heading-numbering schemes.

4. Verify that your document headings are numbered correctly. If you don't like the look of the numbering scheme, click the Undo button on the Quick Access toolbar.

Tip

If a paragraph that you want to number as a heading isn't included when you use a heading-numbering scheme, you haven't assigned it the proper outline level. To correct this problem, you can either modify the style and assign it the correct outline level, or switch to Outline view, click in the paragraph, and select the outline level on the Outlining tab.

The Multilevel List button

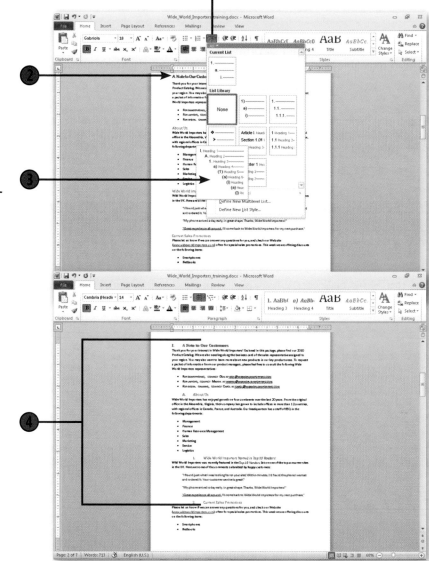

Number the Lines

1. On the Page Layout tab, click the Line Numbers button, and choose the type of line numbering you want from the drop-down menu.

2. If you want to change the starting number or the interval at which line numbers are shown (every fifth line, for example), click Line Numbers again, choose Line Numbering Options from the menu, and, on the Layout tab of the Page Setup dialog box, click the Line Numbers button to display the Line Numbers dialog box.

3. Select the Add Line Numbering check box, if it isn't already selected, to turn on line numbering.

4. Specify the options you want.

5. Click OK, and then click OK in the Page Setup dialog box.

Tip

If there's a paragraph whose lines you don't want to be included in the line-numbering process, click in the paragraph, click the Line Numbers button on the Page Layout tab, and choose Suppress For Current Paragraph.

Tip

The line numbers are visible on your screen only in Page Layout view and Print Preview.

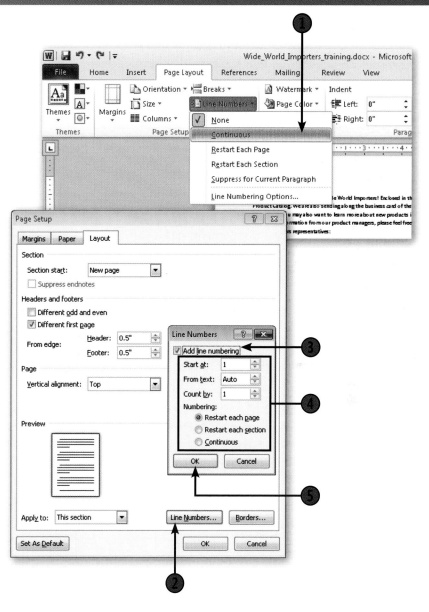

Inserting a Cover Page

When you've spent time and energy making the inside of your report look great, you may want to add a professional cover page to give the entire document a polished look. A well-designed cover page makes a good first impression and gives readers important information about what they'll see inside your document.

Insert the Cover Page

① On the Insert tab, click the Cover Page button, and in the gallery that appears click the cover page you want.

② Switch to Print Layout view if you aren't already in that view, press Ctrl+Home to move to the beginning of your document, click in an area that needs to be completed, and type the required information. Repeat these actions for all the other areas that need to be completed.

③ If you're not happy with the design of the cover page, do any of the following:

- On the Insert tab, click Cover Page, and choose another design.

- On the Page Layout tab, click Themes, and choose a different theme.

- Add a picture, a drawing, fields, text, or other items to customize the page.

- On the Insert tab, click Cover Page, and choose Remove Current Cover Page to delete the cover page.

④ Save your document.

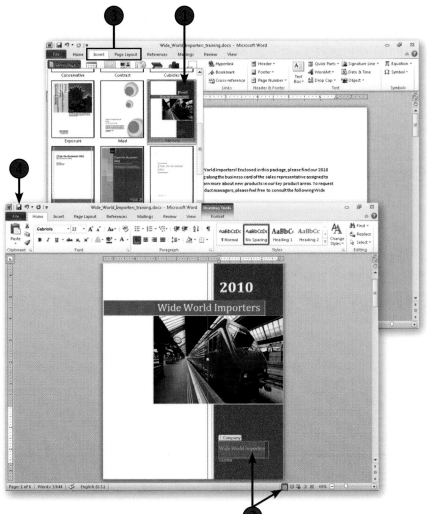

Inserting Information with Additional Actions

Word 2010 is a smart program, and it can help you do more with the information in your document by providing action items you can use to carry out specific tasks that are tied to the word or phrase. For example, suppose that you include the name of a coworker in your document. Word 2010 offers an additional action when you right-click that enables you to send an e-mail message, schedule a meeting, or display the person's contact information. When you right-click a paragraph that includes a company name. You can specify the actions you want Word 2010 to be able to take depending on the type of information it finds in your document. In versions of Word prior to Word 2010, Additional Actions were known as *smart tags*.

Contact a Colleague

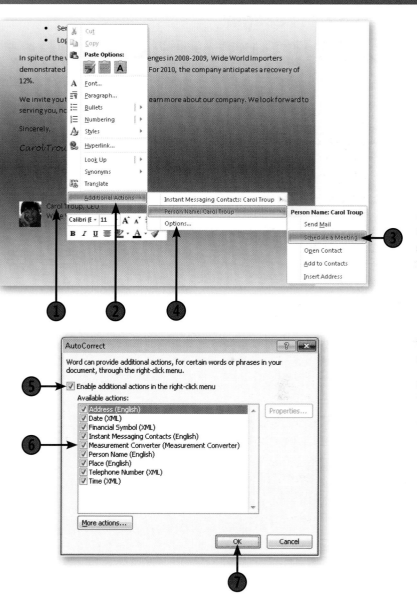

1. Look through your document and right-click a person's name.

2. In the context menu that appears, click Additional Actions.

3. Click the action you want to perform.

Or

4. Click Options.

5. Click Enable Additional Actions In The Right-Click Menu if necessary.

6. Click the check boxes of the items you want to include.

7. Click OK.

Inserting an Equation

If you create documents in which you need to display accurate mathematical equations, you'll be pleased with the equation improvements in Word 2010. The enhanced tools now enable you to create sophisticated custom equations, choose and modify predesigned equations, and add all the elements you need to create the equation the way you want it. What's more, you can save your equation to the Equation gallery so that it's there the next time you need it.

Insert the Equation

1. Click in the document where you want to insert the equation.

2. On the Insert tab, click the down arrow at the right of the Equation button, and in the gallery that appears click the equation you want.

3. Edit and format the equation as desired.

Or

4. Use the tools on the Equation Tools Design tab to add to the equation.

5. Click outside the equation when you've finished working with it.

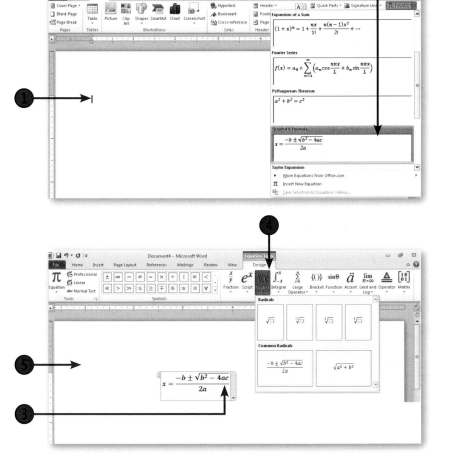

Adding a Sidebar or a Pull Quote

When you want to add a special design element that reinforces key ideas, adds extra information, or spotlights phrases in your text, sidebars and pull quotes help you present the text in a special way. Word 2010 offers a variety of sidebar and pull quote styles you can add for that distinctive look.

Insert a Predesigned Text Box

1. Switch to Print Layout view if you aren't already in that view.

2. On the Insert tab, click the Text Box button, and in the gallery that appears click the text-box design you like.

3. Select any sample text in the text box, and paste or type your replacement text.

4. Click the outer boundary of the text box, and drag it to the location you want.

5. Use any of the tools on the Text Box Tools Format tab to modify the text box itself, or use the formatting tools on the Home tab to modify the text.

6. Click outside the text box to resume working on the main content of your document.

Tip

To create your own custom text box, click Draw Text Box in the Text Box gallery, and use your mouse to drag out the dimensions of the text box.

Tip

You can change the way the text wraps around a text box you add by right-clicking the box and choosing Wrap Text from the context menu. Click the option reflecting the way you want the text to flow around the text box.

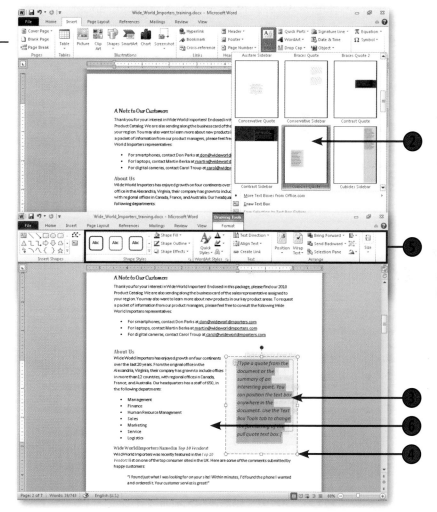

Inserting a Watermark

A *watermark* is a picture or some text (a company logo, for example) that appears subtly "behind" the main text in your document. Watermarks can help identify your document as *your* document and give readers additional information about how they can use the piece (for example, some watermarks say "Do Not Copy." The watermark in your Word 2010 document appears on every printed page as though it were part of the paper. You can create a picture watermark or a text watermark, but you can't have both in the same document.

Create the Watermark

1. On the Page Layout tab, click the Watermark button, and choose the watermark you want from the gallery that appears.

2. If none of the existing watermarks is what you want, choose Custom Watermark from the gallery to display the Printed Watermark dialog box.

(continued on next page)

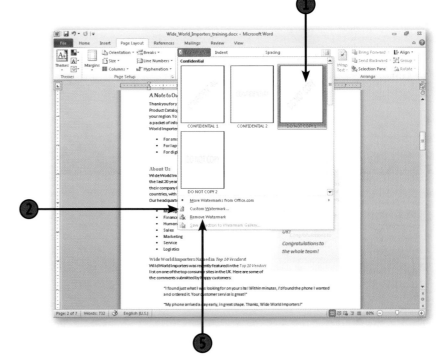

Tip

To have the same watermark appear automatically in every document that you create using a particular template, add the watermark in that template. To make sure a specific watermark is available for all your documents, add it to the Watermark gallery.

Create the Watermark (continued)

- To create a text watermark, select Text Watermark, type the text, choose your formatting options, and click OK.

- To create a picture watermark, select Picture Watermark, click the Select Picture button and locate and select the picture file you want to use, choose your formatting options, and click OK.

- If you decide you don't want a watermark after all, click the Watermark button on the Page Layout tab, and choose Remove Watermark from the gallery.

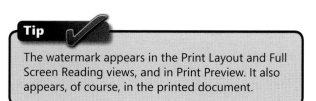

Tip

The watermark appears in the Print Layout and Full Screen Reading views, and in Print Preview. It also appears, of course, in the printed document.

Creating Footnotes and Endnotes

If you are creating a document in which it's important to cite your references and add notes that support your text, you'll love the footnote and endnote features in Word 2010. Word automatically positions footnotes at the bottom of the page or places endnotes at the end of the document or section, whichever you specify. Word numbers both the footnotes and the endnotes, giving each a unique numbering format. Whenever you add or delete a footnote or an endnote, Word automatically renumbers the appropriate series. For a footnote, Word also figures out how much space is required at the bottom of the page for the footnote, and when a footnote is too long for the page Word automatically continues it on the next page.

Insert the Footnote or Endnote

1. In Print Layout view, with the insertion point located where you want the footnote or endnote reference mark to appear in your document, click the Insert Footnote button on the References tab for a footnote or the Insert Endnote button for an endnote.

2. Type your footnote or endnote text.

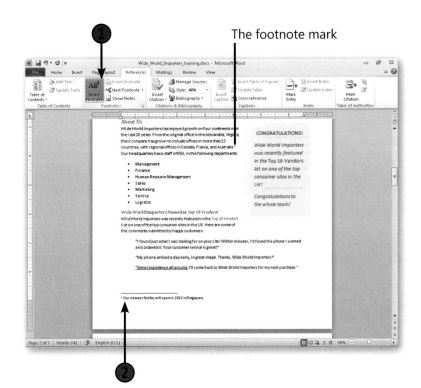

The footnote mark

Change the Reference Mark

Click if you want to convert endnotes to footnotes, or vice versa.

1 On the References tab, click the Footnote & Endnote dialog launcher.

2 Specify where you want the footnotes or endnotes to appear, and click the numbering format you want.

3 Click to display the Symbol dialog box, choose a symbol for the footnote or endnote reference mark, and click OK.

4 Click Apply to change the location of the footnotes or endnotes and/or the number format, or click Insert to use the selected symbol as the reference mark for this footnote or endnote.

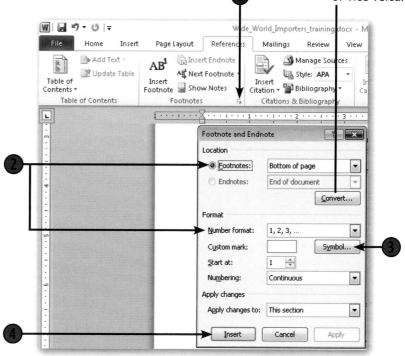

Inserting a Citation

When your writing references outside sources and/or works by other people—including books, articles, legal decisions, or other items—you'll need to cite these sources. Word provides a rich environment for entering, compiling, formatting, and inserting citations into your documents. If you're working in a company, a school, or an agency that frequently creates documents that include citations, you probably already have the data entered in bibliographies, ready to be dropped in. If not, however, you can type the information as you go and save it for future documents. You can insert individual citations and manage the sources you use as references in your Word 2010 documents.

Add Existing Citations

① On the References tab, click the Manage Sources button to display the Source Manager dialog box.

② If the default source file isn't the one you want, click Browse. Use the Open Source List dialog box to locate the source file you want, and then click OK. You can use numerous source files to copy citations into your document.

③ If citations exist in the source document that aren't already in your document, and you'll eventually want to add them, select the citations you want, and click Copy. Use the Sort and Search tools if you need to find citations in a large source file, and add those you want to your document.

④ Select any citation you're not sure of to inspect the information, and then decide whether or not to add it to your document.

⑤ Click Close when you've finished.

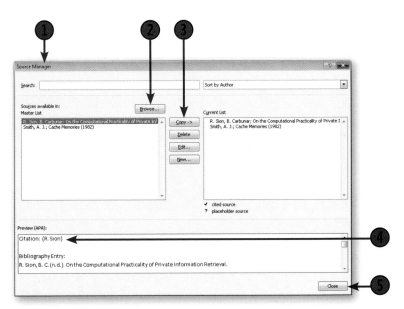

Insert a Citation

1 Select the citation style you want for all of your citations.

2 Click in your document where you want the citation to appear.

3 On the References tab, click the Insert Citation button, and if the citation you want is listed, click it.

4 If the citation isn't listed, click Add New Source to display the Create Source dialog box.

5 Select the type of citation you want.

6 Enter the information for the citation.

7 Either use the proposed citation tag name or enter a unique name.

8 Click OK.

9 If you want to insert a bibliography of your citations or a list of works cited, place the insertion point where you want the item to appear, click the Bibliography button, and click the item you want in the gallery that appears.

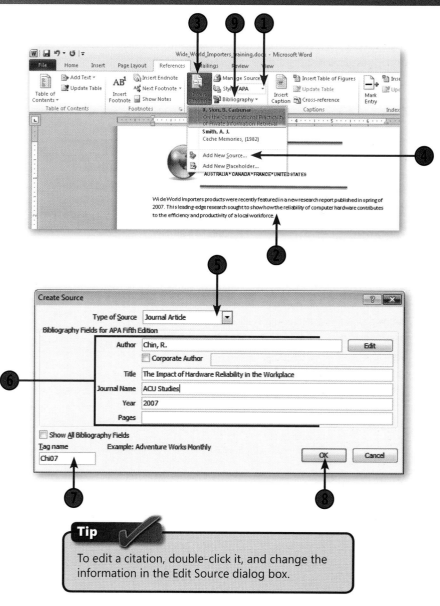

Tip ✓

The citation is placed inside a *content control* in your document. To edit the citation or the source, or to convert the citation into static text, point to the content control, click the down arrow that appears, and choose what you want to do from the drop-down menu.

Tip ✓

To edit a citation, double-click it, and change the information in the Edit Source dialog box.

Creating a Table of Contents

For long documents, adding a table of contents is a great reader service, making it easy for those reading your document to turn just the page they want to see. Word 2010 provides a number of predesigned tables of content so that you can choose one you'd like to use or modify it to fit your document. Word 2010 will automatically include all headings you've styled as Heading 1, Heading 2, and so on as it compiles the table of contents. After you add the table, you can easily update it, change its style, or update only the page numbers, which enables you to make sure the table of contents is accurate if one or more headings get moved during editing.

Set the Outline Text

1 In Outline view, scroll through the document, verifying that any paragraph you want to appear in the table of contents has a style that uses the appropriate level 1, level 2, or level 3 outline level, and that any paragraph you don't want to include has an outline level of 4 or below or a Body Text outline level. If a paragraph you want to include doesn't have a style with the appropriate outline level assigned to it, click in the paragraph and apply the appropriate style.

(continued on next page)

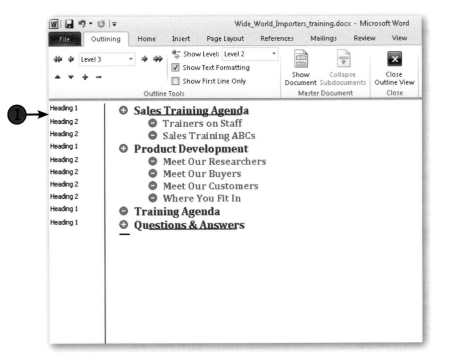

Set the Outline Text   *(continued)*

● Switch to Print Layout view, and click in the document where you want the table of contents to appear.

● On the References tab, click the Table Of Contents button, and select the style and type of table of contents you want to insert.

● If you make changes to the document that affect the pagination or the heading content, click the Update Table button on the References tab.

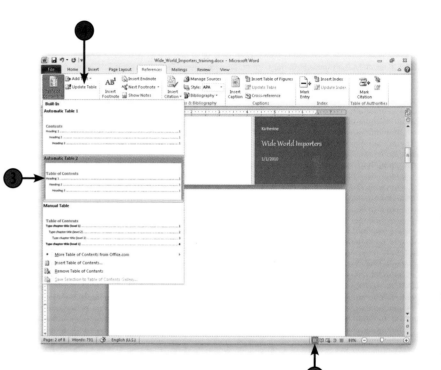

Tip

If you want to include or exclude a paragraph but don't want to change its style, click the Add Text button on the References tab, and click the outline level you want to apply.

Tip

After you've added the table of contents to your document, you can update it easily by clicking the table and pressing F9. Word helps you keep the table of contents up to date so that the page numbers and headings are correct, even after you've added text, moved sections around in the document, or edited the headings in the file.

Printing an Envelope

Sometimes a printed envelope conveys just the look and feel you're looking for when you send a document. Suppose, for example, that you've just created a great proposal that you want to deliver to a top client. Creating a printed envelope in the same font and style as the proposal helps your work look consistent and professional. With Word, you can easily create crisp, businesslike printed envelopes. You can add your return address, and, in the United States, you can add electronic postage. If you already have the mailing address in your letter, Word usually detects it and copies it to the Envelopes And Labels dialog box. You can also type the address directly in the dialog box.

Add the Address

1. On the Mailings tab, click the Envelopes button to display the Envelopes And Labels dialog box.

2. If a delivery address is displayed on the Envelopes tab, verify that it's correct.

3. If no delivery address is shown, or if you want to use a different address, type the address. If the address is in your Microsoft Outlook Contacts list, click the Insert Address button.

4. Verify that the return address is correct. If you're using an envelope with a preprinted return address, select the Omit check box so that the return address won't be printed.

5. Click Options to display the Envelope Options dialog box.

(continued on next page)

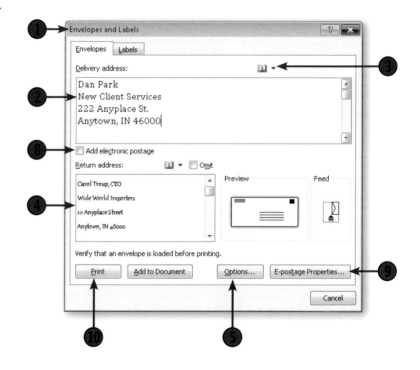

Add the Address *(continued)*

(6) On the Envelope Options tab, specify the envelope size and the fonts and positions for the addresses.

(7) On the Printing Options tab, specify how the envelope is to be loaded and printed. Click OK.

(8) If you have electronic postage (e-postage) software installed, select this check box to use electronic postage.

(9) If you need to make changes to your e-postage setup, click the E-Postage Properties button.

(10) Click Print to print the envelope.

Printing a Mailing Label

Printing mailing labels is much easier than it used to be. Today you can purchase labels at almost any office supply store and find that you can easily print what you need—one label or sheets of labels—in Word 2010. You choose your label type, enter the address, and select how you want the label to be printed, and Word does the rest. Nice.

Print the Label

① Make a note of the manufacturer and the design number of the labels you'll be using. If you're planning to print only one label, figure out which label on the sheet of labels is the one you're going to use. Later in the process, you'll need to specify the label by row (the horizontal line of labels) and by column (the vertical line of labels). Insert the sheet of labels into your printer (usually into the manual feed tray, if there is one).

② On the Mailings tab, click the Labels button to display the Envelopes And Labels dialog box.

③ On the Labels tab of the Envelopes And Labels dialog box, use the proposed address, type a new one, or click the Insert Address button to insert an address from your Outlook Contacts list. To insert your return address, select the Use Return Address check box.

④ If the type of label shown isn't the one you're using, click Options to display the Label Options dialog box, specify the label you're using, and click OK.

⑤ If you're using a full sheet of labels, click the appropriate option to print a whole page of identical labels or only one label on the sheet of labels. If you want to print only one label, specify the label by row and column.

⑥ Click Print to print the label or labels.

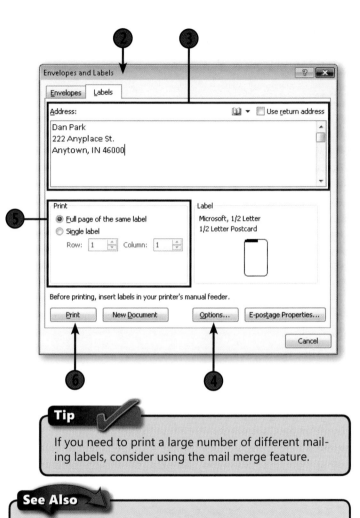

Tip

If you need to print a large number of different mailing labels, consider using the mail merge feature.

See Also

Read "Managing Your Contacts" on pages 296–297 for information about adding or modifying address information in your Outlook Contacts list. Read "Changing Your User Information" on page 399 for information about modifying your return address.

Mail Merge: The Power and the Pain

If you've ever had to send the same letter or catalog to more than one person, you know what a time-saver mail merge can be. Mail merge saves you the trouble of typing numerous names and addresses by merging your contacts list with the document you're creating. In Word 2010, mail merge uses a *master document* and a *data source* to accomplish the task. The master document is the template (although not a template in the Word-document sense) that lays out your document and contains text or other items that never change. This might be the sales letter, for example, that you want to send out to all your customers. The master document also contains instructions for inserting data from a data source into each document. The *data source* is your contact list, Microsoft Excel 2010 spreadsheet data, or other file containing the name and address information you want to merge with the document.

The goal of mail merge is simple: to produce many different documents that are personalized to go to many different individuals—without a lot of extra work from you. The process of putting together a mail merge document may seem a bit complicated at first, but it's really just a matter of telling Word where to substitute the different data items. (For example, the *name* goes here, and the *address* goes there.) Once you use the mail merge feature a time or two, it will seem intuitive. After you master the basic mail merge process, you can get a little fancier by adding conditional expressions, which enable you to create a mail merge letter for a customer if a certain condition is true.

It's More than Letters

The mail merge feature can do more than create form letters and address envelopes. You can save the merged documents as a file so that you can edit them or send them by e-mail. You can create almost any type of document by using a specific template or designing the document from scratch. All Word needs is a data document with some data fields in it. You can create mailing labels and address books, awards, parts lists, different versions of exams, and catalogs designed for specific geographical areas or demographic populations. The uses for mail merge are limited only by your creativity, your willingness to experiment with different data fields and Word fields, and your decision as to whether mail merge would be faster than manually creating individual documents.

> **Tip** ✓
>
> There's one change for Microsoft Works users who plan to use their Works database as the data source for a Word 2010 mail merge. Now you need to export your data and then create a new data source before importing the information into Word. Word 2010 no longer directly imports Works databases.

Setting Conditional Content

Mail merge offers you a flexible way to produce content based on what your customers want to see. You can easily tailor the content according to the data stored in your mailing list. For example, you might offer one promotion to individuals who live in the western region, but offer a different promotion to those who live in the southern U.S. If you have an entry in your data file that tracks the region in which the customer lives, you can use that data to control the content of your document. To add this kind of conditional content, you use the IF field, available in the Rules tool in the Mailings tab. You can tell Word to insert one set of content IF the contact lives in the western region, or insert a different set of content IF the contact lives in the southern region.

Creating a Form Letter

If the idea of creating a form letter sends a shudder of apprehension down your spine, relax; it's no more difficult than writing a simple note to a coworker. Once you create the letter, you can customize it by adding the mail merge fields you want—and then it's just a few short steps to the final merge process.

Set Up Your Letter

- Create and save your letter.
- Click the Start Mail Merge button, and choose Letters.
- Click Select Recipients and choose one of the following:
  - Type New List to enter your data.
  - Use Existing List to use data that exists in a file Word can read.
  - Select From Outlook Contacts to use data from your Outlook Contacts list.
- Click Edit Recipient List.
- Select or clear check boxes to choose recipients.
- Click OK when you've finished.

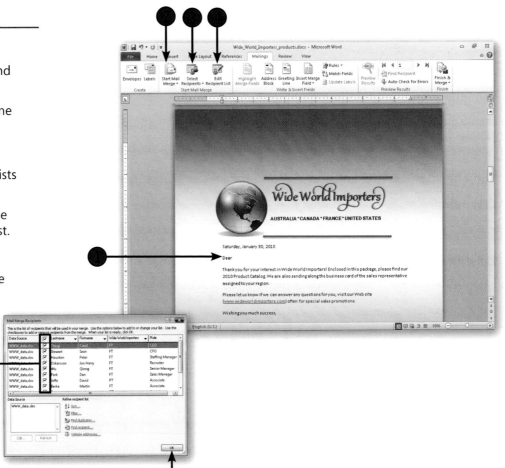

Specify the Data to Be Merged

① In your document, click where you want to add information from your data source.

② In the Write & Insert Fields group, click the type of information you want to insert.

③ In the dialog box that appears, specify the options you want, and then click OK. Continue adding items to the letter.

④ Click Preview Results.

⑤ Click to preview the letters.

⑥ Click Edit Recipient List to make changes to the data list.

⑦ Click Auto Check For Errors.

⑧ Click Finish.

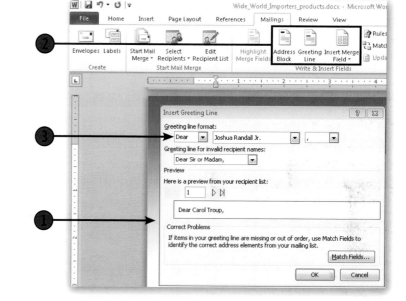

If you're familiar with conducting a mail merge using the Mail Merge Wizard that steps you through the process, and if you want to use the wizard, click the Start Mail Merge button, and choose Step By Step Mail Merge Wizard from the drop-down list.

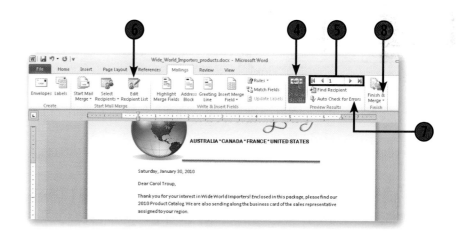

Finalizing Your Document

Word 2010 includes a Document Inspector that helps you assess your document before you send it to ensure that you aren't including any sensitive information—personal or business—that should stay inside the company. Additionally, the Document Inspector can help you prepare the file for distribution and ensure that it isn't edited against your wishes.

Prepare Your Document

1 With your document completed and saved, click the File tab.

2 In Backstage view, in the Prepare For Sharing area, click Check For Issues.

(continued on next page)

Tip

If you don't want other people who have access to your document to edit it, click File, click Protect Document in the Permissions area, and click Mark As Final.

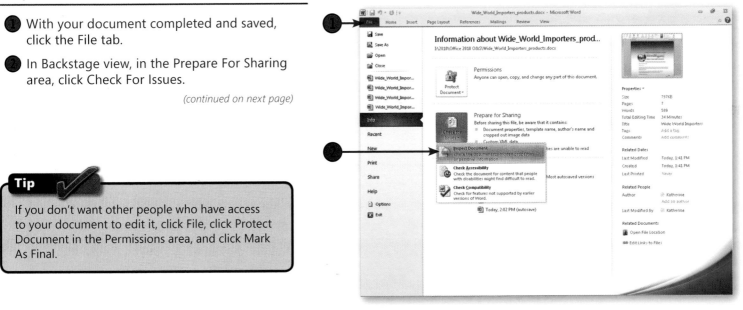

Prepare Your Document *(continued)*

③ In the Document Inspector dialog box, clear the check boxes for the items you want to keep in the document and select the check boxes for the items you don't want to appear in the document.

④ Click the Inspect button at the bottom of the dialog box.

⑤ In the Document Inspector dialog box, click the Remove All button for each type of item you want to remove.

⑥ Click Close when you've finished.

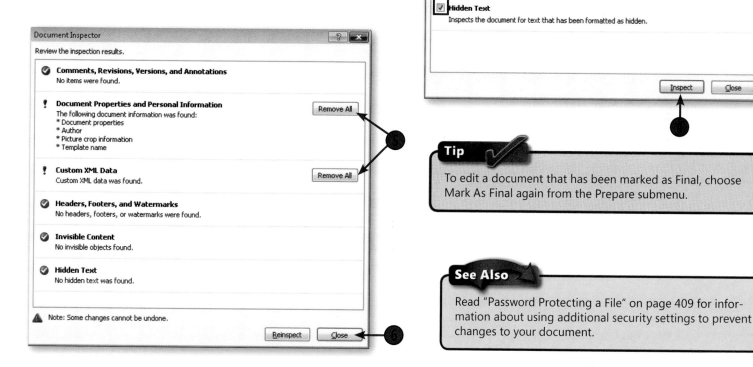

Tip ✓

To edit a document that has been marked as Final, choose Mark As Final again from the Prepare submenu.

See Also

Read "Password Protecting a File" on page 409 for information about using additional security settings to prevent changes to your document.

7 Working in Excel

If you're a numbers person, you will enjoy the way Microsoft Excel 2010 helps you organize your financial information, perform calculations, and display results in different ways. If you're *not* a numbers person, you'll appreciate the way Excel 2010 provides help all along the way as you learn how to use the various features in the program. Whether you have previous worksheet experience or not, Excel 2010 provides the tools you need to do both simple and complex calculations, reports, charts, and more—whatever you need to share financial information with others.

This section of the book introduces you to spreadsheet basics and shows you how to enter and edit data as well as add visual appeal and clarity to your worksheets. You learn how to format your data using fonts, colors, and borders, and how to help others understand the trends and values in your worksheet by adding sparklines to worksheet cells. You'll also learn how to format numbers in various ways—as currency, percentages, or decimals—for readability—and discover how to update, change, move, or copy your data. In other words, if you want to learn the basic Excel tasks that help you to create and manage worksheets, you'll find what you're looking for in this section.

What's Where in Excel?

Microsoft Excel 2010 is a spreadsheet program that makes it easy for you to gather and work with numeric information in many different ways. The Excel window is designed to give you all the tools you need to create, format, enhance, and calculate your data. Like all programs in Microsoft Office 2010, the ribbon offers a set of tabs, each of which includes tools related to a specific task you want to accomplish with the program.

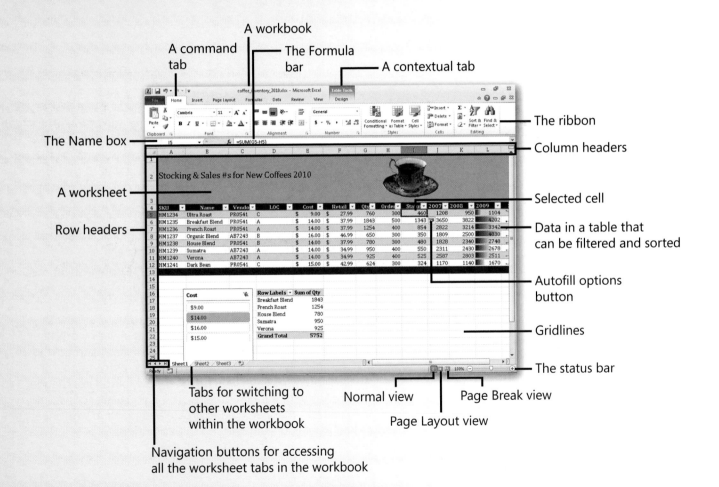

- A command tab
- A workbook
- The Formula bar
- A contextual tab
- The ribbon
- The Name box
- Column headers
- A worksheet
- Selected cell
- Row headers
- Data in a table that can be filtered and sorted
- Autofill options button
- Gridlines
- The status bar
- Tabs for switching to other worksheets within the workbook
- Normal view
- Page Break view
- Page Layout view
- Navigation buttons for accessing all the worksheet tabs in the workbook

Excel 2010 Basics

Excel 2010 may be much easier to use than you think, even if you've shied away from spreadsheet programs in the past. The program is designed to enable you to enter, edit, and format data easily. You can create simple or complex formulas to perform calculations on that data; you can create charts to illustrate your data. You can search, sort, and reorder the data in the worksheet easily.

Knowing the basic lay of the land and understanding terms you'll see used in the program is a good way to begin to build a comfort level with the program. Here are some of the terms you'll see:

- An Excel worksheet is organized in rows and columns for your data. The columns are lettered (A, B, C, and so on) and the rows are numbered (1, 2, 3, and so on).

- The intersection of each row and column is called a *cell*. You add your data (cell values and labels or formulas, for example) in each cell.

- Each cell has its own unique *cell address*, which includes both the column letter and the row number. For example, B6 is the address of the cell at the intersection of column B and row 6.

- Each Excel workbook can contain multiple worksheets, which you access by clicking the tab at the bottom of the worksheet area. You can name the different tabs to help you remember the content of each worksheet.

- You can format the data in the Excel worksheet in many ways. Numbers might represent values that you want to use in calculations; text might serve as data labels in your columns and rows. You'll learn about the various ways you can format and work with cell values in this section.

- Excel enables you to group and name sets of cells so that you can use them in calculations you create. This is known as *naming a range* of cells.

- You can use several features to illustrate the data in your worksheet. Charts display data and help you make comparisons; sparklines are a feature new in Excel 2010 that displays in a single cell a trend or value in your data; and conditional formatting enables you to add visual elements (such as data bars or icon sets) to help others understand the ideas your data presents.

Tip ✓

The important thing to remember about Excel 2010 is that you can create worksheets that are as simple or as complex as you like. Throughout this section and the one that follows, you'll learn about the basic features you are likely to want to use with Excel.

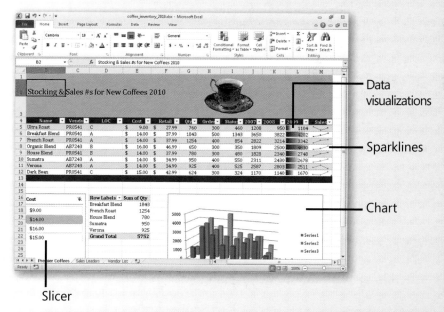

Data visualizations

Sparklines

Chart

Slicer

Using a Predefined Workbook

Wouldn't it be great to have a workbook all set up and ready for you so that all you have to do is enter your information? Well, your wish has been granted. When you use one of Excel's existing templates, you don't have to worry about structure and formatting—they're already taken care of for you. Not only that, but many templates provide an extensive array of formulas and relationships already built in that provide some powerful methods of data analysis.

Open and Use a Template

1. Click the File tab to display Backstage view.

2. Click New to display Excel's available templates.

3. If you see a template you want, select it to preview it, and then click Create.

4. If you don't see a template you want, do any of the following:

    - Click Sample Templates to see a small collection of Microsoft templates installed on your computer, and double-click the one you want to use.

    - Click My Templates to display the New dialog box and choose a custom template. Double-click the template you want to use, and a worksheet opens.

    - Click New From Existing to open an existing workbook as a template.

    - In the Office.com Templates area, click a topic to see templates of that type that are available for download, and double-click the one you want to use.

5. Click Create. In the new workbook that appears, replace any placeholder text or data with your own, and add any other elements you want.

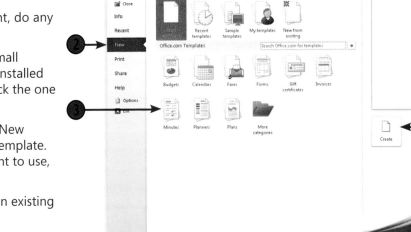

Tip

To change the number of worksheets included in the new workbook, the default font and font size, and the default view, click File and in Backstage view, click Options. Click General, and change the value in the Include This Many Sheets box.

Choosing a Theme for Your Worksheet

Themes are available throughout Office 2010, enabling you to define the look of your entire file—as well as other files you create in other applications—with a similar look and feel. When you choose a theme for your worksheet, the color scheme, fonts, and effects for shapes and graphics are all coordinated for that theme. You can add cell data, format headings, include charts, and more—and all the formatting choices you make are connected to the theme. The beauty of this is that if you later want to apply a different theme to your worksheet, all the coordinated elements change automatically to reflect the color, font, and effects choices of that new theme. This helps you keep the formatting in your worksheets consistent and makes changing the look easy if you decide to do that later.

Apply a Theme

1 On the Page Layout tab, click the Themes button to display the Themes gallery.

2 Do any of the following:

- Point to a theme to see how your worksheet will look if you use that theme.

- Click the theme you want to use.

- Click Browse For Themes to display the Choose Theme Or Themed Document dialog box. Select a theme, or select a document that contains the theme you want, and click Open.

3 Use the tools on the Home and Insert tabs as you normally would, selecting from the theme fonts and colors shown or selecting non-theme fonts and colors for special effects.

Tip

You're not limited to the fonts or colors of your theme. The theme fonts and colors are suggested and usually appear at the top of your formatting choices, but you can choose any fonts and colors you want. Any font, color, or effect choices you make that aren't part of theme won't change automatically if you choose a different theme at a later time, however.

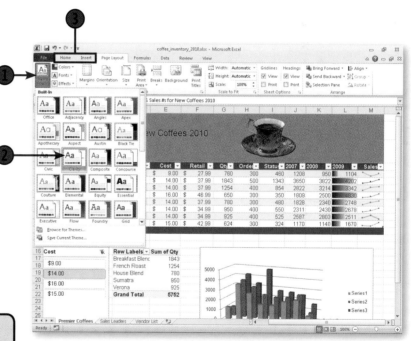

Entering the Data

Whether you start with a template or begin with a blank worksheet, Excel makes it easy for you to add to and format your data. You can begin the process by clicking the cell you want to update and typing the information. You can also copy and paste information from other sources into your Excel worksheets so that you can spend more time number-crunching and less time typing.

Enter Your Data

1 Start a new workbook if necessary.

2 Save the workbook with a new file name by clicking Save in the Quick Access toolbar and entering a name for the worksheet, and clicking Save.

(continued on next page)

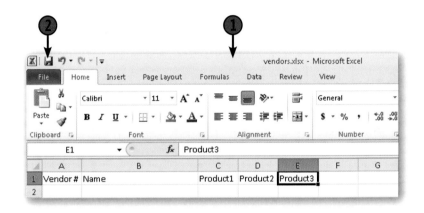

Tip

You can also import data from a text file, a Web source, or a Microsoft Access 2010 database into your Excel worksheet. Click the Data tab, and click your choice in the Get External Data group; then navigate to the file you want to use and click Open to add your data at the selected cell.

Enter Your Data *(continued)*

3 Type the header for the first column, press Tab, and type the header of the next column. Continue across the top row to enter all column headers. Press Enter after you've typed the last item.

4 Click in the beginning of the second row, and enter your data. Press Tab, and continue entering your data. Press Enter after you've typed the last item.

5 Continue entering your data row by row, and be sure to save the file periodically. Use the keys in Table 7-1 to navigate through your worksheet data.

Navigating the Worksheet

Key	Description
Tab	Selects the cell to the right
Shift+Tab	Selects the cell to the left
Enter	Selects the cell one row down
Shift+Enter	Selects the cell one row up
Right arrow	Selects the cell to the right
Left arrow	Selects the cell to the left
Up arrow	Selects the cell one row up
Down arrow	Selects the cell one row down
Home	Selects cell A1
Ctrl+right arrow	Selects the cell farthest right in the current row
Ctrl+left arrow	Selects the cell farthest left in the current row

Editing the Data

Often you need to go back and make changes to your data after you've entered it. You can correct and update the data quickly and easily, either by replacing the contents of an entire cell or by editing the existing content.

Replace the Data

1 Click in the cell you want to change, or use the arrow keys to select the cell whose data you want to replace.

2 Type the new data, and press Enter.

Or

3 Highlight the entry in the Formula bar and type the new data.

Edit the Existing Data

① Double-click the cell to activate it for editing, or select the cell and press F2.

② Press Backspace, Delete, or any other key you need to use to correct the information.

③ Press Enter to add the corrected information.

Tip

You can change the direction the selection moves when you press Enter if you like. Click File to display the Backstage view, and then click Advanced. At the top of the Advanced tab, click the Direction arrow and choose the direction you want the selection to move when you press Enter. Click OK.

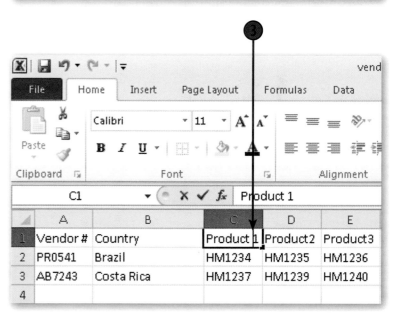

Formatting Cells

You can dramatically improve the look of your worksheet by using Excel's many formatting features. Formatting your data serves a number of purposes: first, it helps others reviewing your data see easily what's most important on the worksheet. Next, it helps you organize your data so that you can easily find what you need later.

You can use Excel's predefined formats to choose a look for your cells that makes the data stand out. The cell styles available in the Styles group of the Home tab are coordinated with the theme you select for the worksheet, so all the colors and fonts available are consistent with the overall theme you have chosen.

Format Some Cells

1. Select the cells you want to format. The following table offers different ways to select multiple cells.

2. On the Home tab, click Cell Styles in the Styles group to display the gallery.

3. Point to the styles you would like to preview on the worksheet. Click the style you want to apply.

4. Add your own formatting, if desired, by clicking the tools in the Font and Alignment groups of the Home tab.

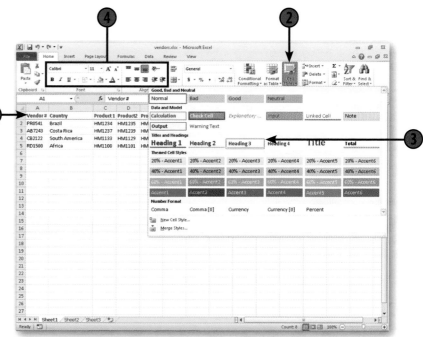

Selecting Cells in the Worksheet

To Select	Click
A column	Click the column header.
A row	Click the row header.
Adjacent cells	Click in the first cell, and drag the mouse until the cells you want are highlighted.
Nonadjacent cells	Select the first group of cells, and then press and hold Ctrl while dragging over the other cells.
All data in the worksheet	Click one of the data values, and press Ctrl+A.

Tip

To select a large range of cells, select the first (top-left) cell of the selection, scroll down and/or over to the end of the area to be selected, hold down the Shift key, and then click the last (bottom-right) cell of the selection.

Formatting Numbers

When you look at columns and rows stacked full of numbers, it might not be clear what those numbers represent. Are the values showing dollar amounts? Are they percentages of something? You can improve the readability of your workbook by using standard numeric formatting to make everything as clear as possible for those viewing your worksheet.

Format Some Numbers

1. Select the columns, rows, or cells that contain numbers you want to format.

2. In the Number group of the Home tab, click the Number format arrow to select the formatting you want to use.

3. Use the buttons in the Number group to choose the numeric style you want to apply.

4. If the formatting isn't what you want, click the Format Cells: Number dialog launcher to display the Format Cells dialog box.

5. On the Number tab of the Format Cells dialog box that appears, select the type of formatting you want.

6. Select any available options you want to use to customize the formatting.

7. Click OK when you've finished.

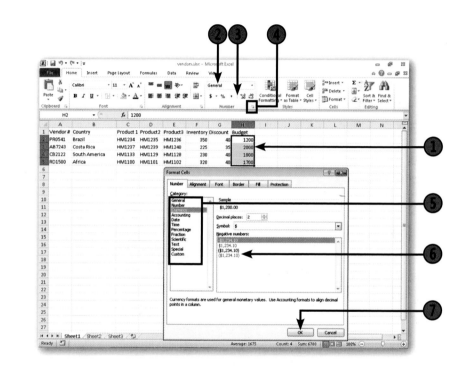

> **Tip** ✓
>
> The tool with the dollar sign is the Accounting Number Format tool. You can change the format of the currently selected text by clicking the arrow to the right of the tool and clicking the type of currency format you want from list.

Moving, Copying, and Pasting Data

As with all Office 2010 programs, you can move data around in Excel by copying or cutting it. However, when you copy data in Excel, you'll need to have a blank area ready to receive the data; otherwise, Excel will overwrite any existing data. You can also tell Excel to copy the contents of a cell to a group of adjacent cells.

Excel 2010 includes the new Paste with Live Preview feature to see how your information will look when pasted using different paste options. You can choose how you want the information to be pasted both before and after you add it to your worksheet.

Move Data

1. Select all the cells you want to move.

2. Move the mouse pointer to the edge of your selection. The pointer turns into a four-headed arrow.

3. Drag the selection to a blank location.

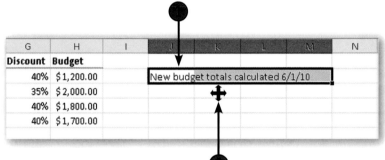

See Also

Read "Adding and Deleting Columns and Rows" on pages 158–159 for information about adding blank columns or rows.

Copy or Cut Data

1 Select the cells you want to copy or cut.

2 Click Copy (or press Ctrl+C) or Cut (or press Ctrl+X) in the Clipboard group of the Home tab.

3 Click in the first cell of the destination, and press Enter to paste a single copy of the copied content. Click Paste or press Ctrl+V to paste multiple times.

Copy and Paste Data to Adjacent Cells

1 Select the cell whose content you want to copy.

2 Move the mouse pointer to the bottom-right corner of the cell until the pointer turns into a cross (the Fill handle).

3 Drag the Fill handle either vertically or horizontally.

4 If the results aren't what you expected, click the AutoFill Options button, select the Copy Cells option, and click outside the selection to have the contents of the first cell copied to all the other selected cells instead of creating a calculated series.

See Also

Read "Creating a Data Series" on page 161 for information about having Excel insert a series of values based on the first selected cell instead of just copying the contents of that cell.

Adding and Deleting Columns and Rows

As you continue building your worksheet and work with it over time, chances are that at some point you'll need to add or delete columns and rows. You might need to move one row to make room for another, for example, or remove columns of data you plan to move to another worksheet. Whatever your reason, you can remove data only or remove both the data and the column or row, depending on your needs.

Add a Column

Right-click the column header to the right of the point you want to add the new column.

Click Insert from the context menu.

To add or delete several rows or columns at one time, or to clear the contents of multiple rows or columns at one time, select multiple column or row headers before you right-click. To select nonadjacent rows or columns, hold down the Ctrl key as you click each row or column header.

Add a Row

Right-click the row header below where you want the new row.

Choose Insert from the shortcut menu.

Excel will create a new row 3.

Excel will create a new column F.

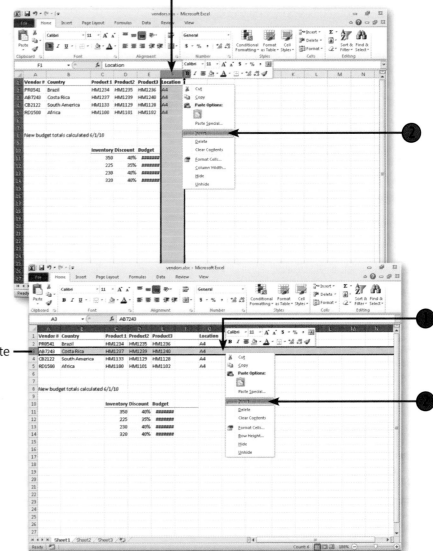

Delete a Column or a Row

① Right-click the column header or the row header.

② Choose Delete from the shortcut menu.

See Also

Read "Hiding Columns and Rows" on page 160 for information about hiding columns or rows without deleting them.

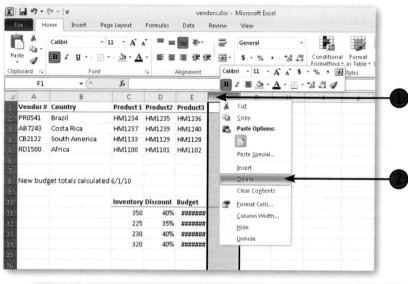

Delete Some or All Content of Cells

① Select the cells to be cleared.

② On the Home tab, click the Clear button and, from the submenu, choose what you want to delete.

Tip

To quickly clear the content of a selected cell or cells without removing any formatting, press the Delete key. Remember that you can use the Undo button on the Quick Access toolbar (or press Ctrl+Z) to restore any content that you delete unintentionally.

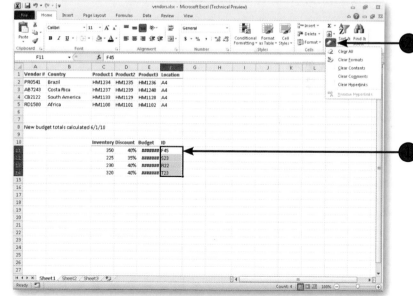

Hiding Columns and Rows

When you create a worksheet, it sometimes contains columns and rows of data that aren't relevant for every review or for every use of the worksheet. You can suppress the display of data you do not want displayed for general view by hiding columns and rows. Later you can reveal the data once again easily to return the data to normal view.

Hide Columns or Rows

① Select the columns or rows that you want to hide.

② Right-click one of the selected headers, and choose Hide from the shortcut menu.

Reveal Hidden Columns or Rows

① Select the columns or rows that are adjacent to the hidden columns or rows.

② Right-click one of the selected headers, and choose Unhide from the shortcut menu.

See Also

Read "Finalizing Your Document" on pages 142–143 for information about using the Document Inspector.

Tip

To make sure that you don't accidentally distribute a workbook that contains information you don't want to share with others, make sure there are no hidden rows or columns in your final version of the workbook. To check for hidden rows or columns, run the Document Inspector by clicking the File tab, and clicking Check For Issues in the Prepare For Sharing group. Click Inspect Document in the list.

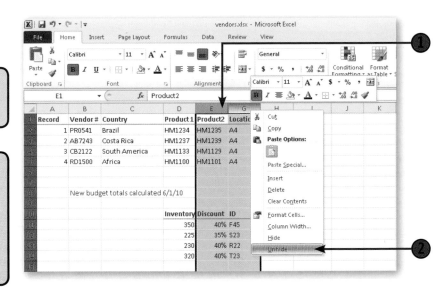

Creating a Data Series

When you're working with a *series*—that is, a particular set of data such as a series of dates or a list of consecutive numbers—numbering or labeling all the items in the series can be time consuming. You can put your time to better use by letting Excel do the work for you. All you need to do is make sure that Excel recognizes the data as a series.

Create a Series

① Type the first item in the series.

② Point to the bottom-right corner of the cell until the mouse pointer turns into a cross (the Fill handle).

③ Drag the Fill handle to fill the cells that you want to be included in the series.

④ If Excel copied the cell instead of creating a series or didn't fill the series as you expected, click the AutoFill Options button, and select Fill Series or any other appropriate option.

⑤ Make sure the series is correct. If it isn't, click the Undo button on the Standard toolbar and try again.

Tip ✔

If the Fill Series option isn't listed on the AutoFill Options shortcut menu, Excel doesn't recognize the data as a series. You can define your own series by clicking File and choosing Options; then click the Advanced tab and in the General area, click Edit Custom Lists. In the Custom Lists dialog box, define your list, and click OK.

	A	B	C	D	E	F	G
1	Record	Vendor #	Country	Product 1	Product2	Product3	Location
2	1	PR0541	Brazil	HM1234	HM1235	HM1236	A4
3		AB7243	Costa Rica	HM1237	HM1239	HM1240	A4
4		CB2122	South America	HM1133	HM1129	HM1128	A4
5		RD1500	Africa	HM1100	HM1101	HM1102	A4
6							

	A	B	C
1	Record	Vendor #	Country
2	1	PR0541	Brazil
3	1	AB7243	Costa Rica
4	1	CB2122	South America
5	1	RD1500	Africa
6			
7		◉ Copy Cells	
8		○ Fill Series	
9			
10		○ Fill Formatting Only	
11		○ Fill Without Formatting	
12			

	A	B	C
1	Record	Vendor #	Country
2	1	PR0541	Brazil
3	2	AB7243	Costa Rica
4	3	CB2122	South America
5	4	RD1500	Africa
6			

Formatting Cell Dimensions

You can adjust the height and width of cells, rows, and columns to accommodate the formatting you want to use in your worksheets. As you enter information, you might find that some columns are too narrow, resulting in truncated content. In other columns, you might find that some columns are too wide, resulting in wasted space. Similarly, you might want to

increase the height of the rows to increase the readability of the content. Although a row will automatically increase in height if you increase the font size of its content, you might want to increase the height of the row and then change the vertical alignment of the text to add space above or below the content.

Set the Column Width

① Select the columns whose widths you want to change.

② Right-click one of the selected column headers (F, in the figure) and choose Column Width from the shortcut menu to dislpay the Column Width dialog box.

③ Specify the width of the columns, calculated by the number of characters of the default font that can be displayed on one line.

④ Click OK.

Tip ✓

To change the vertical alignment of text in one or more rows, select the cells to be adjusted, and then click the Top Align, Middle Align, or Bottom Align button in the Alignment section of the Home tab.

Tip ✓

To select the entire worksheet, click the blank header between the "1" row header and the "A" column header. If the cells in the area you want to format are contiguous—that is, all the cells are adjacent to one another—just click in any one of the cells before you choose AutoFormat, and Excel will figure out the area to be formatted.

Try This!

Select alternating columns in your worksheet (click the first column, press and hold Ctrl, and click the third column, for example). Click the Fill Color tool in the Font group of the Home tab. Click a color from the Theme Colors section of the palette. The color is applied to the selected color.

Set the Row Height

1. Select the rows whose heights you want to change.

2. Right-click one of the selected row headers, and choose Row Height from the shortcut menu to display the Row Height dialog box.

3. Specify the height of the rows in points.

4. Click OK.

Adjust the Height or Width to Fit the Content

1. Select the cells that you want to format.

2. On the Home tab, click the Format button, and choose AutoFit Row Height from the drop-down menu.

3. Click the Format button again, and choose AutoFit Column width from the drop-down menu.

Organizing Your Worksheets

Up to this point, you've learned how to add and work with data on your worksheet. Excel also includes features that help you organize the various worksheets you create. As you know, each worksheet appears on its own tab in your workbook. You can customize the worksheets, rename the tabs, reorder the worksheets, and add new ones as needed, all from within your current workbook.

Name Your Worksheets

1. Double-click a worksheet tab, type a descriptive name for the worksheet, and press Enter.

2. Repeat these actions for any other worksheet tabs you'd like to rename.

Tip

To change the color of a worksheet tab, right-click the tab, choose Tab Color from the shortcut menu, and click the color you want in the gallery.

Change Their Order

1. Click the tab of the worksheet you want to move.

2. Drag the tab to the desired location.

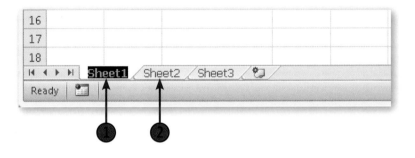

Insert a Worksheet

 Click the Insert Worksheet button.

② Rename the new worksheet, and move it to a different position among the tabs if you want.

> **Tip**
>
> To hide a worksheet from view instead of deleting it, right-click the tab, and choose Hide from the shortcut menu. To display the worksheet again, right-click a tab, choose Unhide from the shortcut menu, and, in the Unhide dialog box, select the worksheet to be displayed.

Delete a Worksheet

① Right-click the tab of the worksheet you want to delete, and choose Delete from the shortcut menu.

② When you're asked to confirm the deletion, click Delete.

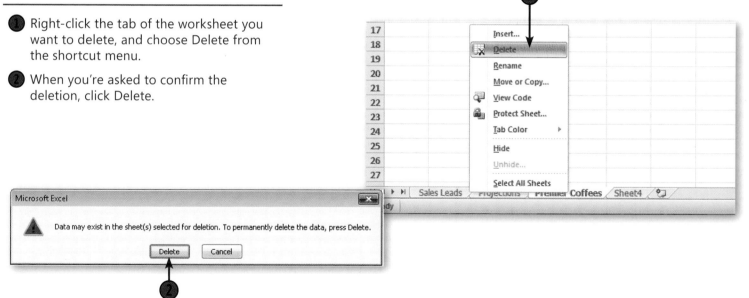

Preparing for Printing

You don't really need to worry about page setup in Excel until you're ready to print or distribute your worksheet, but at that point it's crucial that you attend to several details so that you get the results you want.

Set Page Dimensions

1. Display the worksheet in Page Layout view.

2. On the Page Layout tab, click Margins, and select the margin settings you want. To create different margins, click Custom Margins, make your settings on the Margins tab of the Page Setup dialog box, and click OK.

3. Click the Orientation button, and click either the Portrait (longer than wide) or Landscape (wider than long) printing orientation in the gallery that appears.

4. Click the Size button, and select the paper size you'll be using.

5. Specify the scaling to change the size of the printed worksheet or to force the worksheet to fit onto a set number of pages.

6. Specify whether you want to display and/or print the gridlines and the headings.

Tip

If you're going to print more than one worksheet at a time, step through these procedures for each worksheet.

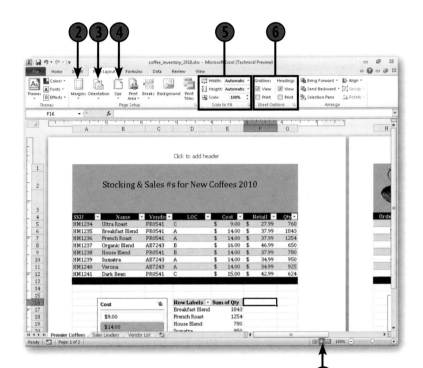

Set the Header and Footer

① Display the worksheet in the Page Layout view.

② On the first page of your worksheet, click in a section of the header.

③ On the Header & Footer Tools Design tab, specify whether you want to have a separate first-page header and/or different odd-page and even-page headers.

④ Click the Header tool if you want to choose one of the predesigned headers from the gallery.

⑤ Type your information, and use the tools in the Header & Footer Elements tab to complete the header.

⑥ Click the Go To Footer button, and add your content to the three sections of the footer.

⑦ Click in your worksheet. If you chose to have a different first-page header and/or different odd-page and even-page headers, move to the next page, click in the header area, and repeat steps 2 through 6. Repeat these actions for any other headers that you want to add.

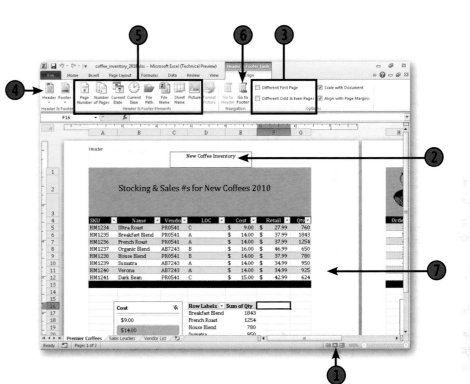

Printing a Worksheet

When you print a worksheet, the big part of getting the result you want involves setting things up properly; if you don't, you may find yourself wasting paper and printing only pieces of the worksheet you want to print. You can avoid unwanted results by setting a print range and pre-viewing your worksheet in Excel's improved Print Preview.

Specify the Print Area

① Select the area to be printed.

② On the Page Layout tab, click the Print Area button, and choose Set Print Area from the list.

Repeat Row and Column Titles

① To repeat headings on each page, click the Print Titles button on the Page Layout tab to display the Sheet tab of the Page Setup dialog box.

② Click the worksheet button and select the rows you want to be repeated on the printed page. Press Enter.

③ Click the Columns To Repeat At Left button. Select any columns that you want to repeat at the left side of each printed page, and press Enter.

④ Select the check boxes for the items you want to print, and clear the check boxes for the items you don't want to print.

⑤ Select the way you want the worksheet to be printed.

⑥ Click OK.

Check the Layout and Print the Worksheet

① Switch to Page Layout view, and examine the way the pages will appear.

② Click Page Break Preview to check page breaks.

③ Drag the dotted line to a new position if you want to change where the page breaks. Drag a page break to a new position, and adjust other page breaks if necessary.

④ Click File to display Backstage view, and click Print. Enter your print options and click Print to print the worksheet.

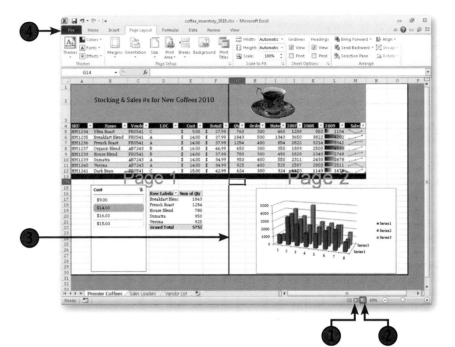

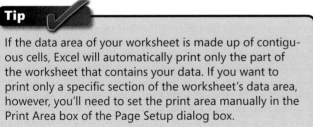

Tip

If the data area of your worksheet is made up of contiguous cells, Excel will automatically print only the part of the worksheet that contains your data. If you want to print only a specific section of the worksheet's data area, however, you'll need to set the print area manually in the Print Area box of the Page Setup dialog box.

Adding and Viewing Comments

You can use comments in a workbook in a couple of ways. You can add an explanatory comment to an item to track what you did or clarify it to others, or you can use a comment when you're reviewing a worksheet to add any concerns or suggestions.

Create a Comment

1 Click the cell to which you want to attach your comment.

2 On the Review tab, click the New Comment button.

3 Type your comment. Press Enter only if you need to start a new paragraph in the note. Click outside the note when you've finished it.

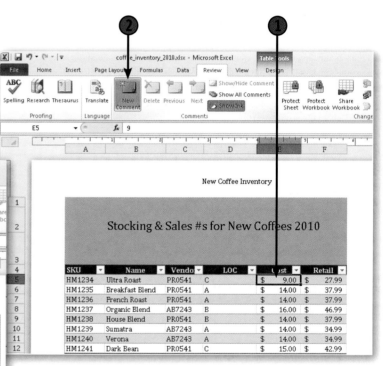

Review the Comments

1 Move the mouse pointer over a cell that contains a red triangle in the top-right corner. Read the comment that appears.

2 If you can't find a comment, or if you want to review several comments, on the Review tab, do any of the following:

- Click Previous or Next to find and display a comment.

- Click Show All Comments to display all the comments in the worksheet.

- With a comment displayed, click Edit Comment to modify the comment. (The New Comment button changes to the Edit Comment button when a comment is selected and displayed.)

Working with the Excel Web App

Excel 2010 is now available to you anywhere you go, as long as you have access to the Internet. Using the Excel Web App, you can view, edit, format, save, and share the worksheets you create. What's more, when you have saved an Excel 2010 worksheet to your Microsoft SharePoint Workspace 2010 or Windows Live SkyDrive account, you can co-author your worksheets in real time and communicate with your co-authors while you work.

Use the Excel Web App

1. Access your Windows Live SkyDrive account or SharePoint site.

2. Select the Excel worksheet you want to use.

3. Click Edit.

4. Make your changes as needed.

5. Save the worksheet.

> **Tip** ✓
>
> If you have a smartphone that runs Microsoft Windows Mobile 6.5, you can also work with your Excel worksheets using Office Mobile 2010. You can view, edit, format, and even create conditional formatting and work with pictures and charts, all in the small interface optimized for the phone screen. Office Mobile 2010 is available separately from Office 2010.

8

Analyzing and Presenting Data in Excel

There's more to working with your data than entering information in worksheets and making it look nice—although that's important, too. As you discover how to analyze and share the ideas your data suggests, you get in touch with the real power of Microsoft Excel 2010. The calculations you perform—whether they are simple or complex—enable you to carry out statistical, financial, and mathematical computations with ease. With Excel's help, you can use functions and create formulas you can use again and again. And by adding tables, PivotTables, and slicers to your worksheet, you can choose the way in which you want your data to be analyzed and presented to others who view your work.

You'll find some fairly advanced tasks in this section: adding sparklines to showcase the data trends and values in worksheet cells, using conditional formatting to spotlight key items in your data, working with functions and formulas to create complex calculations, and designing PivotTables and slicers that enable you to filter the data you choose to show at any given time. This section also shows you how to create charts that illustrate your data in ways that rows and columns cannot.

Applying Conditional Formatting to Cells

Excel 2010 includes a number of features that help you call attention to important features or trends in your data. You might highlight specific data values, for example, when your sales figures pass a certain mark. Or you might add a special icon to a cell that indicates the highest enrollment totals in a district. The conditional formatting choices in Excel enable you to highlight cells, add data bars, or display icons in the cells to help others viewing your worksheet understand the information you're presenting.

When you add this kind of conditional formatting to your worksheet, you tell Excel to apply special formatting to any cells that meet the specific criteria you've set. Excel will add the cell formatting only when the conditions you indicate are found to be true.

Highlight Specific Cells

1. Select the cells, columns, or rows to which the formatting will apply.

2. On the Home tab, click the Conditional Formatting button, point to Highlight Cells Rules or Top/Bottom Rules and, in the gallery that appears, click the item you want.

3. Specify the formatting you want.

4. Click OK.

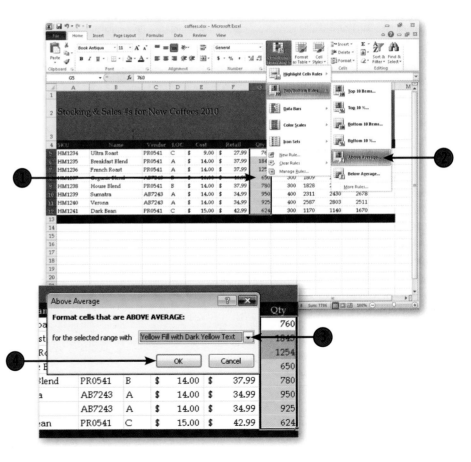

Tip ✓

You can apply multiple conditions and formatting to a selection of cells. Make sure, however, that you use different formatting for each criterion so that you're able to distinguish between the different conditions.

Add Data Bars

1 Select the cells in which you want the data bars to appear.

2 Click Conditional Formatting in the Styles group of the Home tab.

3 Point to Data Bars.

4 Click the data bar style you want to apply to the cell data.

Tip

You can choose to apply a gradient so that the edge of the data bar fades in the cell. (This sometimes makes it easier for others to read the values in the cell.) You can also choose to display the data bars as solid bars, which applies the data bar color you select without grading it.

Apply Icon Sets

1 Select the cells in which you want to add the icons.

2 Click Conditional Formatting in the Styles group of the Home tab.

3 Point to Icon Sets.

4 Click the icon set you want to apply to the cell.

Tip

Another style of conditional formatting enables you to choose a color range for the cells you select. For example, you can choose a two-color or three-color range that displays the low, mid-range, and high values in different colors. To apply this formatting style, choose Conditional Formatting, point to Color Scales, and click the color scale you want to apply.

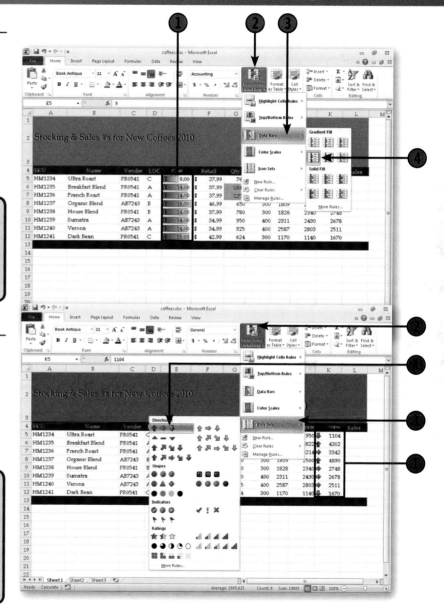

Customizing Conditional Formatting

Excel's preset conditional formatting is great for most conditions, but if you want to set your own parameters and formatting, you can do so by creating a new rule.

Create a Rule

① Select the cells to which you want to apply your conditional formatting.

② On the Home tab, click the Conditional Formatting button, and choose New Rule from the gallery to display the New Formatting Rule dialog box.

③ Select the type of rule you want to use.

④ Enter the information required for that rule, using the values and formatting you want. Each rule requires different types of information.

⑤ Select the formatting you want to apply to the cells that meet the conditions you've set. If the dialog box contains a Format button, click it, and in the Format Cells dialog box that appears, specify the formatting you want.

⑥ Click OK.

⑦ Apply any additional rules to the selection.

Tip

To remove conditional formatting, click the Conditional Formatting button on the Home tab, point to Clear Rules, and from the submenu, choose where you want to remove the rules.

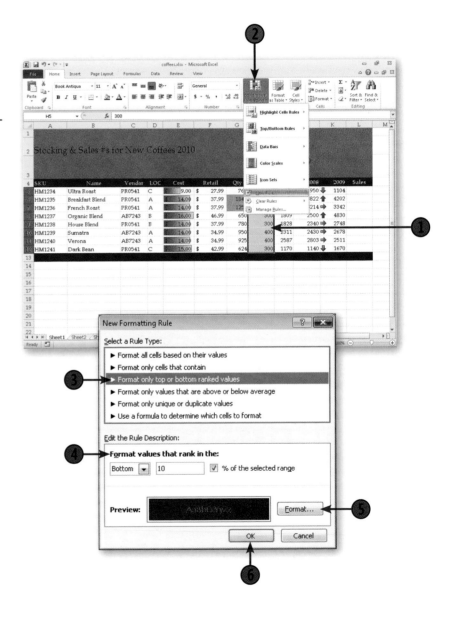

Cell References, Formulas, and Functions

When you begin to add formulas and functions to your worksheets, you need to know a little more about how to reference cells in the calculations you create. Understanding how to reference individual cells and ranges of cells will help you get the results you want from the functions and formulas you use.

A Little More About Cell References

As you learned in Section 7, every cell in an Excel worksheet has its own address, created from the intersection of the column and row where the cell is located (for example, C3). To quickly determine a cell's address—also known as a *cell reference*—click in the cell, and look in the Name box at the left of the Formula bar.

When you select a block of cells, the block is called a *range*. Ranges are written with the top-left cell first and the bottom-right cell last, separated by a colon—for example, when you select the range C5:E7, the selected cells appear as shown in figure.

Because workbooks can contain more than one worksheet, it's possible to refer to the same cell reference on different sheets when you're copying or moving data from one sheet to another. For this reason, Excel will include the worksheet name in cell references when necessary. For example, you might see Sheet1!C3 as a cell reference, to show that this cell is a different one from cell C3 in Sheet 2.

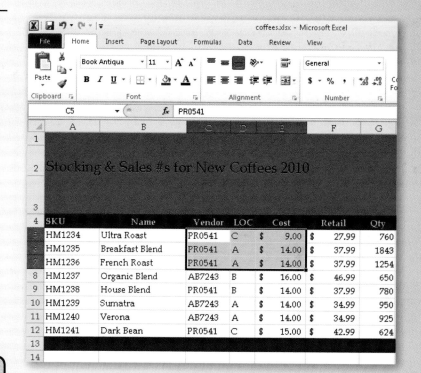

Tip

If you are working with a worksheet in which the column headers show numbers instead of letters, that workbook has been set up to use the R1C1 reference style, which is an old style of cell referencing. You can change the column headings to letters by clicking File, clicking Options, and clearing the R1C1 Reference Style check box in the Formulas tab.

Tip

You can give ranges, tables, and entire worksheets specific names that you can then use with your formulas and functions instead of the cell references.

Adding Sparklines

An exciting new feature in Excel 2010 called *sparklines* enables you to show cell-based illustrations of data trends or values in your worksheet. This enables you to show, for example, how sales in a certain region are trending (up or down?), how a particular product sold during a promotion, or how your inventory levels changed during a specific timeframe. Sparklines are easy to create and customize in your Excel worksheet.

Create Sparklines

1. Click in the cell in which you want to create the sparkline.

2. Click the Insert tab, and choose the type of sparkline you want to create.

3. When the Create Sparklines dialog box appears, drag to select the cells you want to use for the sparkline. Click OK.

(continued on next page)

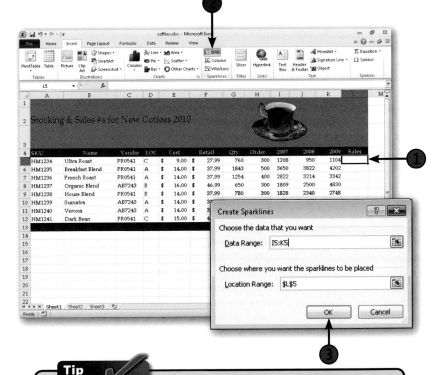

Sparkline Styles

Style	Name	Description
Line	Line	Adds a line chart to the current cell depicting the data in the range you select
Column	Column	Inserts a column chart contrasting the data values in the cells you specify
Win/Loss	Win/Loss	Displays a win/loss chart of the selected cell values

Tip

You can copy the sparkline to a column or range of cells by clicking the small handle in the lower right corner of the sparkline cell and dragging the cell border across the columns or rows you want to display sparklines. Sparklines are added in the original sparkline's style and the sparkline display in each cell is adjusted to reflect the range in that row or column.

Create Sparklines *(continued)*

④ In the Show area, click the markers you want to add to the sparkline

⑤ Click the More button in the Style group to display a palette of sparkline styles, and click the style you want to apply.

⑥ Customize the line and marker color as needed.

Edit Sparklines

① Click in the cell containing the sparkline you want to change.

② Click the Sparkline Tools Design tab.

③ Click Edit Data in the Sparkline group if you need to change cell data.

④ Change the sparkline type by clicking a new option in the Type group.

⑤ Modify the Show settings, and change Style if necessary.

Tip ✔

If you want to delete the sparklines you've added to your worksheet, select the sparklines, and in the Group group of the Sparklines Tools Design tab, click Clear and then click Clear Selected Sparklines.

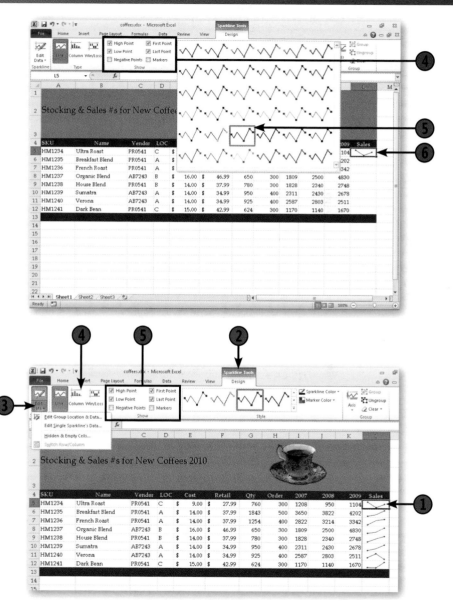

Introducing Formulas

You'll use cell references frequently in Excel—when you designate the area of a worksheet you want to print, for example. One of the most important uses of cell references, however, is in *formulas*. A formula can be just a simple calculation based on numbers you enter (=4*8.5), or you can have Excel plug in the values automatically by including the cell references in the formula (=C3*E7).

The benefit of using cell references is that the calculations continue to be accurate and update as the information in your worksheet changes. You can use both *absolute* and *relative* cell references to refer to the cells in your worksheet. Absolute references always refer to the same cell—for example, cell C3—no matter where you may move the data currently in that cell. You indicate an absolute reference by putting a currency symbol in front of the cell address (for example, $C3). A relative reference, on the other hand, causes Excel to keep track of where the information in that cell moves. So if you copy and move the content of C3 to D4, the formula adjusts automatically, replacing the cell reference C3 with D4. You don't need to do anything to indicate a relative reference—this is the default referencing style in your worksheet. Once you get the formulas working properly, you can rest assured that the right calculations are being done no matter how often your data may change.

Note that all formulas begin with an equal sign (=). The asterisk (*) symbol indicates multiplication; the forward slash (/) symbol indicates division. Your formulas can be as simple or as complex as you need, and a number of features in Excel help you create smart, effective formulas.

Caution

You are not likely to need to use absolute cell references often in your worksheets, especially when you are first starting out. Check your calculations carefully in the worksheet when you do use them so that you can be sure your formulas are working properly and your information updates the way you expect it to.

See Also

For information about calculating totals, see "Summing the Data" on pages 184–185. For more information about creating formulas with AutoFill and about using absolute references, see "Creating a Series of Calculations" on page 188. For information about displaying formulas, see "Troubleshooting Formulas" on pages 189.

Formula for current cell

Result displayed in cell

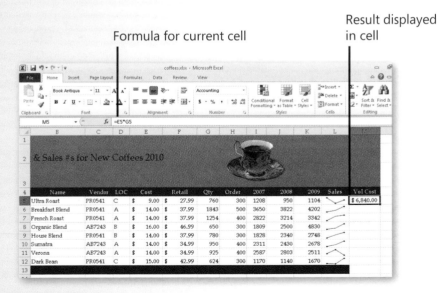

Understanding Functions

In addition to the cell references in a formula, which tell Excel which values you want to work with, you use functions to tell the program what kind of calculation you want to perform. For example, if you want to add the values in cells C3:E7, you use the SUM function by entering the formula in the cell where you want the result to appear, like this:

=SUM(G5:G12)

Excel 2010 includes a large range of functions that cover just about any type of calculation you want to perform. You can see the whole list of functions by clicking the Insert Function tool to the left of the Formula Bar and choosing the type of function you want in the Category list.

Doing the Math

Working with math in Excel is similar to figuring out a sum on paper except that you actually do less work! All you have to do is type the values and the arithmetic operators and then leave it to Excel to do all the calculations. You can easily change the values you've entered if necessary, or make the values equal to a value in another cell or series of cells.

Calculate a Value

1 Click in the cell in which you want the result of the calculation to be displayed, type an equal sign and then type the numbers and operators for your calculation.

2 Press Enter to see your result.

Arithmetic Operators

Action	Operator
Addition	+ (plus sign)
Subtraction	− (minus sign)
Negation	− (minus sign)
Multiplication	* (asterisk)
Division	/ (forward slash)
Percentage	% (percent sign)
Exponentiation	^ (caret)
Set order of actions	( ) (opening and closing parentheses)

The formula is also displayed in the Formula bar.

Excel highlights the cells in the formula

Tip

Excel makes its calculations based on the standard order of precedence for arithmetic operators—that is, negation, percentage, exponentiation, multiplication and division, and addition and subtraction. If two operators have the same precedence, Excel makes the calculation from left to right. To change the order of calculation, you use parentheses to group portions of the formula.

Try This

In an empty cell, type **=10+5*30+6/3** and press Enter. Copy the formula to a new cell, and then press the F2 key to activate editing of the cell. Add a pair of parentheses to the formula so that it's now **=(10+5)*30+6/3** and press Enter. Note that adding the parentheses changed the order of the operations and thus the result. Continue adding, moving, or deleting pairs of parentheses in the formula to see the effects on the final result.

Calculate the Value of Cells

① In the cell where you want the result to be displayed, type an equal sign.

② Click in the cell whose value you want to use.

③ Type the arithmetic operator you want to use.

④ Click in the next cell whose value you want to use in the calculation.

⑤ Continue typing the operators and clicking in cells until you've completed the formula, and then press Enter.

Tip

You can mix cell references and numeric values in a cell—for example, a formula might be =C1+C3+10. You can also reference cells in other worksheets or in other workbooks.

Caution

Don't assume that a formula contains an error just because it uses different operators from those you're familiar with. Some formulas are logical tests that return a true or false value, while others are used to manipulate text. For example, a formula of =C3=10 would display TRUE if the value in cell C3 was equal to 10, and would display FALSE otherwise.

11	Verona	AB7243	A	$ 4.00	$ 34.99	925	400	2587	2803	2511	
12	Dark Bean	PR0541	C	$ 15.00	$ 42.99	624	300	1170	1140	1670	=E12

11	Verona	AB7243	A	$ 14.00	$ 34.99	925	400	2587	2803	2511	
12	Dark Bean	PR0541	C	$ 15.00	$ 42.99	624	300	1170	1140	1670	=E12*

11	Verona	AB7243	A	$ 14.00	$ 34.99	925	400	2587	2803	2511	
12	Dark Bean	PR0541	C	$ 15.00	$ 42.99	624	300	1170	1140	1670	=E12*G12

M12			fx	=E12*G12							
	B	C	D	E	F	G	H	I	J	K	L	M
1											
2	& Sales #'s for New Coffees 2010										
3											
4	Name	Vendor	LOC	Cost	Retail	Qty	Order	2007	2008	2009	Sales	Vol Cost
5	Ultra Roast	PR0541	C	$ 9.00	$ 27.99	760	300	1208	950	1104		$ 6,840.00
6	Breakfast Blend	PR0541	A	$ 14.00	$ 37.99	1843	500	3650	3822	4202		$ 25,802.00
7	French Roast	PR0541	A	$ 14.00	$ 37.99	1254	400	2822	3214	3342		
8	Organic Blend	AB7243	B	$ 16.00	$ 46.99	650	300	1809	2500	4830		
9	House Blend	PR0541	B	$ 14.00	$ 37.99	780	300	1828	2340	2748		
10	Sumatra	AB7243	A	$ 14.00	$ 34.99	950	400	2311	2430	2678		
11	Verona	AB7243	A	$ 14.00	$ 34.99	925	400	2587	2803	2511		
12	Dark Bean	PR0541	C	$ 15.00	$ 42.99	624	300	1170	1140	1670		$ 9,360.00
13												

Summing the Data

Likely one of the most frequent calculations you'll make in Excel is to *sum,* or add up, a series of numbers. Luckily, summing is also one of the easiest calculations, with the AutoSum feature just a click away.

Sum the Numbers

1 Click in a cell below or at the right of the series of cells you want to sum.

2 On the Formulas tab, click the AutoSum button.

(continued on next page)

Sum the Numbers *(continued)*

③ Make sure the selection rectangle encloses all the cells you want to sum. If you've accidentally included any unwanted cells or omitted any desired cells, move the mouse pointer over a corner of the selection until a two-headed arrow appears, and then drag the selection rectangle to resize it so that it includes all the cells you want. You can also move the entire selection rectangle by pointing to a side of the rectangle and dragging it to a new location.

④ Press Enter to sum the cells and see the result.

Tip

To quickly find the average, count, and sum of a series, select the series, and note the values on the status bar.

Making Calculations with Functions

Excel includes a fascinating array of functions that can help you create just about any kind of calculation you may need. Do you want to know the standard deviation of a series of numbers? What about the sum of the squares? How about calculating the number and amount of the payments needed to retire a loan over a certain period? If you're a real stickler for precision, you can even use a function that returns the value of *pi*, accurate to 15 digits.

Find a Function

1. Click in the cell in which you want the results of the function to be displayed.

2. Click the Insert Function button. If the Formula bar isn't displayed, click the Insert Function button on the Formulas tab.

3. In the Insert Function dialog box, type the name of the function or a description of the action you want to take, and press Enter.

4. Select the function you want in the list.

5. If the function isn't listed, select a different category, and then select the function in the list.

6. Verify that the function will do what you want it to do.

7. Click OK.

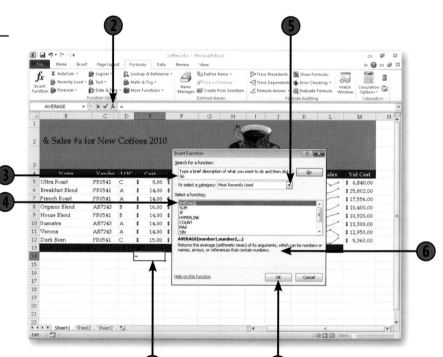

> **Tip** ✔
>
> If you know the name of the function you want to use, click the button on the Formulas tab for the type of function, and then choose the function from the drop-down menu. To use a function that you used recently, click the Recently Used button on the Formulas tab, and choose the function from the drop-down menu.

Add Arguments

1 In the Function Arguments dialog box that appears, if a range is proposed, make sure it's the one you want. If it isn't, type any values that you want to enter directly or type the cell references.

2 To select cell ranges, click to minimize the dialog box and return to the worksheet. In the worksheet, select the cell or range of cells you want to use as an *argument,* or parameter, for the function, and then click the button again to restore the dialog box to its normal size.

3 Complete any other arguments that are required for the function.

4 Click OK.

Tip

You can integrate more than one function into a formula, or you can include other elements—for example, standard arithmetic operations such as adding or multiplying by a number or a value in another cell.

Tip

Numerous functions don't return a value but are logical tests instead. The powerful IF function, for example, returns one value you've set if the logical test is true and a second value if the logical test is false. Many other functions, such as ISBLANK, return true or false values only.

Tip

A function requires specific types of data, delivered in a specific order; these are the arguments for the function. Some functions don't have any arguments—for example, NOW( ); some have a single argument—SQRT(*number*); and some have multiple arguments—NPER(*rate,pmt,pv,fv,type*). For information about the arguments for a function, click Help On This Function in the Function Arguments dialog box.

Creating a Series of Calculations

When you reference cells in a formula and then use the AutoFill feature, Excel modifies the reference to cells relative to the newly filled cells. That means you can create a whole series of calculations simply by creating a single calculation and then filling cells with the formula. And if you need to use a single constant value in all the calculations, you can use an absolute reference to a cell instead of a relative reference.

Create the Series

1. Create the first formula, referencing the cells.

2. Drag the Fill handle to fill adjacent cells.

3. Click in a filled cell.

4. Verify that the formula is correct.

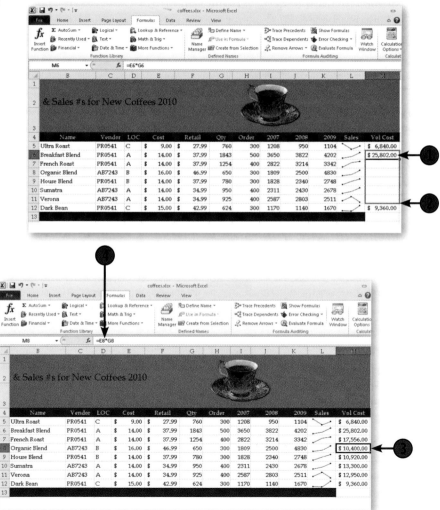

Tip

To include a reference to the same cell in all the formulas, make the reference to the cell absolute instead of relative. Press F4 to switch from a relative reference to an absolute reference.

See Also

Read "Cell References, Formulas, and Functions" on page 177 for information about the difference between relative and absolute references.

Troubleshooting Formulas

Formulas are powerful tools that you can use to create simple calculations or very complex and sophisticated equations. If you are just getting started creating formulas, start simple and build more involved calculations as you go along. Excel provides a number of formula-auditing tools that can help you find and fix errors as you learn to create more complicated formulas. Common errors in formulas include circular references, incorrect formula syntax, and cell references in a formula that have been deleted.

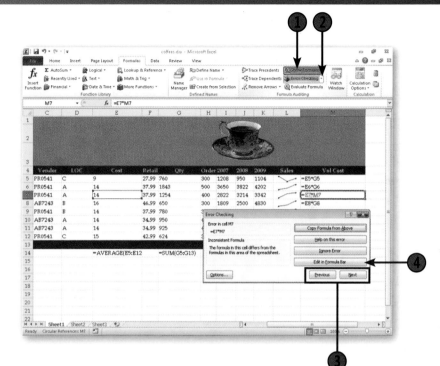

Check for Formula Errors

 On the Formulas tab, click the Show Formulas button to display all the formulas in the worksheet.

2 Click the Error Checking button.

3 In the Error Checking dialog box, use the Next and Previous buttons to find and review the errors in your worksheet.

4 Click the Edit In Formula Bar button if you see the mistake and want to correct the formula.

Creating a Table

Excel gives you many different ways to work with your data, but data can include more than just numbers. Excel's column-and-row format lends itself smoothly to creating and reviewing lists by placing them in tables. Excel provides special features that make it easy for you to sort your table by specific criteria. You can also filter the data to show only part of the list or summarize the data in the list.

Create a Table

1. In a worksheet, enter the data for your table, making sure that you add descriptive titles for the columns and saving the file as you work.

2. Select your entries.

3. On the Home tab, click the Format As Table button.

4. In the gallery that appears, click the table style you want to use.

5. In the Format As Table dialog box that appears, confirm the range of cells that you want to be included in the table.

6. Select this check box if your list has column headings; otherwise, clear the check box if you want Excel to insert generic headings.

7. Click OK.

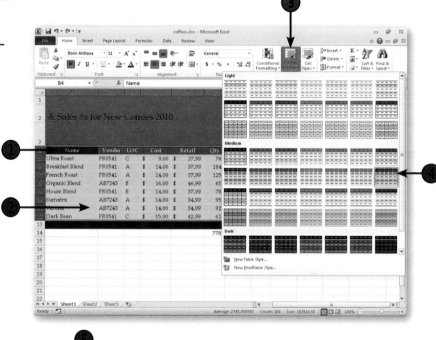

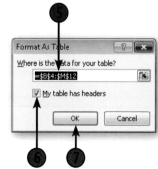

Use the Table

1 Click in the table, and on the Table Tools Design tab, select the check boxes for the items you want displayed and clear the check boxes for the items you don't want displayed.

2 If you've included a totals row, click in the cell that has the totals, click the down arrow that appears, and select the type of total you want. Use the AutoFill feature to copy the totals setting to any other cells that you want to display the total.

3 Click Summarize With PivotTable if you want to create a PivotTable based on the data in the table.

4 Click Remove Duplicates if you want to remove duplicated information from selected columns.

5 Click the down arrow at the top of the column that you want to use to sort or to filter the list; then select the action you want to take. Repeat for any other columns whose data you want to sort or filter.

6 Click Convert To Range if you want to convert the table back to standard data in your worksheet.

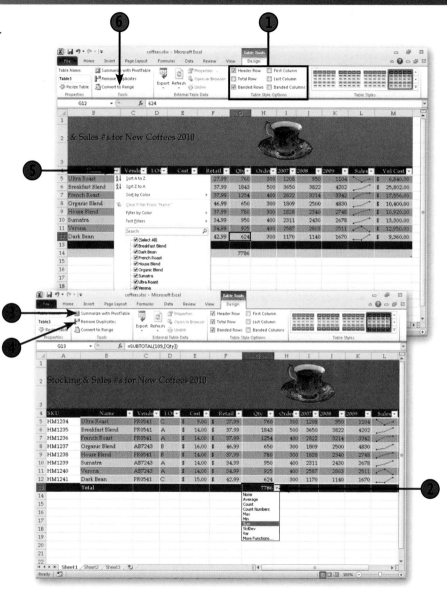

> **See Also**
>
> Read "Creating a Series of Calculations" on page 188 for information about using AutoFill.
>
> Also read "Summarizing the Data with a PivotTable" on pages 196–197 for information about using a PivotTable to examine your data.

Sorting the Data

One of the easiest ways to organize or evaluate your data is to use Excel's Sort feature. There are a couple of ways to control the sort—you can do a simple ascending or descending sort, or you can specify which data you want to sort and the type of sort you want to conduct.

Conduct an Alphabetic or a Numeric Sort

1. Select the columns or the portions of columns whose contents you want to sort.

2. On the Data tab, click the Sort button to display the Sort dialog box.

3. Specify whether or not the columns have header labels.

4. Specify which column you want to sort by.

5. Select Values if it isn't already selected.

6. Specify whether the data will be sorted A to Z, Z to A, or based on a custom list (alphabetic); or from smallest to largest, largest to smallest, or based on a custom list (numeric).

7. If you want to refine the sort by also sorting by a second column, click the Add Level button, and enter the search parameters. Repeat for any further level of search. You can use up to 64 levels in your search.

8. Click the Options button if you want to change to a case-sensitive sort for text or if you want to sort by rows instead of by columns.

9. Click OK to sort the data.

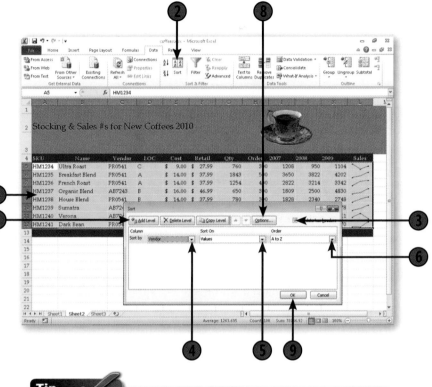

Tip

To do a quick alphabetic sort without setting any sort parameters, click the Sort A To Z or the Sort Z To A button on the Data tab; or, if you've selected numbers, click the Sort Smallest To Largest or the Sort Largest To Smallest button at the left of the Sort button.

Tip

If you've formatted your worksheet as a table, you can sort the data by clicking the arrow to the right of the column label and choosing the way in which you want to sort the rows.

Filtering the Data

When you want to display only data in your worksheet that meets certain criteria you specify—for example, rows that contain specific text, or numbers that are greater than or less than a specific number—you can have Excel filter your data.

Filtering temporarily hides the rows that don't meet your criteria so that you see only the data you want to see. Excel makes it easy for you to filter your data in the current table; you don't need to create another worksheet to apply the filter.

Filter the Data

1. Select the data you want to filter.

2. On the Data tab, click Filter in the Sort & Filter group.

3. Click the down arrow for the column you want to use as the filter, and select the item you want to use as the filter.

4. To filter by another column, click the down arrow for that column, and select the item you want to use as the filter. It's easy to see which columns have filtering applied—they show a little filter icon instead of a black down arrow.

5. When you've finished with the filtered data and want to return it to its unfiltered state, click the Filter button on the Data tab again.

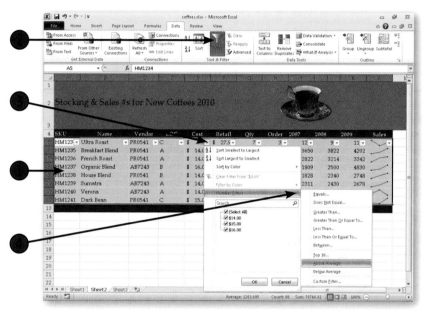

> **Tip**
>
> If your data is arranged so that you want to filter by rows, you must transform the data so that the rows become columns and the columns become rows. To make this happen, select the data and click Copy. Click in a blank area where you want to place the transformed data, click the down arrow at the bottom of the Paste button, and click Transpose in the drop-down list.

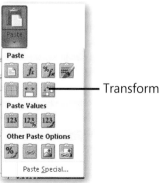

Transform

Separating Data into Columns

You might find that some data has been collected in a way that doesn't fit easily with what you want to do with it. For example, suppose that you've just opened a worksheet that includes coffee names and their types in the same column. What do you do if you want the coffee name in one column and the type in a second column? Easy! You just tell Excel to divide this type of information into separate columns.

Separate the Data

1. Select the data that is to be separated.

2. On the Data tab, click the Text To Columns button to start the Convert Text To Columns Wizard.

3. Specify whether the data is currently separated by a character such as a tab, a space, or a comma (Delimited), or whether the data is in text columns of specific widths (Fixed Width).

4. Click Next, and step through the wizard to specify how you want the data to be separated; whether the data should be formatted as numbers, text, or dates; and where the new column or columns should be placed.

5. Inspect the result. If it's not what you want, click the Undo button on the Quick Access toolbar, and use the wizard again, setting different values this time.

Tip

If you choose to replace the existing data, make sure there's a blank column for each new column that you create.

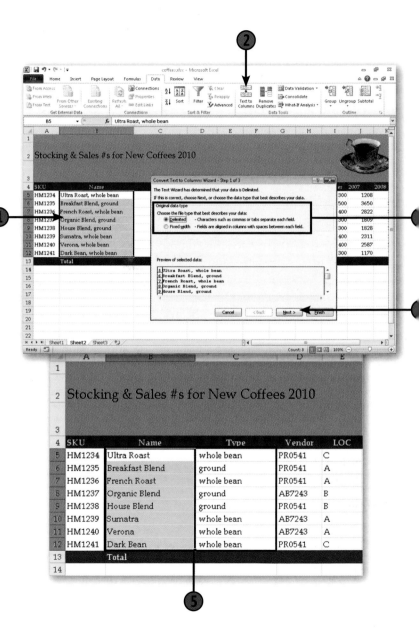

Creating Subtotals

When you've accumulated a mass of data, you can leave it to Excel to calculate the subtotals in your worksheets—how many boxes of crayons you sold in January, for example, or the number of different song-birds you've seen in your back yard. All you need to do is group the data by the items to be subtotaled and tell Excel to outline—that is, to classify and prioritize—your data, and to calculate the subtotals. You'll need to sort the data before you tell Excel to create the subtotals.

Create the Subtotals

1 Select and sort the data by the columns for which you want to create the subtotals.

2 On the Data tab, click the Subtotal tool in the Outline group to display the Subtotal dialog box.

3 Select the column that you want to be subtotaled.

4 Select the function to be used to calculate the subtotal.

5 Select the column or columns in which you want the results to be displayed.

6 Select any other options you want.

7 Click OK.

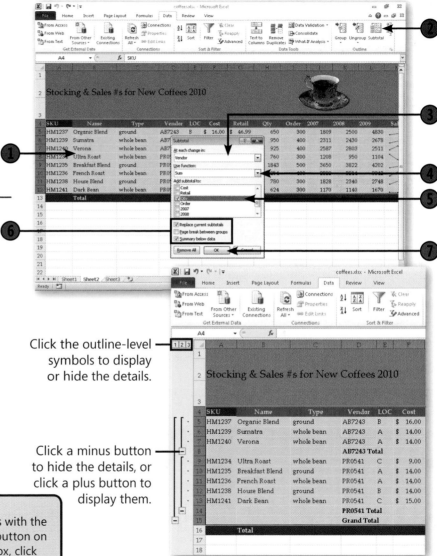

Click the outline-level symbols to display or hide the details.

Click a minus button to hide the details, or click a plus button to display them.

> **Tip** ✓
>
> To remove all the subtotals, select the cells with the data and the subtotals, click the Subtotal button on the Data tab, and in the Subtotal dialog box, click the Remove All button.

Summarizing the Data with a PivotTable

A PivotTable is a dynamic and powerful analysis tool in Excel that lets you look at relationships among your data and display the data you want to see. The PivotTable is named this way because you can "pivot" the data in different ways to show different aspects of your data. It can sometimes be a bit difficult to figure out the proper arrangement of the data fields, but once you've created the PivotTable, you'll find it easy to work with and very useful.

Create the PivotTable

1 Select the range of cells you want to use as the data for the PivotTable.

2 Click PivotTable in the Insert tab. Select the source of the data, specify where you want the PivotTable to appear, and click OK.

3 Select each data field that you want to use.

4 Drag items between the different areas as needed.

5 To change the names or any other display settings for field headings, click the down arrow, choose Field Settings from the drop-down menu, and make your changes in the Field Settings dialog box.

6 To change what type of value is calculated, click the down arrow, choose Value Field Settings, and in the Value Field Settings dialog box, specify how you want to summarize the data. Click OK.

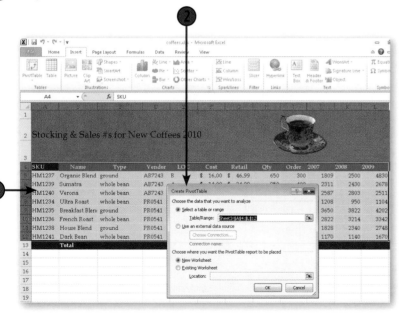

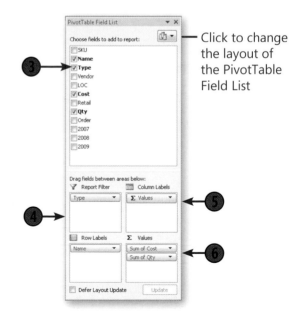

Click to change the layout of the PivotTable Field List

Use the PivotTable

1. Click the down arrow in the Report Filter field, select the item you want to be displayed, and click OK.

2. Click in a Column or Row field, and clear the Select All check box.

3. Select the items you want to be displayed, and click OK.

4. Continue selecting the items you want to be displayed in the other fields.

5. Use any of the tools on the PivotTable Tools Options and Design tabs to modify the PivotTable.

Tip

A PivotChart works just like a PivotTable, except that the data is displayed as a chart instead of as table data. You might find it easiest to create a PivotTable, modify it, and then use it as the source for a chart. The chart will be a PivotChart in which you can change the data that's displayed.

Adding Slicers

Changing the data displayed in a PivotTable can be a bit confusing if PivotTables aren't your thing, but in Excel 2010 a new feature makes changing the table display simple and fast. Now you can use slicers to choose different segments of data you want to display in the resulting table. Slicers are easy to create and use, enabling you to easily compare and evaluate the data on your worksheet from a number of different perspectives.

Create a Slicer

1 First create the PivotTable you want to use with the slicer you create, and click the PivotTable to select it.

2 Click the Insert tab, and click Slicer in the Filter group. You can also click Insert Slicer in the Sort & Filter group of the Pivot Table Options tab.

(continued on next page)

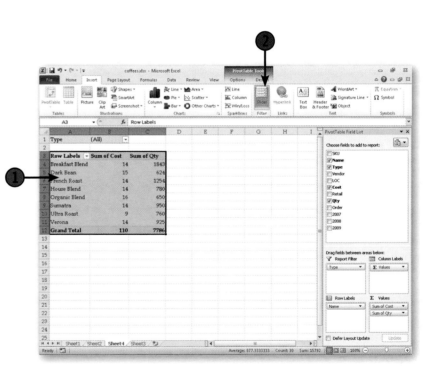

Create a Slicer *(continued)*

③ In the Insert Slicers list box, click the field you want to use to slice the PivotTable data.

④ Click OK.

⑤ Click an item in the list to change the display of the PivotTable data.

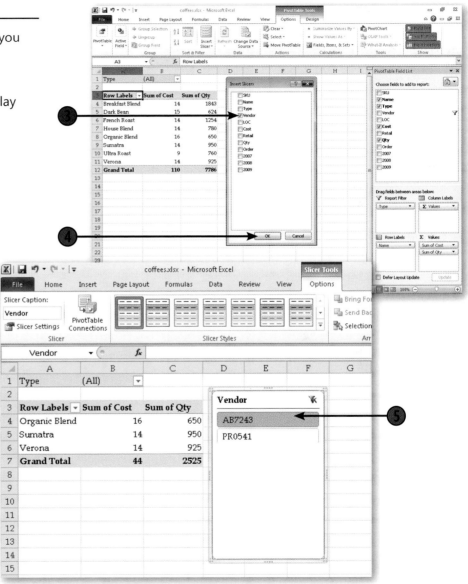

> **Tip** ✓
>
> You can modify the look of a slicer by clicking the Slicer Tool Options tab and changing the slicer caption, style colors and effects, button size and format, and overall size of the slicer window.

Reviewing the Data

If you're working with a lot of data, your worksheet may grow to a point that it seems unwieldy. When you need to review your data in a large worksheet, you can "freeze" certain parts of the worksheet—the column and/or row titles, for example—so that they'll remain in view while you scroll through other parts of the worksheet. You can also split the window into several sections if you want different parts of the worksheet to be visible so that you can compare them.

Freeze the Columns and/or Rows

① Click in a single cell that's at the right of the columns and/or below the rows to freeze the columns and/or the rows.

② On the View tab, click the Freeze Panes tool in the Window group.

③ Choose whether you want to freeze both the rows above and the columns to the left, or to freeze just the top row or the first column.

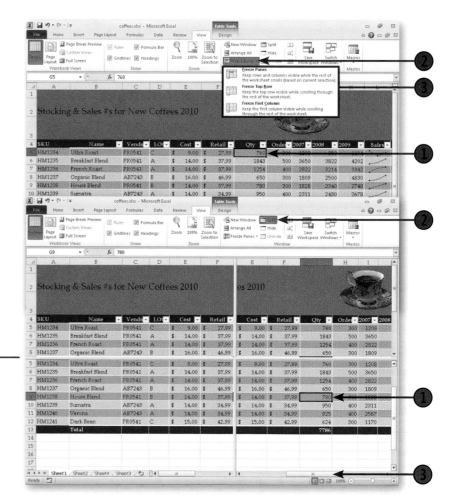

> **Tip**
>
> If your data is contained in a table, the table headings will replace the standard column labels (such as A and B) at the top of the window when you scroll the window and the table headings move off the screen.

View Multiple Sections

① Click where you want to split the worksheet.

② On the View tab, click Split in the Window group.

③ Use the scroll bars to scroll the contents of the different panes.

④ Click the Split button again to remove the multiple panes.

The Anatomy of a Chart

A chart gives you a way to display your data so that people viewing your worksheet can understand at a glance what the data is trying to convey. You can use a chart to compare cookie sales for the members of your scout troupe, plot the results of your annual membership drive, or contrast key items in your household budget.

Excel 2010 enables you to create many types of charts. Column charts and pie charts are the most common, but you can also create line, bar, area, scatter, stock, surface, donut, bubble, and radar charts. In addition to choosing a basic chart type, you can apply a number of formatting effects to create just the look you want. You'll find the tools you need for creating an Excel chart in the Insert tab. The following illustration points out important chart elements.

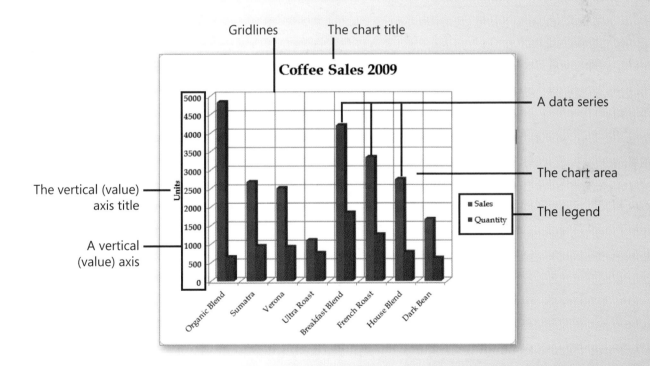

Charting Your Data

One of the best ways to present your data in a clear and understandable form is to use a well-designed chart. You can choose to create a number of different chart types in Excel, depending on what you want to show with the data in your worksheet. First decide which data you want to include in the chart and then select the type of chart that will best illustrate the information.

Create a Chart

1. Select the data you want to use in the chart.

2. In the Charts group on the Insert tab, click the type of chart you want to use.

3. In the gallery that appears, click the chart style you want.

4. Click the chart and on the Chart Tools Design tab, select a layout for the chart.

5. Click the Change Chart Type tool to choose a different type of chart or click the Switch Row/Column tool in the Data group to change the way the data will be plotted.

6. If you want the chart to appear in its own worksheet, click Move Chart in the Location group, and in the Move Chart dialog box, select New Sheet. Click OK.

Tip

Your data doesn't have to be contiguous. To select noncontiguous data, hold down the Ctrl key while you're dragging over the data.

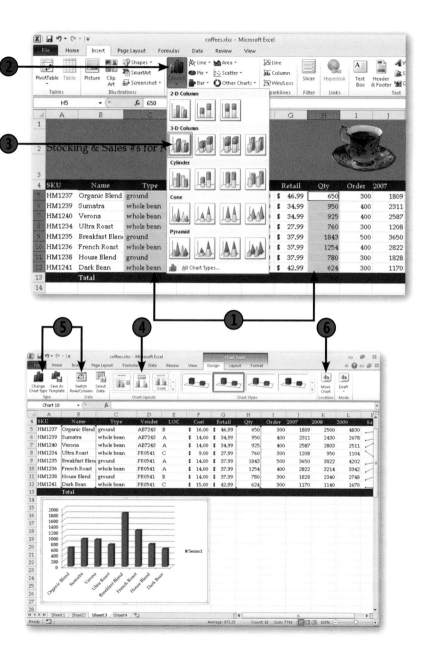

Complete the Layout

① On the Chart Tools Layout tab, with the chart selected, click any of the Labels buttons. Specify whether you want a label and, if so, where you want it. Type the text for any labels you've created.

② Click the Axes button, and select the style and/or scale for any axis you want to modify.

③ Click the Gridlines button, and if you want to display gridlines for an axis, specify the types of gridlines you want.

④ Click any of the Background buttons, and choose to hide or display background elements or to modify the 3-D rotation.

⑤ Click to show a trendline, drop lines, up/down bars, or error bars. Note that not all line types are available for all chart types.

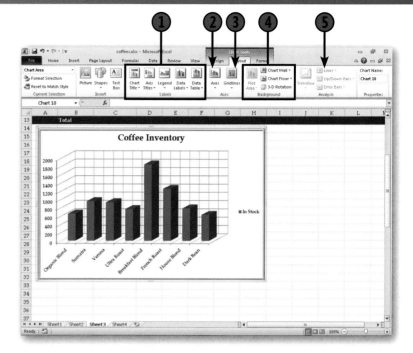

Tip

The numbers and/or the text on the chart's axes are based on the worksheet data you're using. To make changes to these elements, you'll need to make the changes in your worksheet.

Tip

There are numerous types of lines you can display. For example, the trendline can be linear, exponential, linear forecast, or a two-period moving average. The error bars can be based on standard error, percentage, or one standard deviation. Make sure that you choose the correct type of line for the information that you're presenting.

Formatting a Chart

When you create a chart, Excel uses the default settings for the chart design. You can change the overall appearance of the chart by changing the chart style or by changing the theme. You can also modify the appearance of individual parts of the chart.

Change the Chart Style

1 Click the chart to select it.

2 On the Chart Tools Design tab, click the style you want for the chart.

Change the Theme

1 On the Page Layout tab, with the chart visible, click the Themes tool, and point to the different themes to see how the appearance of the chart changes with each theme.

2 Click the theme you want for your chart.

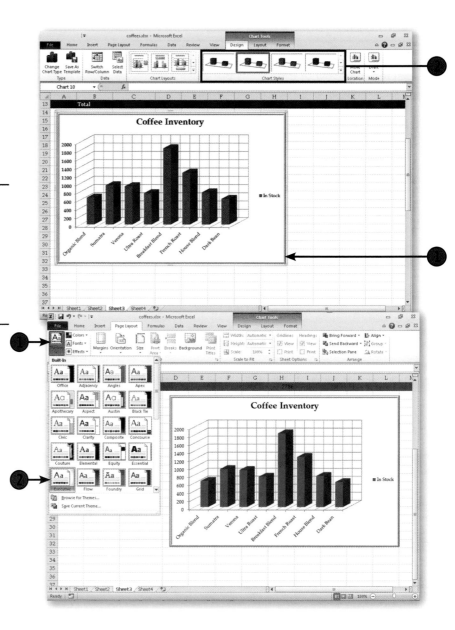

Format an Element

1 On the Chart Tools Format tab, select the chart element you want to format.

2 Select the style you want to apply to that element.

3 Click the appropriate tool to modify the formatting applied by the style.

4 If the selection contains text that you want to format using WordArt, click the WordArt style you like. Click the appropriate button to modify the formatting.

5 Use the Size tools to adjust the dimensions of the selected element.

6 Click the Format Selection tool in the Current Selection group, and in the Format dialog box, click the various categories to make changes to the formatting of the element.

7 Click Close when you've finished.

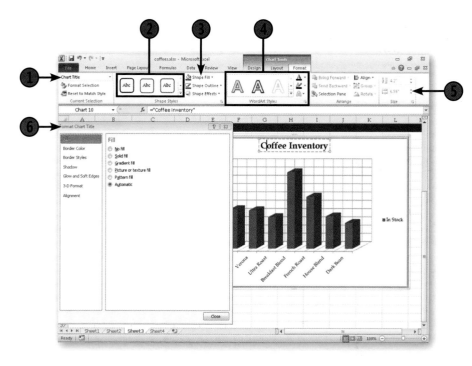

Tip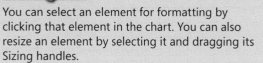

To format text without using WordArt, use the font and alignment tools on the Home tab.

Tip

You can select an element for formatting by clicking that element in the chart. You can also resize an element by selecting it and dragging its Sizing handles.

Customizing a Chart

In some situations, you may want to combine different chart types to create the best approach for displaying your data.

You can even add one or more axes so that your data can be presented with different scales.

Change a Data-Series Chart

1. Click to select the chart.

2. On the Chart Tools Design tab, click Change Chart Type in the Type group to display the Change Chart Type dialog box.

3. Select the chart type that you want to use for the selected series.

4. Click OK.

Caution

Some chart types are incompatible, so Excel might not allow you to add one type of chart to another. In this case, you'll need to experiment with different combinations of chart types to find out which ones work together.

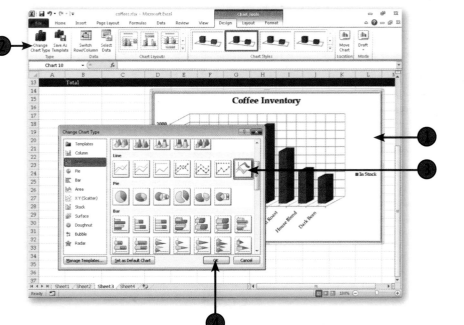

9

Creating a PowerPoint Presentation

Anytime you present information—whether you're talking to a group of salespeople, sharing a school presentation, introducing a product, or outlining plans for your gardening club—you need a simple tool that helps you put your thoughts and images together in a way your audience understands. Microsoft PowerPoint 2010 makes it easy for you to create slide presentations and deliver them in person or over the Web. You can also incorporate video clips, apply video styles, animate slide elements, and choose from an expanded collection of transitions.

As with most Office programs, you can use one of Power-Point's existing layouts or you can create your own slide presentation from scratch. You can choose a theme to create a unified design throughout all the slides in your presentation; modify a theme; or design your own customized theme, choosing the background, colors, and fonts to complement the mood of the presentation. You can add tables and SmartArt graphics to your slides and make them sparkle with some WordArt or animation. You can easily add narration or music, perhaps adding a CD soundtrack to your presentation. And if you need to do a bit of editing and tweaking, you'll find PowerPoint's Outline view and Slide Sorter helpful and easy to use.

What's Where in PowerPoint?

Microsoft PowerPoint 2010 is designed to help you create and present professional slide presentations. Your presentation can include slides, text, pictures, videos, charts, and more. You can create a simple informational presentation—just the facts, please—or an elaborate presentation with video, audio, and segments that you hide or display depending on your audience. Your presentation can include animated elements, sophisticated transitions, and other effects that will keep your audience engaged and interested.

You'll do much of your work in Normal view, adding text and pictures, adjusting and enhancing content, and adding new slides.

The ribbon

A preview of the slides in the presentation

The PowerPoint work area

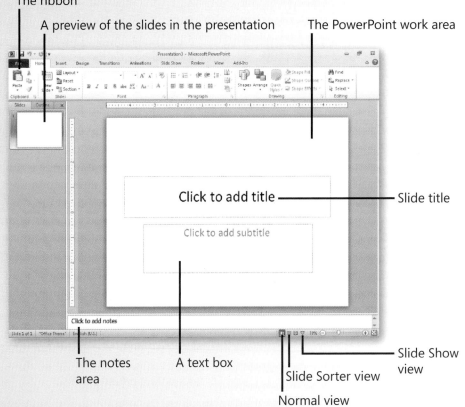

Slide title

The notes area

A text box

Slide Sorter view

Normal view

Slide Show view

Ways to View Your Presentation

After you add content to your slides, you can use Slide Sorter view to organize your entire presentation and to make sure that all the elements you've added have a consistent look. You can also use Slide Sorter view as a kind of storyboard for reviewing your presentation: just double-click a slide in Slide Sorter view, and the slide will open in Normal view, ready for editing. Slide Sorter view is also the view to use when you want to see, for example, which theme you've selected or which transition is being used for a particular slide.

There are other views—Slide Show view and Notes Page view, as well as the view of the slide master, handout master, and notes master—that aren't shown here. Slide Show view is self-explanatory, and Notes Page view is similar to Normal view except that it's formatted as a printed page. Notes Page view shows a printed version of the slide and includes an area where you can type your notes. The three master views allow you to set up the overall layout and coordinate the look of your slides, handouts, and notes.

Presentation slide

Use tools on the ribbon to set the slide layout, theme, backgrounds, animation, and transitions.

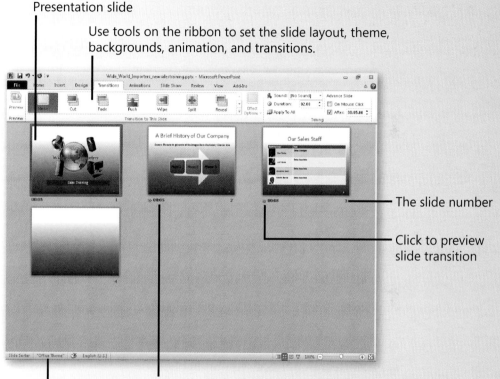

The slide number

Click to preview slide transition

The length of time the slide is displayed before advancing

The status bar shows the selected theme.

Creating a Presentation

When you start PowerPoint 2010, the program displays a blank title slide by default. You can begin to add text and pictures on that slide, choose a different slide layout, apply a design, and much more. If you prefer, you can choose a PowerPoint template and build your own presentation using the professional design already put together for you. When you're ready to begin working on the presentation, you can set up the slide size, orientation, and background styles you want so that all slides you create will have a similar look and feel.

Choose a Template

1. Start PowerPoint.

2. Click File, and click New.

3. Click the folder of the type of presentation you want to create.

4. Or, if the template is stored on your computer, click My Templates.

5. To view predesigned presentations, click Sample Templates.

6. Click the template you want to use.

7. Click Create.

Tip

After you find a template you like on Office.com, you can save it to your computer so that you can use it again later. After you open the template, click File and choose Save As; then save the file as a PowerPoint Template (*.potx). The template will appear in your My Templates folder.

Set Up the Presentation

 Display the new presentation.

 If you need to customize settings for your slides, click Page Setup in the Page Setup group of the Design tab to display the Page Setup dialog box, change your settings, and click OK.

 Point to the various themes to preview the way your slides will look with each theme. Click the theme you want to apply to all the slides in your presentation.

 Click the Background Styles button, and in the gallery that appears, point to the different styles to preview the effect each has on your slides. Click the style you want.

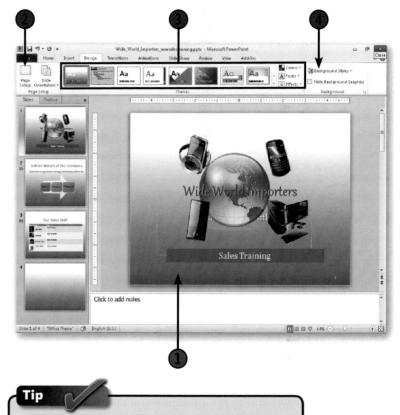

> **Tip** ✓
>
> Every presentation has a default theme that defines the color scheme, default fonts, and graphics effects.

> **Tip** ✓
>
> If you're creating a presentation using an existing template, the slides in the New Slide and Layout galleries will probably look different from those you see when you start a blank presentation because custom templates contain modified master slides, which control the layout.

Set the Page Background

The color and texture you choose for the background of your slides say a lot about the personality of your presentation. You can easily apply styles to individual slides or to the entire presentation so all your slides look professionally designed.

Format the Background

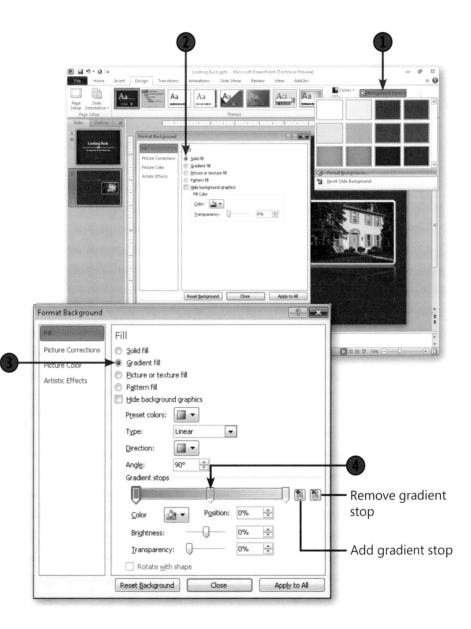

1. On the Design tab, with the slide you want to modify selected, click the Background Styles button, and click Format Background in the gallery to display the Format Background dialog box.

2. If you want to use a single color, select this option and specify the color and the degree of transparency you want.

3. If you want to use a gradient fill, select this option and specify the colors, the type of gradient, and the direction and angle of the gradient.

4. Use these settings if you want to create a customized gradient.

(continued on next page)

Remove gradient stop

Add gradient stop

Format the Background   *(continued)*

5 If you want to use a texture or a picture file, select this option and specify the source you want to use.

6 Select this check box if you want to use multiple copies (tiling), or clear the check box if you want to use a single copy that's resized to fit the slide (stretch).

7 Set the tiling or stretch options.

8 If you choose to use a picture for the background, you can click Picture Corrections, Picture Color, or Artistic Effects to fine-tune the picture.

9 Click Close to use the settings on the selected slide, or click Apply To All to use the settings on all the slides in your presentation.

Entering Content

Adding content to your presentation really is as simple as pointing and clicking in a text box on a slide. You can add different text items and add pictures, video, and more, depending on the layout you choose for your slide.

Add Your Content

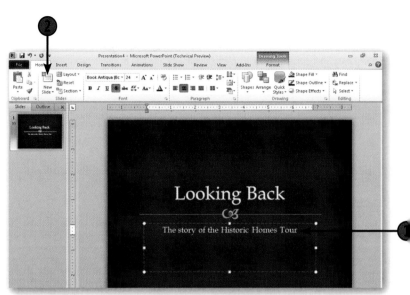

1. Click in a text box and type your text. Use the tools on the Home tab and the Drawing Tools Format tab to modify any text or paragraph formatting. If there are other text boxes, click in each, and add and format your text.

2. When you're ready to create the next slide, click the bottom part of the New Slide button, and in the gallery that appears, select the layout you want for the new slide.

3. If you don't like the current layout, click the Layout button and choose a different layout for the slide.

4. If your slide contains content boxes, either type the text you want or click one of the buttons to add a table, chart, SmartArt graphic, picture, piece of clip art, or media clip.

5. Continue clicking the bottom part of the New Slide button, selecting the layout you want for each slide and adding content to each slide until your presentation is complete.

6. Click the Save button, and name and save your presentation.

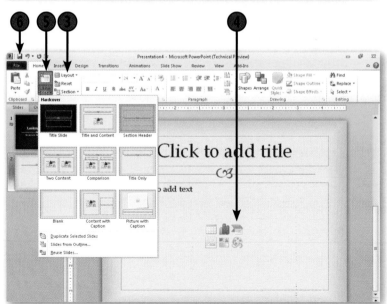

See Also

Read "Inserting Pictures" on pages 32–33, "Adding Shapes" on page 43, "Adding Clip Art" on pages 40–41, "Creating Stylized Text" on pages 46–47, and "Inserting a SmartArt Diagram" on pages 48–49 for information about inserting these elements into your slide presentation.

Formatting a Slide

Although the theme that you choose for your presentation applies the default color and font schemes, you can modify the individual elements and change the background to customize the appearance of each slide. The content boxes on the slides are text boxes, which are just another type of Shape.

Format the Content

1 Click a text box to select it.

2 Use the Sizing handles to resize the text box or the Rotation handle to rotate it, and then drag it to the location you want.

3 On the Home tab, with the text box selected, click the Quick Styles button, and in the gallery that appears, click the style you want for the text box.

4 To format a shape, click Shape Effects in the gallery that appears, point to the various types of effects, and then click the one you want.

5 Select the text you want to modify, and use any of the font tools to change the font and its size or color, and to add or remove any emphasis.

6 Select any paragraphs you want to modify, and use any of the paragraph tools to change the horizontal or vertical alignment, the line spacing, or the text direction; to add or remove bullets or numbering; or to create multiple columns.

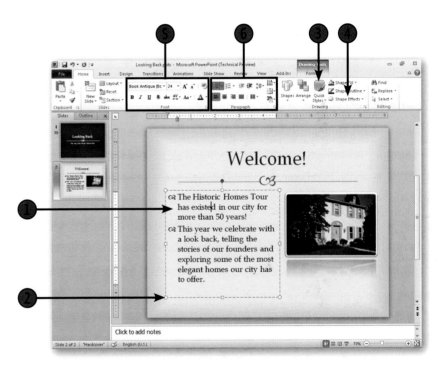

Tip ✓

If you want to include some identifying content that will appear on each slide—a company logo or a watermark, for example—you can do so by using a background picture file. If necessary, increase the transparency value to prevent the background from interfering with the slide's content.

Editing a Presentation

You'll probably go back into your slide presentation many times to add, delete, or tweak a few elements until you're satisfied that your show is ready for prime time. PowerPoint provides two extremely helpful organizational tools that make editing and modifying your presentation a breeze: Outline view and Slide Sorter view.

Change the Content of the Slides

1. In Normal view, with your presentation open, click the Outline tab.

2. Click a slide to preview it.

3. Select any text you want to change, and type the new text. Select and delete an entire entry if you want to remove it from the slide.

4. Click at the left of an item to select it, and using the four-headed-arrow mouse pointer, drag the item to a new location on the slide, to a new location on a different slide, or to the left or right to promote or demote the item in a list.

5. Make any changes to nontext items directly on the slide.

6. Continue through the text and the slides to modify the content as desired.

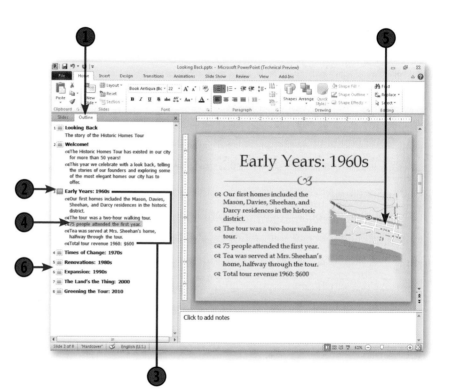

Change the Order of the Slides

(1) Click the Slide Sorter View button to switch to Slide Sorter view.

(2) Drag a slide that you want to display in a different part of your slide presentation to the spot where you want it.

(3) If there's a slide that you don't want to include in this presentation but that you don't want to delete, select it, and on the Slide Show tab, click the Hide Slide button. To return the hidden slide to the presentation, select it and click the Hide Slide button again.

(4) To permanently delete a slide, select it and press the Delete key.

(5) To add a blank slide, click the slide that will precede the new slide in the presentation and, on the Home tab, click the New Slide button.

Tip

You can change the order of slides in Normal view by selecting a slide on either the Slide tab or the Outline tab and then dragging the slide to a new location on that tab. Slide Sorter view, however, lets you see more of your slides at one time than are visible in Normal view.

Adding Headers and Footers

If you want to add information to all your slides for your audience to see (such as the slide number, the date, your name, or any other information), you can create a footer—that is, an area at the bottom of the slide in which to put the item.

Add the Footer

1. If you want to add the footer to only a single slide, select the slide. If you want to add the footer to all the slides, you can select any slide.

2. On the Insert tab, click the Header & Footer button to display the Header And Footer dialog box.

3. On the Slide tab, select this check box if you want the date to appear.

4. Select this option if you want the date to be updated automatically for each slide show. Select the format for the date.

5. Select this option if you want to enter a specific date and have that date always displayed.

6. Select this check box if you want the slide number displayed.

7. Select this check box, and enter your text if you want to customize the text in the footer.

8. Select this check box if you want the footer to appear on every slide except the title slide, or clear the check box if you want the footer to appear on all slides.

9. Click Apply to have the footer appear only on the selected slide, or click Apply To All to have it appear on all slides.

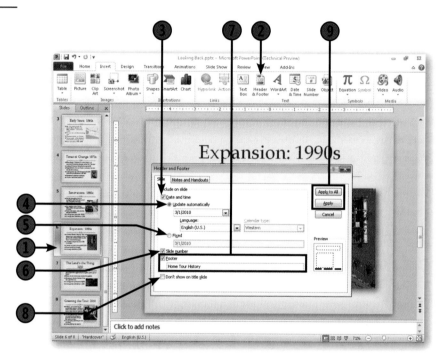

See Also

Read "Format the Background" on pages 212–213 for information about adding a background graphic, and "Modifying the Default Layout" on pages 220–221 for information on how to add the same content to different presentations.

Reusing Slides

PowerPoint makes it easy for you to save slides you really like so that you can use them in other presentations. You can also insert into the current presentation slides you've previously saved. You can choose the Reuse Slides tool at the bottom of the New Slide list to begin the process. Here's how.

Reuse a Slide

① On the Home tab, click the bottom part of the New Slide button, and click Reuse Slides in the gallery to display the Reuse Slides pane.

② Click the Browse button, and choose Browse File from the drop-down menu. In the Browse window, locate and select the presentation that contains the slide you want to copy, and click Open.

③ In your current presentation, click the slide that you want to precede the slide or slides to be inserted.

④ Select this check box if you want the slide to retain its formatting from the original presentation, or clear the check box if you want the slide or slides to take on the formatting of the current presentation.

⑤ Click the slide or slides that you want to add.

⑥ Repeat steps 2 through 5 to insert any slides you want from other presentations.

⑦ Close the Reuse Slides pane when you've finished.

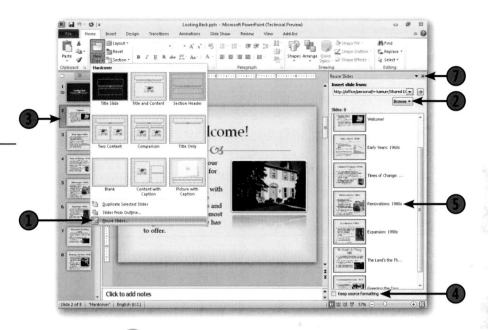

Tip

You can use the same slide more than once in a presentation. To do so, select the slide or slides to be duplicated, click the bottom part of the New Slide button, and click Duplicate Selected Slides in the gallery.

Tip

If you use PowerPoint 2010 with SharePoint Server 2007 or 2010, you can create a slide library to store slides you want to reuse in other presentations. Each slide is stored as a separate file that you and others with permission to use the server site can access and insert in your PowerPoint 2010 presentations.

Modifying the Default Layout

The layouts of your slides are based on the layouts of your slide master and your layout master. If you want to create your own designs, you can modify the slide master and the layout and then save the design as a template for future use. The different slide layouts are the basis for the various slide types you see in the New Slide gallery.

Modify the Layout

1. On the View tab, click the Slide Master button to display the Slide Master tab.

2. Click the first slide, which is the slide master. Changes you make to this slide will be used by the other layout slides that are shown below the slide master.

3. Use the tools on the Slide Master tab to set the slide dimensions, the theme, and the background styles.

4. Click in the title text box, and use the tools on the Drawing Tools Format tab and the Home tab to modify the text style.

5. Click in the content text box, and modify the styles for the different levels of text.

6. Click a slide layout, and modify the contents of the slide, including adding or deleting any text boxes or placeholders. Most changes will apply only to the selected slide, but theme and page setup changes apply to all slides.

7. Continue modifying the layouts to create your design.

8. If there's a slide layout you don't want, select it and then click Delete on the Slide Master tab.

Tip

You can also modify the default layout for your handouts and notes. To do so, click the Handout Master button or the Notes Master button on the View tab, and modify the handout master or the notes master.

Create a New Layout

1. Click the Insert Layout button to insert a new slide.

2. Modify any content in the slide to the way you want it.

3. Click the Insert Placeholder button, and select the type of placeholder you want. Drag out the placeholder, adjust its size if necessary, and move it to the location where you want it. Add any other place-holders you want, and format the slide and the slide elements.

4. With the slide selected, click the Rename button; in the Rename Layout dialog box that appears, type a descriptive name and click Rename.

5. Continue adding and modifying any slide layouts you want.

6. Click the Close Master View button when you've finished.

7. If you want to use this layout for future presentations, click File and click Save As in Backstage view. In the Save As dialog box, type a file name, save the file as a PowerPoint template, and click Save.

Tip

If you want to create a second series of slide layouts based on a new slide master, click Insert Slide Master on the Slide Master tab, and then add the slide layouts.

Inserting a Table

If you want to insert a large table into a slide, it's a good idea to create it in Microsoft Word 2010 or Microsoft Excel 2010 and then copy it into your PowerPoint presentation. However, you can easily create a small table directly on the slide.

Create the Table

1. On the Insert tab, in a slide with a content box, click the Table button and choose Insert Table.

2. In the Insert Table dialog box that appears, specify the number of rows and columns you need for your table. Click OK.

(continued on next page)

Tip

You can also draw your own freeform table by clicking the Insert tab, clicking Table, and choosing Draw Table. Drag to draw the table on the slide. Click the Draw Table tool in the Draw Borders group of the Table Tools Design tab, and add rows and columns by clicking on the border of the table and drawing a line to the opposite edge of the table border. Continue adding lines until you have the number of rows and columns you want, and then click outside the table to add it to the slide.

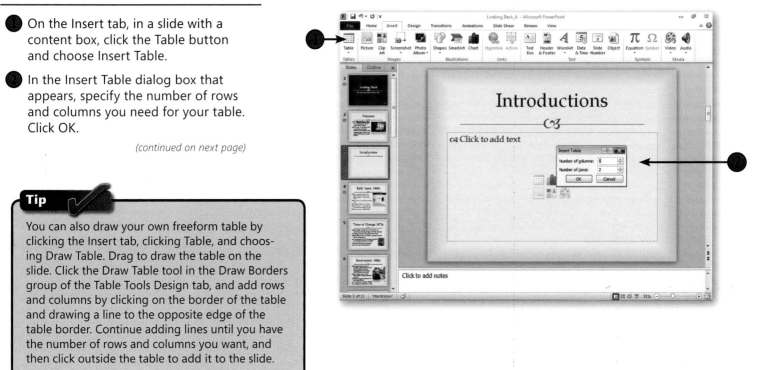

Create the Table *(continued)*

3 Use the tools on the Table Tools Layout tab to modify the table as you want.

4 On the Table Tools Design tab, select the items you want to include in the table.

5 Use any of the Table Styles to format the table.

6 Use the Shading, Borders, and Effects buttons to customize the table.

7 Enter your content in the table.

8 Apply styles and settings to your text if you want.

9 Drag the borders of the table if you need to resize it, and then drag it to the location you want.

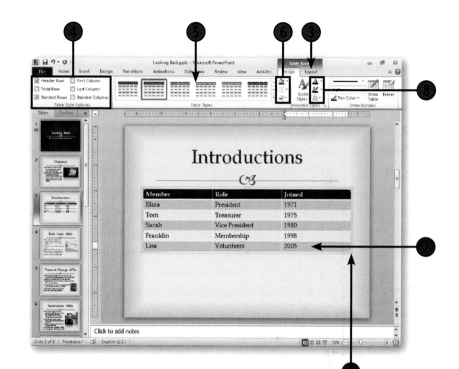

Tip

To insert a table into any slide, click the Table button on the Insert tab, and select the dimensions you want for the table.

Turning Text into SmartArt

An excellent way to improve the appearance of your slides and present information in an easy-to-understand way is to convert headings and bulleted lists into SmartArt graphics. That way, you'll have an organized structure and professional-looking graphics.

Create the Graphic

1. Place all the text that you'll be using in the graphic in one text box, and click in the text box to select it if it isn't already selected.

2. On the Home tab, click the Convert To SmartArt Graphic tool in the Paragraph group, and choose the design you want from the gallery that appears. If you don't see a design you want, click More SmartArt Graphics in the gallery, and use the Choose A SmartArt Graphic dialog box to select the graphic you want.

3. Use the SmartArt Tools Design and Format tabs to modify the SmartArt to the look you want.

4. Drag a Sizing handle on the border of the SmartArt graphic if you want to change its size, and then drag a border to move the SmartArt to the location you want.

See Also

Read "Inserting a SmartArt Diagram" on pages 48–49 for information about working with SmartArt graphics.

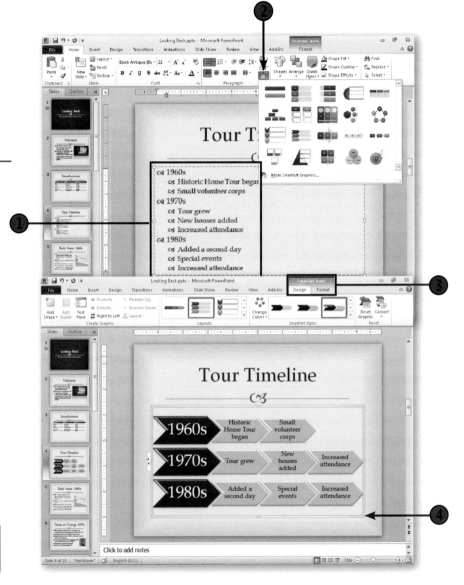

Applying WordArt Styles to Text

Some slide presentations are just fine with plain text that you format using the tools in the Font group of the Home tab, but others can benefit from a little livening up. That's where WordArt comes in. It's easy and fun to add interest to titles or any special parts of your presentation with WordArt formatting. Just don't go overboard with the dazzle factor!

Convert the Text

1. Select the text that you want to convert into WordArt.

2. On the Drawing Tools Format tab, click the More button in the WordArt Styles section to open the gallery. Point to each WordArt style that you might want to apply to your text to see how it will look. Note that the items in the upper part of the gallery affect only the selected text and that the items in the lower part affect all the text in the text box. Click the style you want.

3. Use the Text Fill, Text Outline, and Text Effects buttons to modify the appearance of the selected text.

Tip

If you want to remove the WordArt formatting, select the text and click Clear WordArt in the WordArt Styles gallery.

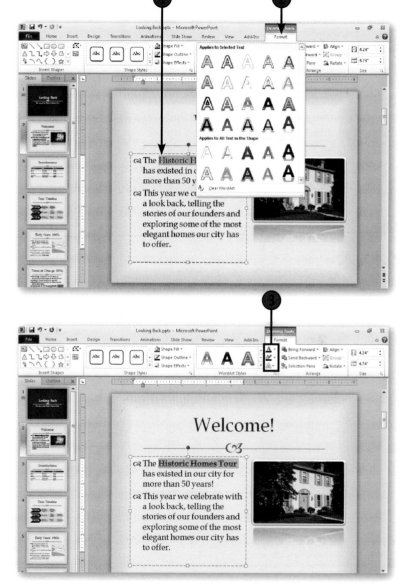

Animating Items on a Slide

Animation can make an onscreen slide presentation come alive with some professional-looking effects. You can animate the appearance of items on your slide—text, shapes, pictures, and more—with just a few clicks. And, when you're presenting your slide show, you can start the animation simply by clicking your mouse, or you can tell PowerPoint to play the animation automatically, triggered by other actions on the slide. PowerPoint 2010 adds some new animation effects, including the Animation Painter tool that enables you to apply animation settings to various items on your slides.

Animate a Slide Element

1. Click the element you want to animate.

2. On the Animations tab, click the More button in the Animation gallery to display the range of animation choices.

3. Point to the animation effect to preview it on the selected text. Click the animation you want to apply.

4. A small number appears where the animation was added. Click it, and click Effect Options to choose the settings for the effect.

Tip

When you select an animation, it runs for you so that you can preview it. To see it again, click the Preview button on the Animations tab.

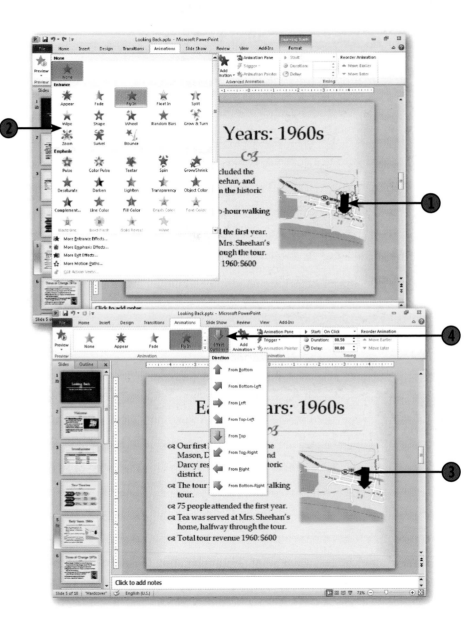

Use the Animation Painter

1. Click the element with the animation settings you want to use.

2. On the Animation tab, click Animation Painter in the Advanced Animation group.

3. Click the element to which you want to apply the animation settings.

Tip

If you want to apply the same animation effects to more than one object on the slide, double-click the Animation Painter before clicking the additional items you want to animate with those settings.

Set the Animation Trigger

1. Click the animated element on the slide.

2. Click the Animations tab, and in the Advanced Animation group, click Trigger.

3. Choose On Click Of, and click the slide element you want to trigger the animation. The animation icon on the element changes to reflect a trigger indicator, which resembles a lightning bolt.

Tip

You can animate a single shape, a table, or a picture. If you're including a chart in your presentation, you can animate an individual data series or individual categories, or you can animate the chart as a single item.

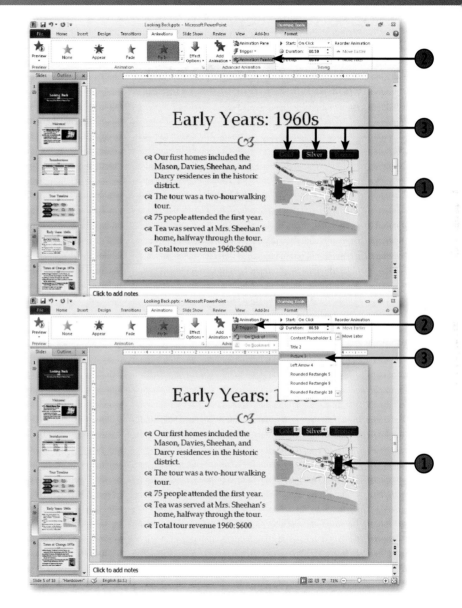

Customizing Your Animation

If you want to control the length of your animation effects and the order in which they occur, add more than one effect, or have access to many types of animations, you can create a customized animation scheme. By customizing your animations, you can make the items do a number of remarkable tricks.

Customize the Animation

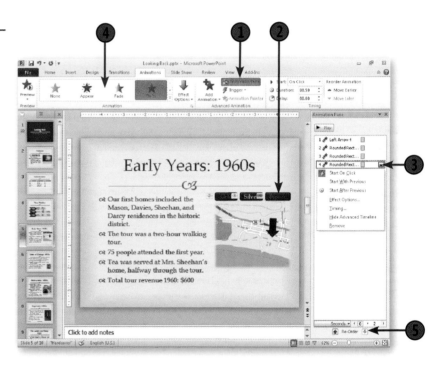

1. On the Animations tab, click the Animation Pane tool in the Advanced Animation group to display the Animation pane.

2. Click the item whose animation you want to apply or change.

3. Click the arrow of the item to display various ways to customize the animation:

   - Start On Click, Start With Previous, and Start After Previous all determine when the animation will play.

   - Effect Options displays the dialog box for that effect so that you can change the settings.

   - Timing enables you to set the start, duration, and repetition of the animation.

   - Hide Advanced Timeline removes the timeline at the bottom of the Animation pane.

   - Remove deletes the animation.

4. If you want to choose a different animation style, you can select it from the Animation gallery.

5. Use the Re-Order buttons if you want to change the order in which the items are animated.

6. Click the Animation Pane button again to close the Animation pane.

Tip

To add sound to the transition, to dim or hide the item, or to animate text by the letter or by the word, click the down arrow for the transition and choose Effects Options from the menu. Choose the sound you want to add in the Effects tab.

Adding an Action to a Slide

Sometimes, in the middle of a presentation, you might want to jump to a different part of the presentation, run a different program as a demonstration, open a file, or even have a little sound clip added. You can do this by assigning an action to the text or to some other item in your presentation.

Assign an Action

1 Select the item you want to use to trigger the action.

2 On the Insert tab, click the Action button to display the Action Settings dialog box.

3 If you want a different slide to appear when you click the item, click this option and choose the page you want to display.

4 If you want to run another program—perhaps to show an Excel worksheet—click this option and choose the program you want to run.

5 Select this check box if you want a sound to play when the item is clicked, and then select the sound.

6 If you want the action to occur when you move the mouse pointer over the item rather than when clicking it, make your settings on the Mouse Over tab.

7 Click OK, and run your slide presentation to make sure the action you want occurs when you click the mouse or move the mouse over the item.

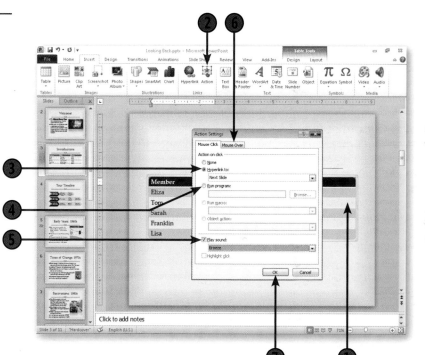

Tip

The Run Macro option is available only if your presentation contains at least one macro. The Object action is available only if you've selected an OLE (Object Linking and Embedding) object, such as an Excel workbook, that was inserted by using the Object button on the Insert tab.

Adding and Editing Video

One of the exciting new features in PowerPoint 2010 is that you now have the ability to edit and style the video clips you add to your slides. You can insert video files from your computer, download them from the Web, or insert video clips from Microsoft Office Clip Art. This enables you to add life to your slides and share compelling stories in a way that's sure to hold your audience's attention.

Insert a Video from a File

① Display the slide that will contain the video, and on the Insert tab, click the Video tool in the Media group.

② Click Video From File.

③ In the Insert Video dialog box that appears, find and select the movie you want and click Insert. Drag the Sizing handles of the image to set the size of your video, and then drag it to the location you want.

④ Play the video by clicking the Play button.

Caution

Remember that copyright laws apply to any content you add to your own creations, so be sure to use only original video clips or have the necessary permission from the copyright owner before you insert other people's clips in your files.

See Also

Read "Adding an Action to a Slide" on page 229 for information about playing any file or running any program from within a PowerPoint presentation.

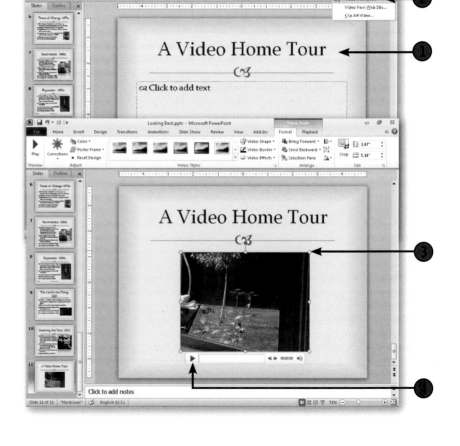

Edit Video Clips in PowerPoint

1. With the video selected, click the Video Tools Playback tab.

2. Click Trim Video in the Editing group.

3. Drag the starting marker to the point on the Timeline where you want the video to begin.

4. Drag the ending marker to the point at which you want the video clip to end.

5. Click OK.

6. Add Fade In and Fade Out values if you want the video to include fade effects.

7. Set Video Options to tell PowerPoint how you want to start the video, whether it should play full screen, and whether you want it to repeat.

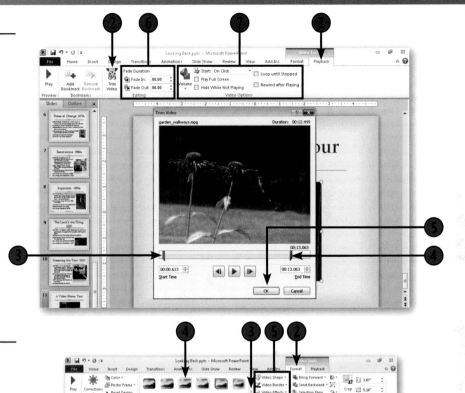

Apply Video Styles

1. Click the video to select it.

2. Click the Video Tools Format tab.

3. Click the Video Styles More button to display the entire gallery.

4. Point to the various styles to preview them.

5. Choose the video effects you want to apply.

6. Click Play.

Tip

The video clip will play during your presentation with the select style intact. For example, if you choose the Reflected Perspective Left style, the entire video clip will play with that style in effect.

Adding Sound to Your Slides

In PowerPoint 2010, you can easily add sound effects, voiceovers, and music to individual slides. You can add a soundtrack and narration to the presentation as well. This section shows you how to add sound to an individual slide.

Insert a Sound

1 Select the slide that will contain the sound, and on the Insert tab, click the bottom part of the Audio tool in the Media group. Choose one of the following sound sources from the drop-down menu:

- Audio From File, to display the Insert Sound window, where you can locate and select the sound file

- Clip Art Audio, to display the Clip Art pane with sound clips displayed

- Record Audio, to display the Record Sound dialog box

2 If you select Audio From File, the Insert Audio dialog box appears. Navigate to the file you want to add and click Insert.

3 If you choose Clip Art Audio, the Clip Art task pane appears so that you can click the clip you want to add to the slide.

(continued on next page)

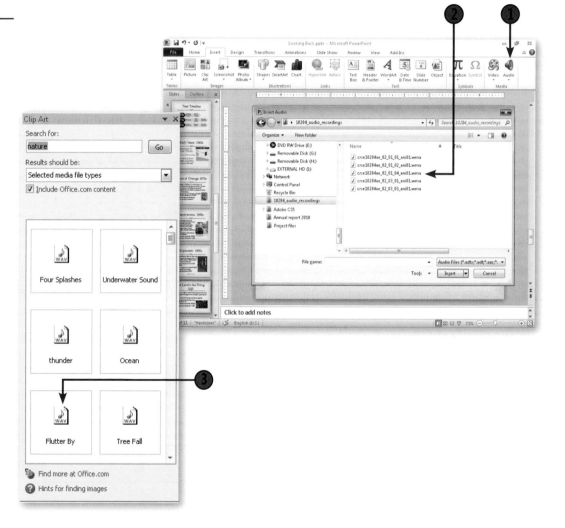

Insert a Sound *(continued)*

4 If you choose to record sound with a microphone or other sound-input setup, enter a name for the recording, click the Record button, record your sounds, and then click the Stop button. Click OK to insert the sound into your presentation.

5 Use the tools on the Sound Tools Options tab or the CD Audio Tools tab Audio Options group to modify your settings if necessary.

Tip

You can easily add a soundtrack or narration to the entire presentation. You'll learn how to do that in Section 10, "Presenting a PowerPoint Slide Show."

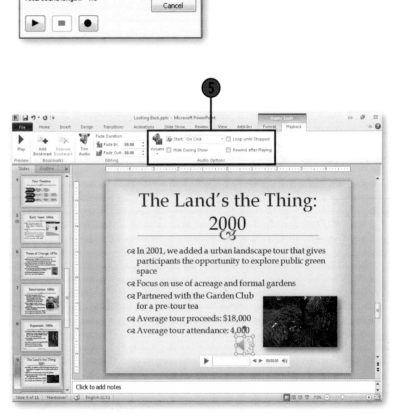

Setting Slide Transitions

When you develop a slide show, you might want to include some special effects as you make the transition from one slide to the next. When a new slide appears, your audience sees a transition effect—for example, a dissolve, a checkerboard, a "newsflash" effect, a sound, or any combination of these. You can also specify whether you want the next slide to advance automatically after a preset time or whether you want to switch to the next slide manually with a mouse-click.

Set the Transitions

1 Display your presentation in Slide Sorter view, and click the slide to which you want to add the transition.

2 On the Transitions tab, point to the various transitions to see how they look and then click the one you want.

3 Click Effect Options to make additional choices about the transition you selected.

4 Select a sound if you want one, and add the duration you want the sound to be played.

5 If you want the slide to advance automatically, clear the On Mouse Click check box and specify how long each slide is to be displayed before it advances.

6 Click Apply To All if you want all the slides in your presentation to have the transition you just selected. If you don't want the same transition for all the slides, repeat steps 1 through 5 to add transitions to the other slides in your presentation.

7 Click Preview to preview the transitions for all the slides.

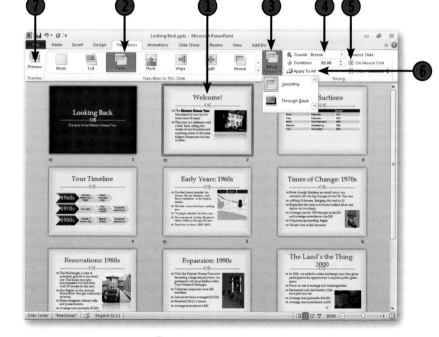

Tip

Although you can add the transition effects at any time, it's usually best to apply them after you've added all the slides to your show.

Caution

As with the text effects, don't use a lot of different transitional effects. They can make your presentation seem chaotic, and an audience might find them quite distracting.

Creating a Photo Album

A PowerPoint photo album gives you a great way to display a collection of pictures. All you need to do is select the pictures and the layout, and PowerPoint will put together a new presentation that contains your photo album. After the presentation is finished, you can save it as a video to CD—and voilà—you have an instant slide show to share with friends and relatives.

Create the Album

1. On the Insert tab, click the Photo Album button to display the Photo Album dialog box.

2. Click the File/Disk button to open the Insert New Pictures window, locate and select the pictures you want to use, and click Insert.

3. Click to include a blank text box in place of a picture.

4. Use the Order buttons to re-order the pictures and any text boxes, or use the Remove button to remove a picture from the album.

5. Use the picture controls to rotate a selected picture or to change its contrast or brightness.

6. Select a layout, the shape of the frame you want for each picture, and a design template if you want to add extra design elements to your photo album.

7. Specify whether you want the file names to be included as captions under all your pictures, and whether you want to convert your color pictures into black-and-white versions. Note that you can't include a caption if the picture is set to fill the entire slide.

8. Click Browse to assign a theme.

9. Click Create to have PowerPoint create a new presentation. Edit the photo album, adding text and changing styles and/or the theme. The completed photo album is now ready to be shown as an onscreen slide show or to be printed and bound.

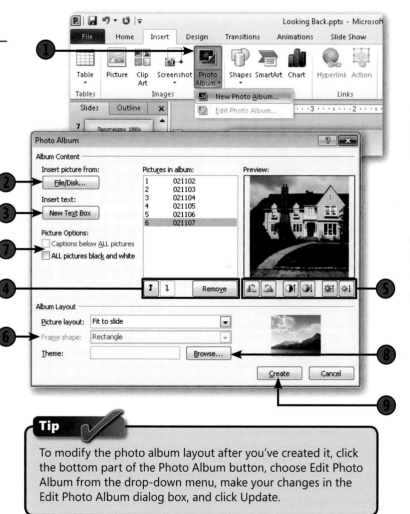

Tip

To modify the photo album layout after you've created it, click the bottom part of the Photo Album button, choose Edit Photo Album from the drop-down menu, make your changes in the Edit Photo Album dialog box, and click Update.

10

Presenting a PowerPoint Slide Show

Now that you've created your slide show, you're almost ready to present it. Microsoft PowerPoint 2010 gives you a number of ways to deliver the presentation, whether you plan to stand up in front of a group, broadcast the presentation on the Web, or save it to a CD so that others can watch it later.

In this section, you learn to finalize your presentation by adding narration, speaker notes, and more. You find out how to print handouts and slide notes so that you can present easily and leave key information in the hands of your audience when you're done. You'll also learn to set the timing of your presentation and practice navigating through the slide show a few times. Finally, you find out how to go live with your presentation—both offering it in a group and broadcasting it over the Web. Fun stuff! And it's easy to present—and look good doing it—with this latest version of PowerPoint.

Exploring Your Presentation Options

Most people aren't too crazy about standing up in front of a group to deliver a presentation. For most of us, preparing a presentation means hours of effort, lots of anxiety, and more than a few dry-mouthed run-throughs before the actual

event. Whether you are new at presenting (and dreading it!) or an old hand who actually *likes* the limelight, you'll find that PowerPoint 2010 includes a number of features that help you present professionally both in person and online.

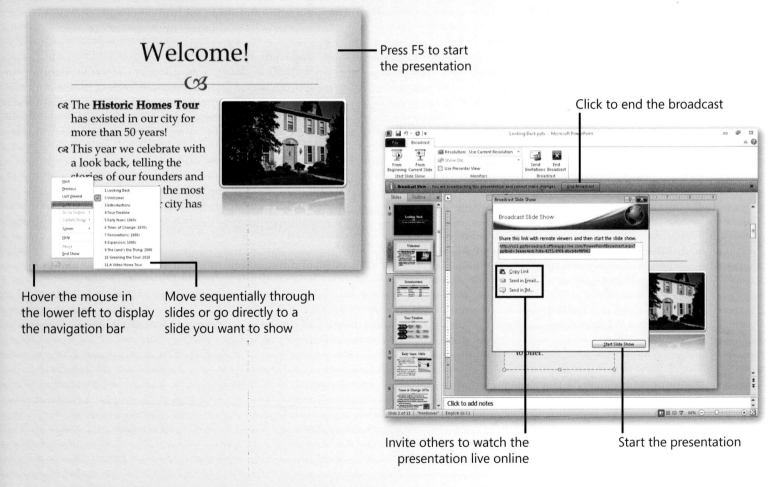

Press F5 to start the presentation

Click to end the broadcast

Hover the mouse in the lower left to display the navigation bar

Move sequentially through slides or go directly to a slide you want to show

Invite others to watch the presentation live online

Start the presentation

Preparing for the Perils of Presentation

Most of us have witnessed the embarrassment of someone who's struggling to get a slide presentation to run from a projector or on a second monitor. Why is there no video signal from the computer to the projector? Why is only part of the screen visible? Or—oops!—once the show finally gets going, a screen saver suddenly pops up or the computer goes to sleep. It's awful! The flustered presenter has to log back on and resume the presentation, only to be sabotaged yet again by the screen saver or the power settings. Here are a few tips to help you get your hardware ready:

■ Turn off your screen saver by clicking the Start button and typing **screen saver** in the search box. Click Turn Screen Saver On Or Off, and in the Screen Saver dialog box, set the Screen Saver setting to (None) and click OK. You can also click Start, click Control Panel, and click Appearance and Personalization. In the Personalization category, click Change Screen Saver and, in the Screen Saver area of the Screen Saver Settings dialog box, click the arrow and choose None. Click OK to save your settings.

■ Prepare your computer to work with a network projector by clicking Start and

typing **network projector** in the search box. Click Connect To A Network Projector and Windows 7 launches a wizard that walks you through the process.

■ If you want to use dual monitors, click Use Presenter View in the Monitors group of Slide Show tab to make sure PowerPoint 2010 is seeing both your monitors.

■ You can also change the screen resolution of the presentation to enhance the quality of the display your audience sees. Use the Resolution setting in the Monitors group to view options and make your selection.

Use to set up dual monitors

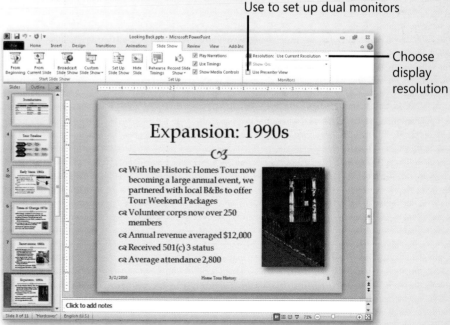

Choose display resolution

Recording a Narration

If you're going to be presenting live to an audience, narrating the presentation in real time is a good idea—it keeps your audience awake and engaged and gives you the chance to tailor your content to the needs of the audience. For those times when you can't be present, however—perhaps you're saving your presentation to CD, broadcasting it online, or making it available on your Web site—you can record the narration so that people viewing the presentation later get the benefit of the whole story.

Narrate Your Presentation

1 Click the first slide to select it.

2 Click the Record Slide Show button on the Slide Show tab to display the Record Narration dialog box.

3 Choose Start Recording.

(continued on next page)

Narrate Your Presentation *(continued)*

④ When the slide show starts automatically, record your narration as you go through the slides. Continue recording your narration until you've completed the slide show.

⑤ Run the slide show to make sure it's being presented exactly the way you want.

Tip

To delete a narration from a slide, in Normal view, click the sound icon at the bottom-right of the slide and press the Delete key.

Tip

The recorded narration for each slide stays with the actual slide, so if you change the timing of the presentation or extend the time by adding animations or other material, the narration will be unaffected.

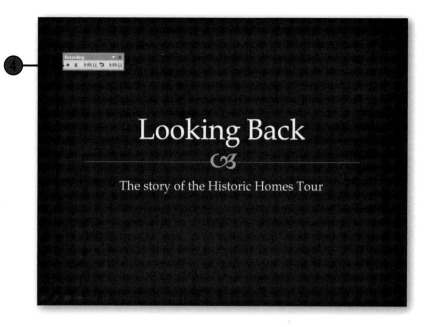

Timing a Presentation

Depending on the place and time you're presenting, you may need to limit your presentation to a specific period of time. Perhaps you have only 30 minutes to present right before lunch, or each of the speakers in the meeting are given a specific timeframe in which to present. To avoid taking too long on some slides and not long enough on others, you can rehearse the presentation and record the amount of time you use for each slide. When you get the presentation timed just the way you want it, you can have PowerPoint save the timing and apply it to the presentation automatically so that the slides advance at just the right time.

Time the Presentation

1. On the Slide Show tab, with your presentation complete and your notes or script in hand, click the Rehearse Timings button to start the slide show and to begin recording the timing.

2. Rehearse the presentation of each slide, noting the elapsed time for each slide and the elapsed time for the entire presentation.

(continued on next page)

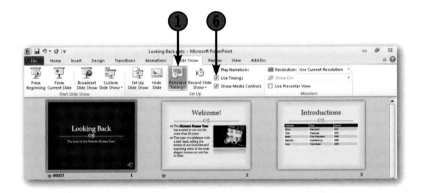

Time the Presentation *(continued)*

3 If you encountered a problem during the presentation of a slide, click the Repeat button to restart the timing for that slide.

4 If you need to suspend your rehearsal, click the Pause button. Click the button again to resume the rehearsal. Continue rehearsing the presentation until you've reached the end of the show.

5 When you've completed the slide show, and if the total time for the rehearsal was within the allocated time, click Yes to keep the recorded timing. Otherwise, click No and keep repeating steps 1 through 5.

6 With the Use Timings check box selected, start the slide show from the beginning, and make sure that the timing for the display of the slides is correct.

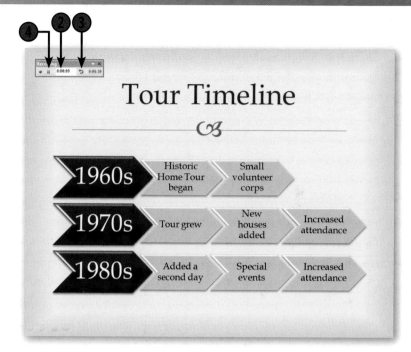

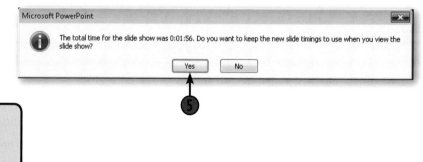

Tip ✓

To pause a timed presentation, right-click in the slide show and choose Pause from the shortcut menu. To resume the timed presentation, right-click again and choose Resume.

Adding Speaker Notes

You can use speaker notes to create prompts that remind you of important things you want to mention during the presentation. The notes could be quick reminders, an outline, or a detailed script—whatever helps you most. You can add notes as you create each slide by entering them in the Notes area at the bottom of Slide view, or you can add them as you review the finished presentation.

In addition to viewing the notes on the screen (either in Normal view or, if you're using two monitors, in Presenter view), you can also print the notes so that you can use them as you present.

Create the Notes

1 In Normal view, click the slide to which you want to add notes.

2 Click in the Notes area, and type your notes as you develop the slide.

3 On the View tab, click the Notes Page button.

4 If you want to change the color scheme for the picture of the slide, select the color setting you want.

5 Verify that the correct slide is shown, adjust the zoom so that you can see your text, and click in the Notes text box. Add, edit, and format the text as you want. You can also format the text box and the background of the notes page if you want.

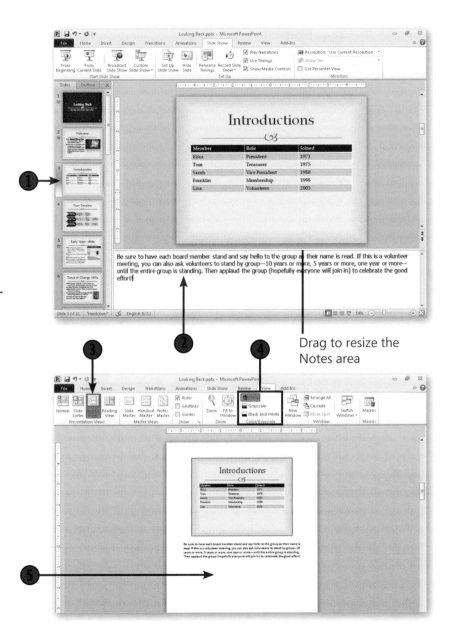

Drag to resize the Notes area

Set Up and Print the Notes

1 On the Design tab, click the Page Setup button to display the Page Setup dialog box.

2 Specify the orientation you want for your notes, and click OK.

3 On the Insert tab, click the Header & Footer button to display the Header And Footer dialog box.

4 On the Notes And Handouts tab, specify what you want to include in your notes, and type any custom header or footer text.

5 Click Apply To All.

6 Click File to display Backstage view, and click Print.

7 Select Notes Pages.

8 Specify whether you want to print your notes in color, grayscale, or black and white.

9 Make whatever other print settings you want, and click Print to print your notes.

Tip

You can page through the presentation to view notes on other slides as well by clicking the Next Page and Previous Page buttons in the lower left corner of the preview pane.

Tip

To print the text of your presentation as it appears in the outline, select Outline View in the Print What list.

Customizing the Presentation

When you've finished putting all the bits and pieces of your slide show together, you'll probably want to make a few tweaks to customize the show so that it will run exactly as you want it to. After you've made your customizations, the settings are saved with the presentation and will be used unless you decide to change them.

Set Up the Show

1. On the Slide Show tab, click the Set Up Slide Show button to display the Set Up Show dialog box.

2. Specify the way you want the show to be displayed.

3. Select this check box to have the slide show run continuously until you (or a presenter) press the Esc key.

4. Select either of these check boxes if you want to omit from the slide show any narration or animation that exists in the presentation.

5. Select the range of slides you want to include in the show, or specify which custom show to use.

6. Specify the way you want each slide to be advanced.

7. If your computer system is equipped with two or more monitors, specify which monitor you want to display the show.

8. Select this check box if you want to use Presenter view and you know that the computer is properly equipped.

9. Click OK.

See Also

Read "Creating Different Versions of a Slide Show" on page 248 for information about creating a custom show.

Reviewing a Presentation

If you are working on your presentation as part of a team effort, you may want to add, review, or remove comments in the presentation. Before you finalize the presentation and prepare it for an audience, you can go through the different slides and resolve any last-minute issues your co-authors pointed out.

Review the Presentation

1 On the Review tab, with the presentation open in Normal view, click the Show Markup button if it isn't already selected. (If the button isn't available, the document doesn't yet contain any comments.)

2 Click or select where you want to insert a comment.

3 Click the New Comment button.

4 Type your comment, and then click outside the comment when you've finished. Continue adding your comments to the presentation.

5 Click the Next or Previous button to find your own or other people's comments.

6 To edit a selected comment, click Edit Comment, make your changes to the comment, and then click outside the comment.

7 To delete a selected comment, all the comments on the slide, or all the comments in the presentation, click Delete, and from the drop-down menu, choose what is to be deleted.

8 Click the Show Markup button when you've finished. Any comments remaining in the presentation will be hidden until you're ready to review them.

> **See Also**
>
> Read "Changing Your User Information" on page 399 for information about changing the initials that are used to identify your comments.

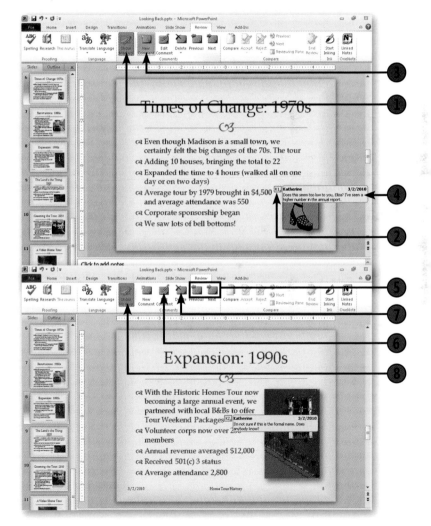

Creating Different Versions of a Slide Show

In some cases, you might want to adjust a slide show to make it suitable for different audiences. For example, you might show one version of the Historic Home Tour presentation for your volunteers and another version for possible donors.

Instead of creating a whole new show—or deleting slides, hiding slides, or rearranging the slide order for a different presentation—you can create one or more custom slide shows while keeping the original presentation intact.

Create a Custom Slide Show

① On the Slide Show tab, with your entire presentation completed and saved, click the Custom Slide Show button, and choose Custom Shows from the drop-down menu to display the Custom Shows dialog box.

② Click New to display the Define Custom Show dialog box.

③ Type a descriptive name for the show.

④ Hold down the Ctrl key, and click the slides that you want in the show to select them.

⑤ Click Add.

⑥ Click a slide, and use the Up or Down arrow button to change the slide's position in the show. Continue moving the slides around until they're in the order you want.

⑦ Click OK.

⑧ Click Show to preview your show.

⑨ The next time you want to view the custom show, on the Slide Show tab, with the original presentation open, click the Custom Slide Show button and choose the show from the drop-down menu.

Printing Handouts

If you want to give your audience members something to remember you by, consider printing handouts. Handouts are printed copies of your presentation that PowerPoint can generate automatically. The handouts show a small image of each slide. You can specify the number of slides you want to be printed on each page, and the slides will be scaled to fit on the page.

Create the Handouts

1. After you complete your presentation, click File to display Backstage view, and click Print.

2. Select Handouts, and specify the number of slides you want per page.

3. Choose other print options as needed for your handouts.

4. Click Next Page, and check the way that page will print. Continue going through the handout pages to verify that the layout appears as you want.

5. Click Print.

Tip ✔

If you want those viewing your presentation to see the notes you used while presenting it, you can print your presentation Notes Pages (which includes one slide on each page) instead of printing handouts. See "Set Up and Print the Notes" on page 245 for more about printing Notes Pages in PowerPoint.

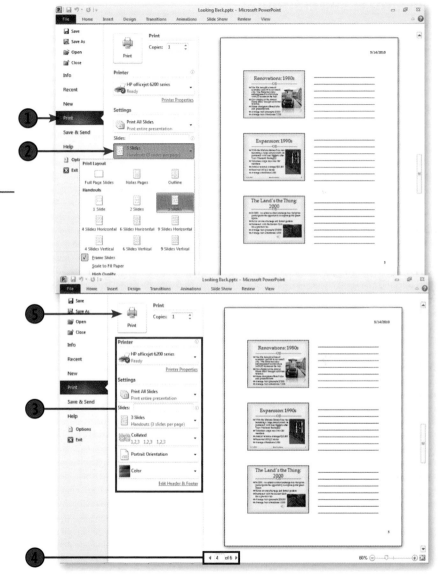

Running a Slide Show

You've finished fine-tuning your presentation and you're ready to show it. The next step involves practicing your presentation so that it is as smooth and polished as possible when you deliver it in front of a live audience. PowerPoint 2010 includes a number of features that help you present the slide show just the way you'd envisioned it.

Run the Presentation

① On the Slide Show tab, with PowerPoint running and your slide show open, select the resolution you want to use.

② If you have more than one monitor attached to your computer, select the one you want to use to show your presentation.

③ Click the From Beginning button (or press F5) or click the From Current Slide button to begin the presentation with either the first slide or the currently selected slide.

④ To display the next animation or—if there are no animations—the next slide, click the left mouse button or press the Right or Down arrow key.

⑤ To move back to the previous animation or—if there are no animations—the previous slide, move the mouse and click the Back arrow, or press the Left or Up arrow key.

Tip

There are multiple keyboard shortcuts to help you navigate your way through your presentation. For a full list, press the F1 key while you're running your presentation.

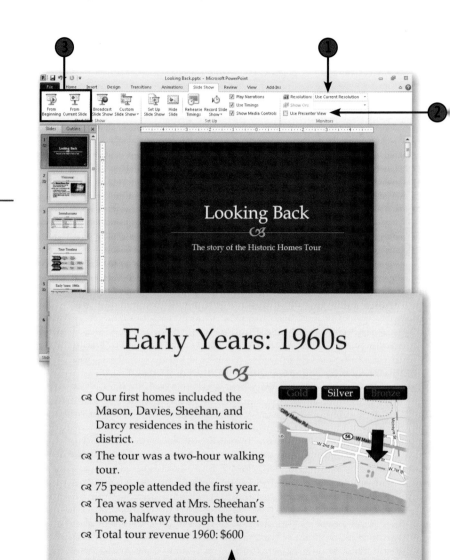

Using Ink While You Present

1 During the presentation, right-click to display the context menu.

2 Click Pointer Options.

3 Choose whether you want to use the Arrow, Pen, or Highlighter.

4 Click Pointer Options again, point to Ink Color, and in the gallery that appears, click the color you want for your annotation.

5 Hold down the left mouse button and drag to highlight or to annotate the slide.

6 Continue to go through the show, making whatever modifications you want. If you want to stop the presentation before you reach the end, press the Esc key, or right-click and choose End Show from the shortcut menu. If you've used any of the annotation tools, choose to save them when prompted if you want the annotations to be saved with the presentation.

The Land's the Thing: 2000

In 2001, we a   rban landscape tour that gives participants   tunity to explore public green space

Focus on use   e and formal gardens

Partnered wi

for a pre tou

Average tour proceed:

Average tour attendance: 4,000

Next
Previous
Last Viewed
Go to Slide
Go to Section
Custom Show
Screen
Pointer Options
Help
Pause
End Show
Arrow
Pen
Highlighter
Ink Color
Eraser
Erase All Ink on Slide
Arrow Options

Theme Colors
Standard Colors

Greening the Tour: 2010

In 2010, we're focusing on sustainable spaces, non-toxic home renovations, and other home ideas that are good for the earth

We are partnering with local environmental groups to provide education and tips for home owners

We are busy planning for our next tour!

Contact Shelby for details!

Sharing a Presentation

PowerPoint 2010 enables you to share the presentations you create in many ways. You can give a presentation in person, of course, or broadcast it over the Web (which you'll learn about later in this section). You can also e-mail the presentation to others, publish the slides to a SharePoint or Windows Live account, or create PDF or XPS files of the slides. You can begin by saving the presentation where you want it to be stored.

Save the Show to SharePoint

1. With your show completed and saved, click File to display Backstage view and click Save & Send.

2. Choose Save To SharePoint.

3. Click the location where you want to save the file.

4. Alternately, click Browse For A Location and navigate to the location you want.

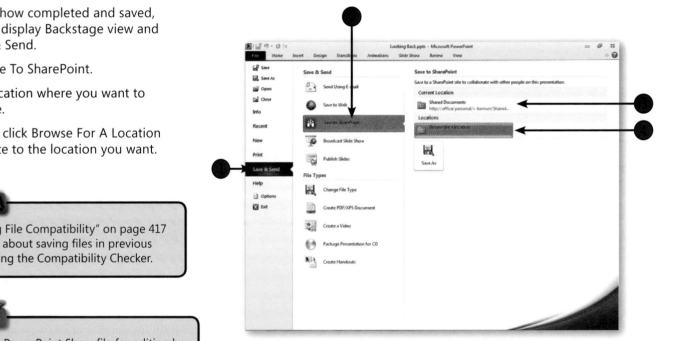

See Also

Read "Checking File Compatibility" on page 417 for information about saving files in previous formats and using the Compatibility Checker.

Tip

You can open a PowerPoint Show file for editing by choosing Open in Backstage view.

Publishing Your Slides

In Section 9, you learned that you can reuse slides you've previously saved in slide libraries that might reside on your computer or on a shared site such as a Microsoft SharePoint Workspace 2010 or a Windows Live account. You can save the files you create to a slide library by using the Publish Slides command in the Save & Send tab of Backstage view.

Add Slides to a Slide Library

① Complete and save your presentation, and click File to display Backstage view.

② Click Save & Send.

③ Click Publish Slides.

④ Click the Publish Slides button.

⑤ In the Publish Slides dialog box, click the check boxes of slides you want to include.

⑥ Click Browse to navigate to the folder where you want the slides to be saved.

⑦ Click Publish.

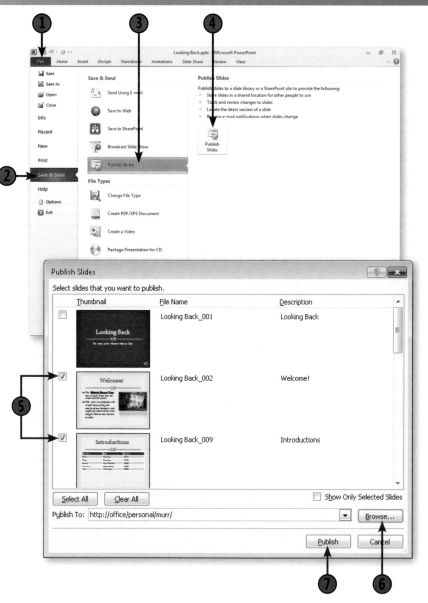

> **Tip** ✓
>
> Before you can save a presentation to a SharePoint folder, you must have the necessary permissions to access the server space. Likewise, before you can save a presentation or slides to a Windows Live account, you need to have created an account and set up the user account and password information you need to access the space.

Packaging Your Presentation

If you need to take your show on the road and run your presentation on a computer other than the one on which you created it, you can package the presentation to include all the different components it uses—slides, video clips, narration, and more. This helps you make sure that the presentation will run properly no matter where you run it.

Package Your Presentation

1 Finish and save the presentation, and click File to display Backstage view.

2 Click Save & Send and choose Package Presentation For CD.

3 Click the Package For CD button.

(continued on next page)

Package Your Presentation   *(continued)*

 Type a descriptive name for the CD.

Click to include any files that you want on the CD, including any other Power-Point presentations.

Click to display the Options dialog box.

Select the files you want to include, and choose whether the presentation should be inspected for inappropriate or private information.

Click OK.

Click either of the following:

- Copy To Folder, to store the files in a folder

- Copy To CD, to copy directly to a CD

Click Close to complete the process.

Caution

If you save the files in the PowerPoint 97–2003 Presentation format, some features, such as the animation of graphics, might be lost.

Creating Pictures of Your Slides

Although pictures of your slides are printed in your notes or handouts, you might need a picture of a slide, or even pictures of your entire presentation, for other purposes—to be included in a report or for a design review, for example. Fortunately, you can save pictures of your slides in just about any picture format you want.

Create the Pictures

1. If you want to create a picture of a single slide, click that slide to select it; to create pictures of all the slides in the presentation, select any slide.

2. Click the File tab and choose Save As to display the Save As window.

3. Type a descriptive name for the picture or pictures.

4. In the Save As Type list, select the picture format you want and then click Save.

5. In the Microsoft PowerPoint dialog box that appears, click the appropriate button:

   • Every Slide, to create a separate picture file for each slide in the presentation

   • Current Slide Only, to create a single picture file for the selected slide

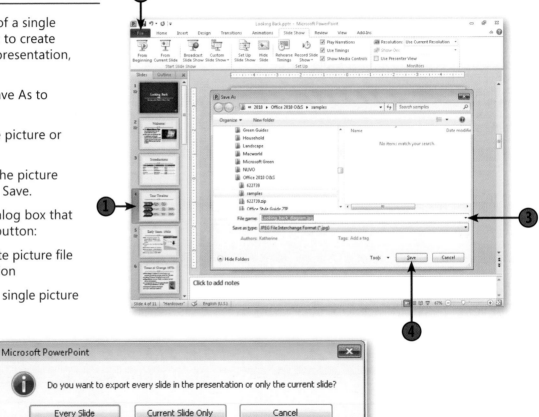

Saving Your Presentation as a Video

If others aren't able to attend your presentation and you want to make it available for them—either on CD or on the Web—you can save the presentation as a video. Whether you plan to post the presentation on YouTube, save it to your Web site, or just e-mail it to friends and colleagues, saving the presentation in this format makes it super easy to share on the fly.

Create a Video

1. Prepare your presentation for sharing by adding content, editing and adjusting slides, and setting timing and transitions.

2. Save the presentation.

3. Click File to display Backstage view, and click Save & Send.

4. Click Create A Video.

5. Click the Computer & HD Displays arrow to choose the size you want the resulting video to be.

6. Choose whether to include timing and narration.

7. Click Create Video.

Tip

You can set the timing in the Share tab by entering a value in the Seconds To Spend On Each Slide box. The default is 5 seconds, but depending on the amount of information on your slides, you may want to increase or decrease this amount. Note that this option is available only if you have selected Don't Use Recorded Timings And Narrations.

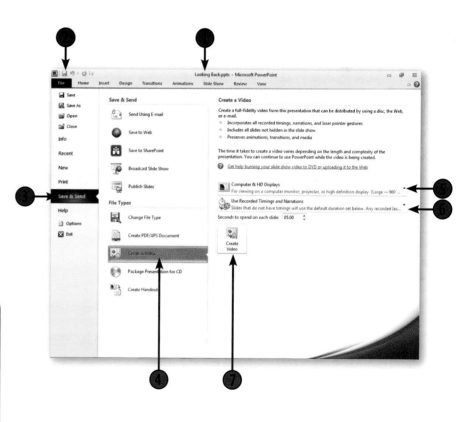

Broadcasting Your Presentation

A big new feature in PowerPoint 2010 enables you to broadcast your presentation—live—to others who are watching online. This enables you to introduce a new product to interested customers, share the latest group news with members who are traveling, or offer training online to those who may work remotely.

Broadcast a Presentation

1 Finish your presentation as normal, and save it.

2 Click File, and choose Save & Send.

3 Click the Broadcast Slide Show option.

4 Click Broadcast Slide Show.

(continued on next page)

Broadcast a Presentation *(continued)*

 Click Start Broadcast.

Click Send In Email to send the link to others you want to view it.

Click Start Slide Show.

Display the presentation normally, and when you're finished, click End Broadcast.

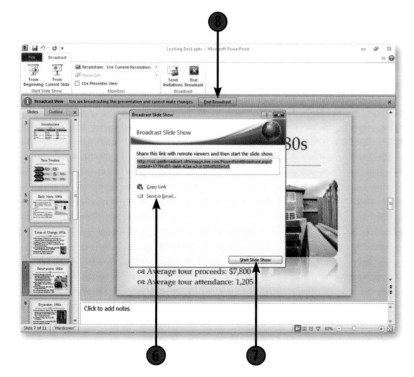

Tip

You can also copy the link and send it via instant message to share it with others on your contact list.

Changing Slide-Show Settings

A PowerPoint slide show is set up to work and look exactly like the slide shows that were created in earlier versions of PowerPoint. However, you can customize the way a slide show appears on your own computer. Note, though, that these changes you make to the PowerPoint options apply only on your computer; they don't affect the way this particular slide show will appear if you show it on another computer.

Change the Settings

1. Click File to display Backstage view, and click Options to display the PowerPoint Options dialog box.

2. Click the Advanced category.

3. Clear this check box if you want to use the right mouse button to move backward in your presentation, or select the check box to display the shortcut menu with navigation and display controls.

4. Clear this check box if you don't want the toolbar that contains the Previous, Pointer, Show, and Next buttons at the bottom of the slide-show screen to be visible. Select the check box if you want those controls to be visible.

5. Clear this check box if you always want to discard any annotations you make during the slide show, or select the check box if you want the option of keeping or discarding the annotations.

6. Clear this check box if you want the slide show to end when you move past the last slide, or select the check box if, at the end of the show, you want to see the black screen displaying a notice that the show has ended.

7. Click OK.

Tip

To change the way PowerPoint appears when you first open it, select the display layout in the Open All Documents Using This View list box.

11

Working with Messages in Outlook

Microsoft Outlook 2010 is designed to help you get a handle on your e-mail, manage your calendar, stay in touch with friends and family, and much more. This chapter shows you the basics of using Outlook to send and respond to e-mail and introduces you to the new Outlook Social Connector, a feature that enables you to see the status updates of your contacts when they post to popular social media sites.

Outlook lets you create e-mail messages containing much more than plain text. You can format the text in your e-mail using a variety of themes and styles and add your own pictures to your messages to create a customized look. You can easily attach a file to your message or share your calendar as an e-mail message with just a few clicks.

In addition to these basic e-mail features, Outlook 2010 now helps you stay in touch with friends and family through the Outlook Social Connector. And if you love receiving news feeds and updates from your favorite sites, you can use Outlook to set up RSS (Really Simple Syndication) subscriptions so that you can receive the content that interests you whenever the sites you are subscribed to update content.

What's Where in Outlook Messages?

The new Outlook message window includes all the tools you need to create attractive and effective e-mail. The Message tab provides the tools for text formatting, copy and paste, finding recipients, attaching files and signatures, and setting the priority of the message. Other tabs contain groups of tools that enable you to include tables, pictures, and more; set permissions and themes; set up delivery receipts and other tracking options; and apply themes and advanced text formatting.

A Look at the New Message Window

- Create, print, export, and manage Outlook items by clicking the File tab to display Backstage view.

- Save a message, undo and redo actions, and page through the messages in a folder with the Quick Access toolbar.

- Use tools on the ribbon to work with the currently selected text or object.

- Choose a tab to display different groups of commands.

- Compose your e-mail in the body of the message window.

- Choose recipients for your message.

- Enter a subject in the Subject field.

- Click the Send button to mail your message.

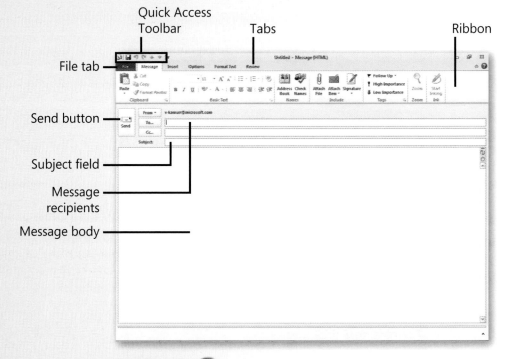

Quick Access Toolbar   Tabs   Ribbon

File tab

Send button

Subject field

Message recipients

Message body

Tip

If you need more text formatting options than the ones you see available on the Message tab, click the Format Text tab. Although many commands are available in both locations, some additional choices, such as Styles, are found only the Format Text tab.

Overview of the Message Window Insert Tab

Creating a message really is as simple as adding text in the message window and clicking Send. But while you're at it, you can add much more than text to your e-mail messages. This message uses commands from several tabs to achieve the effects that you see. The Insert tab offers tools that enable you to add many types of objects to your e-mail messages.

Add a Word table or an Excel spreadsheet using the Table tool.

Insert a picture or another object using tools in the Illustrations group.

Insert Outlook items and files using tools in the Include group.

Add text and text objects like Quick Parts or WordArt with tools in the Text group.

Apply styles to your text.

Insert a picture in your message and use preset frame and shadow effects to enhance its appearance.

Sending E-mail

When you write new messages in Outlook, you use the Message window. This window includes a line for recipients (called the To line), a line for "carbon copied" recipients (the Cc line), a Subject line, and an area for the text of the message. Every new message must have at least one recipient. If you want, you can leave the Cc and Subject lines blank, but it's a good idea to give your messages a subject. This helps the e-mail message get past the spam filter the recipient might be using and gives the receiver information about the content of the message.

Address an E-mail Message

1 In Outlook, click New E-mail in the New group of the Home tab to display a new message window.

2 To open the Select Names dialog box, click To.

3 Click the Address Book drop-down arrow.

4 Click the name of the address book you want to use, and click the name of the person you want to send the message to.

5 Click To, Cc, or Bcc; Outlook copies the name to the specified message recipients list.

6 Repeat steps 4 and 5 until the message recipients list includes all the recipients you want to send the message to.

7 Click OK.

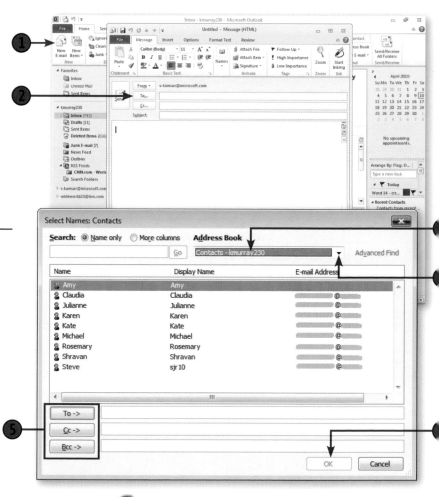

Tip ✓

If you have set up more than one e-mail address with Outlook 2010, the From button enables you to choose the e-mail address from which you want to send the message.

Tip ✓

The e-mail addresses shown in the figure have been grayed out to protect the privacy of the individuals in this e-mail list.

Tip ✓

You can set up several address books to store your e-mail recipients' contact information. For example, you might have a company-wide address book that stores addresses and contact information for all internal employees. A second address book can be set up for external contacts, such as vendors, suppliers, and customers. A third address book could store personal contact information.

Type Your Message Subject and Text

1 After adding the recipient to the To line, type a subject for the new message in the Subject field.

2 Press Tab, or click in the message body area.

3 Type your message.

4 Click Send.

Tip ✓

The small green icon to the left of the recipient's name is known as the *presence icon*. If you are using Microsoft Office Communicator 2007 R2 with Office 2010, you can contact co-authors and colleagues in real-time by clicking the presence icon and starting an instant messaging conversation, sending an e-mail, making a voice call, and more.

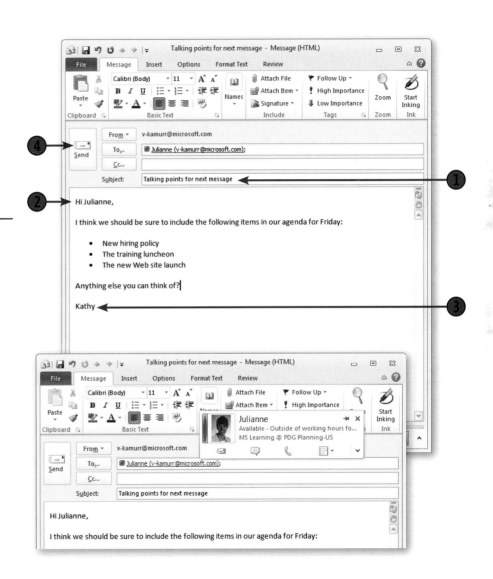

Receiving and Reading E-mail

Outlook makes it easy for you to receive incoming messages and preview them quickly or open them and read their contents. The Inbox folder displays the sender's name, the message subject, the date the message was received, the size of the message, and whether the message has an attachment.

Locate New Messages

1 Click Mail on the Navigation Pane and then click Inbox.

2 Choose Reading Pane in the Layout group of the View tab, and then choose Right from the list.

3 Click the arrow to the left of messages to expand the entire e-mail conversation from that recipient.

> **Tip**
>
> You can use the tools in the Arrangement group of the View tab to arrange the way messages display on the screen. You can sort messages by date, sender, subject, and more.

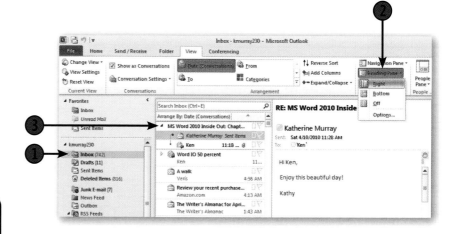

Open Messages

1 Click the Inbox icon on the Navigation Pane to display your new messages.

2 Click the message you want to read to show its contents in the Reading Pane.

3 Double-click the message to open it in its own window.

Replying to and Forwarding a Message

After you receive a message, replying is a snap. If there is more than one recipient on the list, you can also reply to the whole group if you like. You can also forward the message to others easily.

When you reply to a message, Outlook keeps the original message text and lets you add your new text above the original text. The sender's name becomes the recipient name, and the subject line begins with "RE:" to show that the message is a reply.

Reply to an E-mail Message

1. Click the Inbox icon on the Navigation Pane to display messages in your Inbox folder.

2. Click the message to which you want to reply.

3. Click Reply in the Respond group.

4. Click in the space above the original message line, and type your reply.

5. Click Send.

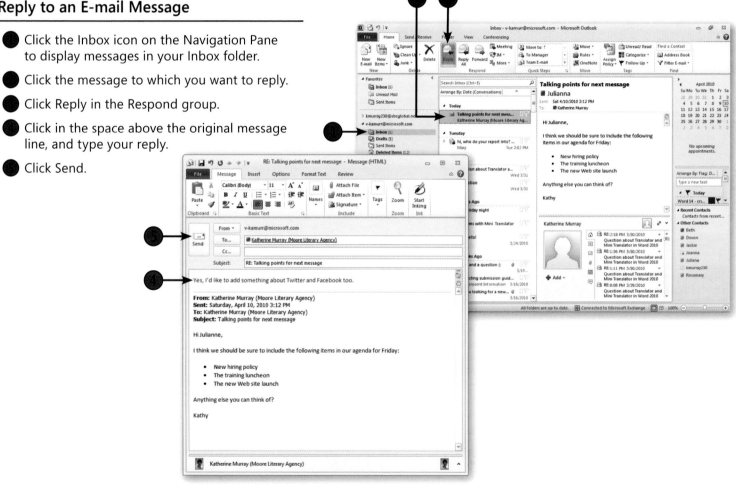

Forward an E-mail Message

① Click the Inbox icon on the Navigation Pane to display messages in your Inbox folder.

② Click the message you want to forward.

③ Click Forward in the Respond group.

④ Add the address to which you want to forward this message.

⑤ Click in the space above the original message line, and type a message, if desired.

⑥ Click Send.

Staying in Touch with Outlook Social Connector

Now in Outlook 2010 you can easily stay up to date with friends and family members who are posting updates on LinkedIn, MySpace, Facebook, or other social networking sites. With Outlook Social Connector (available with Office 2010 Home and Business, Office 2010 Professional Plus, and Office 2010 Professional), you can add social media services to Outlook so that updates and new posts appear in the People Pane at the bottom of the Reading Pane.

Adding a Site to Outlook Social Connector

Display the Outlook 2010 window.

To set up the Outlook Social Connector, click the prompt in the People Pane.

Select the check box of the social media site you want to add.

Enter your user name.

Type your password.

Click Connect.

Tip

When you post updates to the social media site you added, any contacts you have who are using Outlook Social Connector will be able to view your updates. Likewise, when your contacts update their sites, you will see their updates in Outlook.

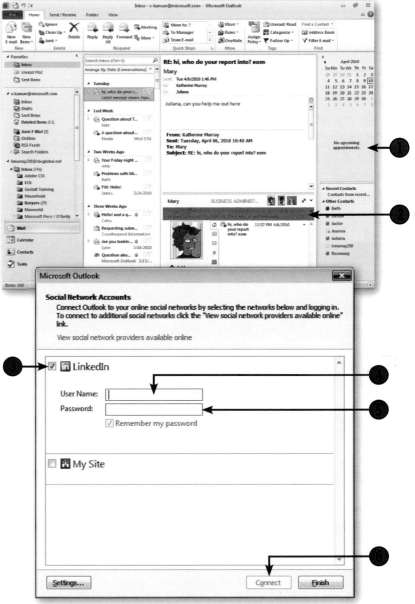

Viewing Social Contacts

 Click Contacts in the Navigation Pane.

Click LinkedIn.

Select the contact you want to work with.

Press and hold Shift, and click additional contacts.

Choose a tool in the Home tab:

- Send an e-mail message to selected contacts.

- Schedule a meeting.

- Create a new group including these contacts.

- Share contacts with others.

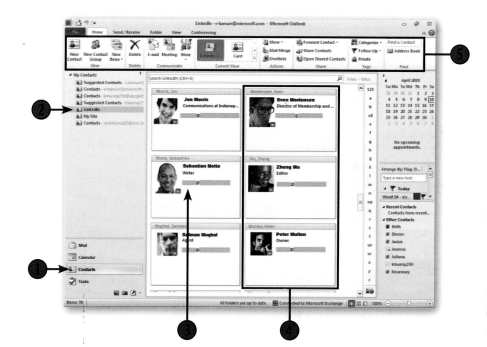

Tip

When you add a social media site to the Outlook 2010 Social Connector, you will be asked for the URL of the services, as well as your user name and password. Outlook 2010 saves this information for you. You can update the information by clicking the View tab and clicking Account Settings in the People Pane group.

Sending or Receiving a File

In some cases, when you create an e-mail message, you will want to send along a file as well. You can easily add a file as an attachment so that when you send the message, the file goes along so the recipient can open it on his or her computer. When you receive an e-mail attachment, you can open it directly from the message, save it to your hard drive and open it from there, or print it straight from the message to a printer. Messages that have attachments show a paper clip icon to the left of the message author's name or below the message-received date, depending on the location of the Reading Pane and the width of the display.

Attach a File

1. Open a new message, and click the Insert tab on the ribbon.
2. Click Attach File on the Include group.
3. Click the file you want to attach.
4. Click Insert.

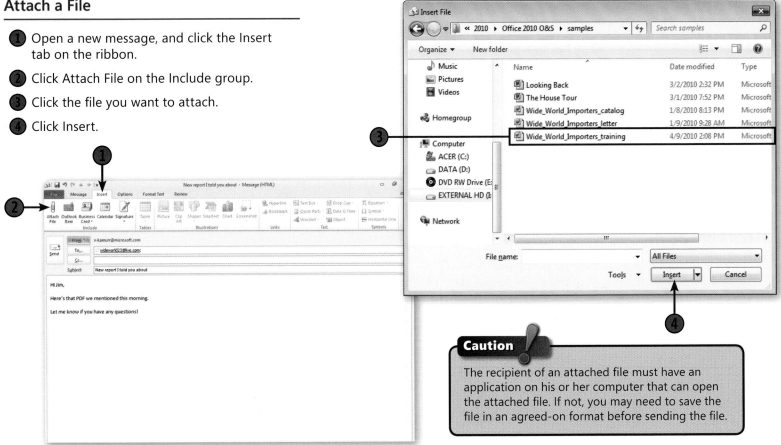

Caution

The recipient of an attached file must have an application on his or her computer that can open the attached file. If not, you may need to save the file in an agreed-on format before sending the file.

Open an Attachment

① Click the Inbox icon in the Navigation Pane to display messages in your Inbox folder.

② Click the message with the attachment.

③ Double-click the attachment in the Attachments field.

④ Depending on whether you have received files from the sender before, the file may appear in Protected View. Click Enable Editing if you want to edit the file normally.

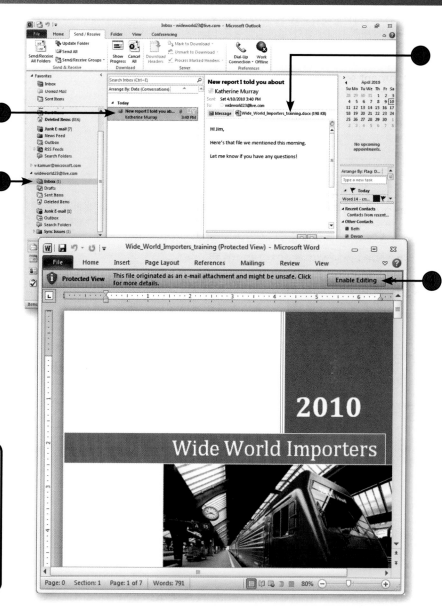

Tip

To open an attachment, you must have an application that supports the attached file. For example, if you receive a Microsoft PowerPoint file (.ppt or .pptx), you must have PowerPoint, the PowerPoint Viewer, or some similar application installed on your system to view the file.

Caution

Some files that you receive from another user—such as programs, Web pages, and script files—might be infected with a computer virus. You should save all executable files to your system and run an antivirus program that checks the file for a virus before you open it. If you receive an attachment from someone you do not know (as happens a lot with junk e-mail), you should never open it. Just delete the message.

Formatting E-mail Messages

Who says e-mail messages have to be boring? Outlook 2010 provides a number of ways you can format text to be both inviting *and* informative. For example, you can apply bold, italic, underline, colors, and other rich formatting to your messages. You also can add HTML formatting to your messages, including tables, hyperlinks, heading levels, and more. You can also apply Office themes to your e-mail messages so that they have the same look and feel as the documents you create in other Office 2010 applications.

Use a Rich Text or HTML Message Format

① Create a new message, and add some text.

② Click the Format Text tab in the ribbon.

③ Choose HTML or Rich Text from the Format group. This makes the formatting tools on the Message and Format Text tabs available.

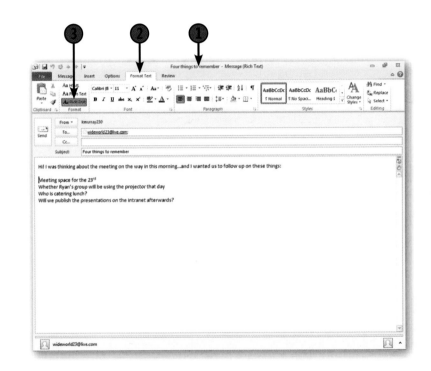

Caution

Some recipients may not be able to handle rich-formatted text. In these cases, the formatted text you see in your message window will appear to your recipients as plain text or be converted to unrecognizable characters.

Tip

To add a hyperlink to an e-mail message, type the hyperlink in your message and Outlook converts it to a live link that your recipient can click. For example, you can add a hyperlink to the Microsoft Web site by typing *www.microsoft.com*.

Add Formatting to a Message

① Select the text you want to format.

② Click the Format Text tab on the ribbon.

③ Click Bold in the Font group to add bold to the text.

④ Click Italic to italicize the text.

⑤ Click Underline to underline the text.

⑥ Select a font name from the Font drop-down list to change the text font.

⑦ Select a color from the Font Color drop-down list to change the text font color.

⑧ Select a value from the Font Size drop-down list to change the text font size.

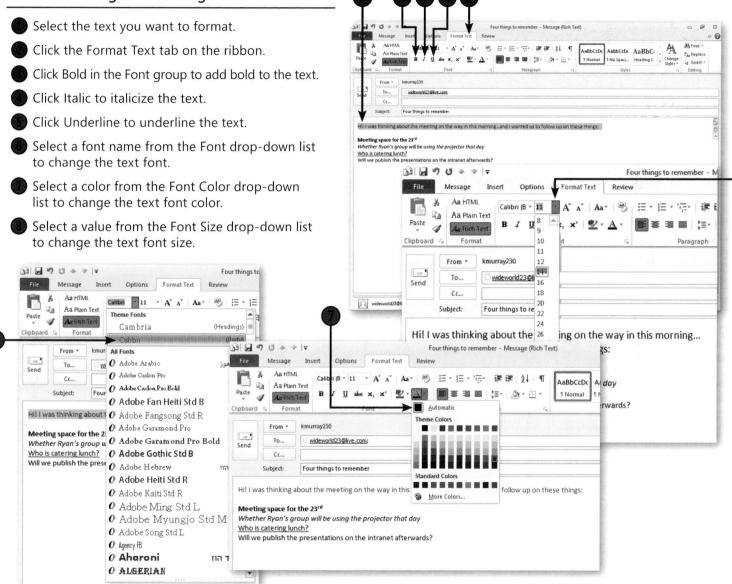

Managing Messages with Quick Steps

One of the big challenges in working with e-mail is managing the huge volume of messages you receive. Chances are you receive messages from friends and family, colleagues, volunteer groups, nonprofits, and all kinds of sales and travel sites.

Outlook 2010 includes a new feature called Quick Steps you can use to manage the messages you receive and stay a few steps ahead of the game. You can also mark, unmark, move, and delete messages using various tools in the Outlook window.

Use a Quick Step to Reply to and Delete a Message

1. Click the message you want to respond to.
2. Click the Home tab.
3. In the Quick Steps group, click Reply & Delete.
4. Type the message you want to send.
5. Click Send.

Tip You can set up different Quick Steps (for example, add the correct e-mail address for the To Manager Quick Step) or edit existing settings by clicking the dialog launcher in the Quick Steps group, choosing the Quick Step you want to change, and clicking Edit.

Create a New Quick Step

1. Click Create New in the Quick Steps gallery.

2. Type a name for the new action.

3. Click the actions arrow, and choose the action you want from the displayed list.

4. Choose the secondary action if necessary.

5. Select a shortcut if you want to add one.

6. Add Tooltip text if desired.

7. Click Finish.

Move Messages Between Folders

1. Drag the message to the destination folder, or

2. Right-click the item, and choose Move.

3. Select the target folder.

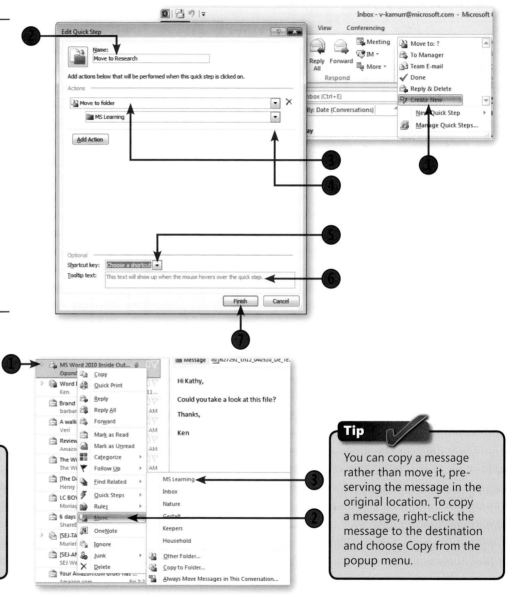

> **Tip**
>
> You can use the various tools in the Folder tab to further organize your message. Among the tools on the Folder tab are those to help you clean up the folders and messages you collect, create new folders, archive past messages, and delete messages and folders you no longer need.

> **Tip**
>
> You can copy a message rather than move it, preserving the message in the original location. To copy a message, right-click the message to the destination and choose Copy from the popup menu.

Signing Your E-mail

A *signature* is boilerplate text or a file that is attached to any new messages you compose. The signature appears at the bottom of your messages, much like the signature that you would write on paper documents. Often, the signature includes your phone number and other information.

Create a Signature

1 In Outlook, click the File tab.

2 Choose Options.

3 Click Mail.

4 Click Signatures to open the Signatures And Stationery dialog box.

(continued on next page)

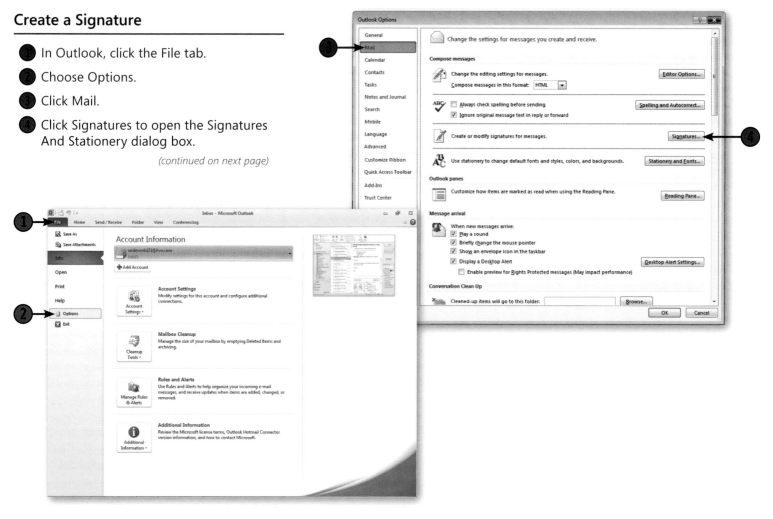

Create a Signature (continued)

5 Click New.

6 Type a name for the signature, and click OK.

7 Click in the Edit Signature box, and type the signature you want to appear.

8 From the E-Mail Account drop-down list, select the account for which you want to assign the signature.

9 Select the signature name from the New Messages drop-down list.

10 Click OK twice, and close the Options dialog box.

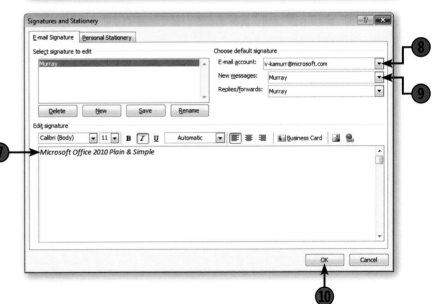

Tip

If you want your signature to appear in messages you reply to or forward, select the appropriate signature from the Replies/Forwards drop-down list.

Tip

You can create custom signatures for different types of e-mail messages you create. For example, you can create a friendly signature for messages intended for family or friends and use a more formal signature for business correspondence.

Reading RSS Items

RSS stands for Really Simply Syndication, and it offers an easy way for publishers to share content with people who subscribe to their information. These subscriptions are known as *RSS feeds*, and you can add RSS feeds directly to Outlook 2010 so that you receive the content you're most interested in seeing.

Who publishes information in RSS format? Just about everyone who wants to build an audience. Whether you want to get the latest content from MSNBC, ESPN, CNN, or any other news, service, or shopping site, you can be sure you'll find an RSS feed on the pages that are updated on the site. Look for the small orange RSS icon.

Add an RSS Feed

1. In the Outlook Navigation Pane, right-click RSS Feeds.

2. Click Add A New RSS Feed.

3. Type the location for the new feed.

4. Click Add.

5. When Outlook asks you to confirm the addition, click Yes.

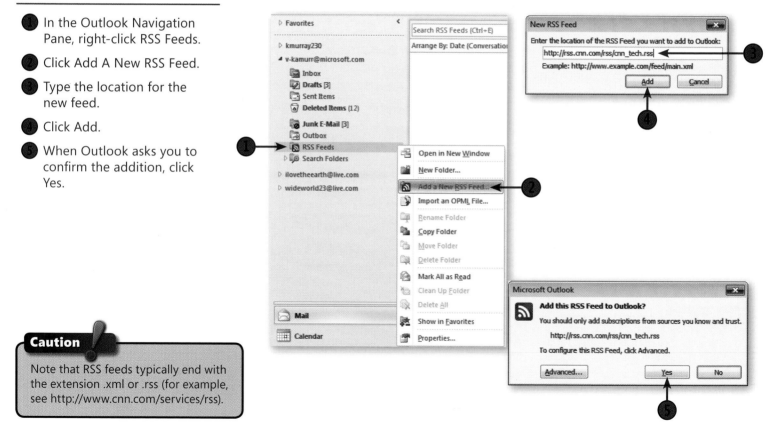

> **Caution**
>
> Note that RSS feeds typically end with the extension .xml or .rss (for example, see http://www.cnn.com/services/rss).

Read RSS Feeds

1. Click RSS Feeds to expand subfolders.

2. Click the RSS folder of your choice.

3. Click the news item you want to view.

4. Read the information in the Reading Pane.

Tip

You can remove RSS feed posts just like you delete e-mail messages you no longer need. Click the item you want to delete, and click Delete in the Delete group, or press Del.

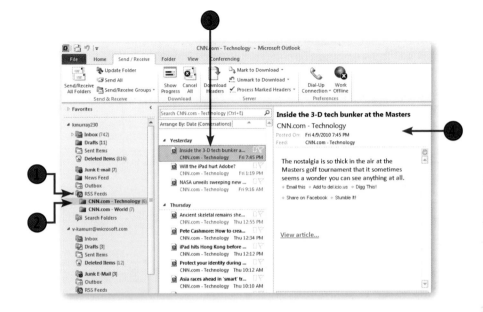

Setting Up E-mail Accounts

One of the great changes in Outlook has been the ease with which you can add e-mail accounts. Now Outlook 2010 can serve as a kind of communications hub for you, integrating a variety of e-mail accounts—including Web-based accounts such as Hotmail and Gmail—along with your social media updates and RSS feeds.

Add an E-mail Account

1. Click the File tab to display Backstage view.

2. Click Add Account.

3. Type your name.

4. Type your e-mail address.

5. Enter your password.

6. Click Next. Outlook sets up the new e-mail account and adds a new folder to your Inbox.

7. Click Finish in the confirmation window.

12 Organizing with Outlook

In addition to providing full-featured e-mail management and a way to connect with friends and peers through social networks, Microsoft Outlook 2010 helps you manage the scheduling of appointments, meetings, and tasks, and keeps track of your tasks, notes, and contacts all at the same time. You can identify your free time (okay, *what* free time?), schedule your appointments, share calendars, and invite people to meetings, as well as quickly determine what is on your schedule for any day, week, or month.

Outlook makes it easy to document your own tasks and assign tasks to others, tracking their progress, and receiving an automatic notification when the task is complete. You can also easily share information about your contacts by creating customized contact business cards that you can attach to your e-mail.

A Quick Look at Outlook's Organizing Abilities

In the last section, you learned how to create, read, and manage e-mail using Outlook, but the capabilities of the program go far beyond basic e-mail management. The Outlook window offers a number of tools you can use to

manage calendars, contacts, tasks, and notes. You can also connect the notes and tasks you create in Outlook with Microsoft OneNote 2010 so that none of the information you need slips through the cracks.

Set appointments

Organize contacts

Set tasks for yourself and others

Check upcoming dates

Review your appointments

See a quick list of tasks you need to complete

Calendar

The Outlook 2010 calendar is a colorful affair that enables you to create and categorize all sorts of appointments and events that fill up your schedule. If you're using Outlook with Exchange Server, you can easily share calendars with others on your team to ensure that you are scheduling meetings when everyone is free. You can also create your own shared calendar, design a calendar group, and list the various tasks that need to be completed on specific days.

Contacts

The Contacts folder acts like an address book but also does much more. Contacts can contain a wide range of information: personal things like birthdays, names of spouse and children; work-related information such as office location, title, and manager's name; and Internet-related information such as IM identity and Web page addresses.

You can also create customized business cards for your contacts, selecting the information and picture to use and then formatting it as you wish. Business cards can be shared with others, making it simple to build a network of business or personal connections.

Outlook lets you view your contacts as a series of single address cards or all at once, moving through your Contacts folder as if it were an electronic phone book or address book. And with the new Outlook Social Connector, you have the option to display the contact information of all the people you've friended on your favorite sites.

View calendars   Daily view   Date Navigator   Contact folders   Individual contact

Tasks for today

Setting an Appointment

Chances are that your life keeps you hopping—and that means you need a way to keep track of the various appointments you have on a daily or weekly basis. Add to that the schedules of your kids, spouse, work, home, and friends, and you've got a lot of information to manage. The Outlook 2010 Calendar can help you stay on top of things by enabling you to keep track of your schedule without getting stuck in the details.

Add an Appointment to the Calendar

1. Click Calendar in the Navigation Pane.
2. Click the date for the appointment you want to set.
3. Click in the appropriate time slot.
4. Type your appointment, and press Enter.

Add Appointment Detail

1. Click Calendar in the Navigation Pane.
2. Click New Appointment in the New group of the Home tab.

(continued on next page)

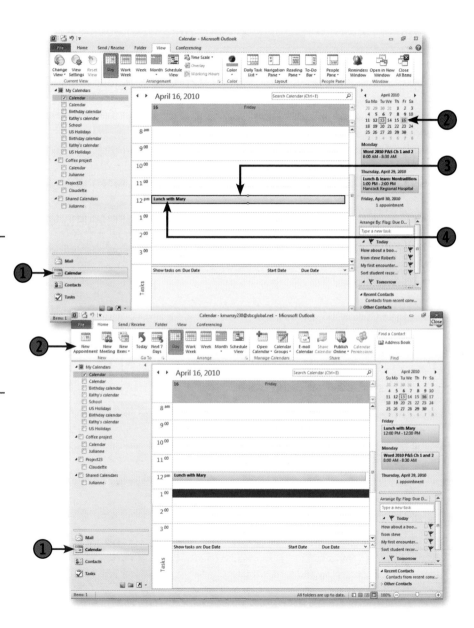

Add Appointment Detail *(continued)*

3 Enter the subject of your appointment.

4 Type the location of the appointment.

5 Choose the start and end times for the appointment.

6 Add any necessary notes.

7 Click Save & Close.

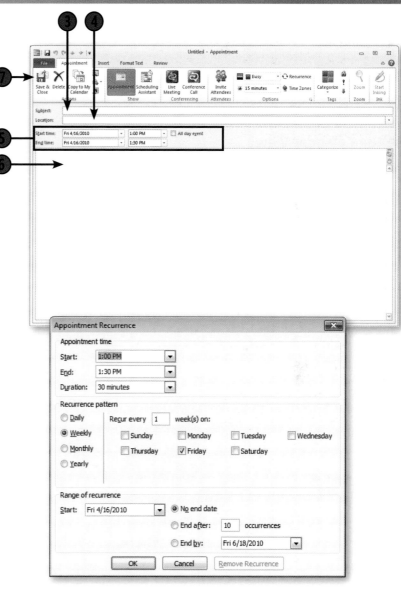

Tip ✓

Will this be a recurring appointment? If so, click Recurrence in the Options group of the new appointment window and enter the start and end times, the way in which the appointment will recur, and the point at which the appointments will end. Click OK to save your settings.

Tip ✓

Do you need reminders about upcoming appointments? You can have Outlook pop up and remind you in advance of a future appointment. Click the Reminder arrow in the Options group of the Appointment tab, and choose when you want to receive the reminder.

Keeping Track of Your Schedule

Outlook 2010's Calendar gives you a number of views from which to choose. The Day view is an hour-by-hour view of your daily schedule, while the Month view shows your schedule for the entire month. The Date Navigator is a small calendar with which you can navigate quickly to a specific day, week, or month, while the To-Do Bar consolidates all the features of the task list, Date Navigator, and appointment list into one task pane. You can also use Schedule View, which is new in Outlook 2010, to add and view all upcoming appointments in a variety of categories.

Use the Calendar View

1. Click the Calendar icon on the Navigation Pane.

2. Click a type of view in the Arrange group of the Home tab, and choose Day, Work Week, Week, or Month.

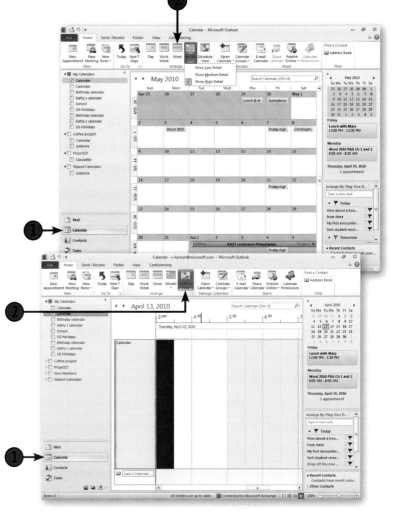

> **Tip**
>
> When you click Month, Outlook offers a list of choices so that you can choose the level of detail you want to display in the view: Low, Medium, or High Detail.

Use Schedule View

1. Click the Calendar icon on the Navigation Pane.

2. On the Home tab, click Schedule View in the Arrange group.

(continued on next page)

> **Tip**
>
> If you see a small calendar icon in the lower right corner of a contact's calendar in Schedule View, you can click it to request permission to view the calendar.

Julianne (v-kamurr@

Use Schedule View *(continued)*

3 Click the check boxes of any category you want to display.

4 Double-click an entry to open the appointment window for that item.

5 Enter a word or phrase to find a specific entry in your schedule.

6 Click to add a calendar to Schedule View.

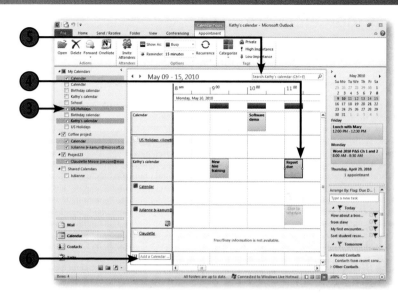

Use the To-Do Bar

1 In either the Mail or Calendar view, click an appointment in the To-Do Bar.

2 In the appointment window, make any necessary changes.

3 Click Actions, and choose Save & Close.

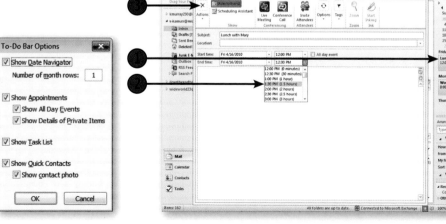

Try This!

Set the options for your To-Do Bar by right-clicking in a blank portion of the Bar and selecting Options. In the To-Do Bar Options dialog box, click the check boxes of items you want to include, and then click OK.

Sharing Calendars

Outlook 2010 has added new features that make it easy for you to set up and share Calendar information with friends, family, and peers. The new Shared Calendar group contains four tools—E-mail Calendar, Share Calendar, Publish Online, and Calendar Permissions—that you can use to manage the way you share your calendar information.

Share Your Calendar

1 Click Calendar in the Navigation Pane.

2 In the calendar list at the top of the Navigation Pane, select the calendar you'd like to share.

3 Click E-mail Calendar in the Share group of the Home tab.

4 In the Send A Calendar Via E-mail dialog box, choose the calendar you want to send.

5 Select the date range for the calendar.

6 Choose the level of detail you want to include.

7 Click OK.

(continued on next page)

Tip ✓

If you are sharing a calendar created with an online Web-based account (for example, Windows Live Mail), clicking Share Calendar will take you to Windows Live, where you can set up your calendar for sharing.

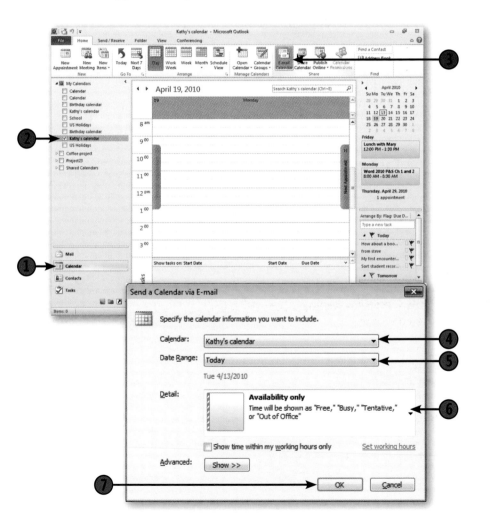

Share Your Calendar   (continued)

8 Click in the To box, and type the e-mail address of the recipient.

9 Click Send.

Tip ✓

If you are trying to find a suitable time for a get-together, you may want to share only your available times with another person; that way you don't have to share your entire calendar. Use the Share Calendar tool in the Share group to send only the times you're available to meet.

Share Your Available Times

1 In the Share group of the Home tab, click Share Calendar.

2 Click in the To box, and type the e-mail address of the recipient.

3 Add any notes you'd like to send with Calendar view.

4 Click Send.

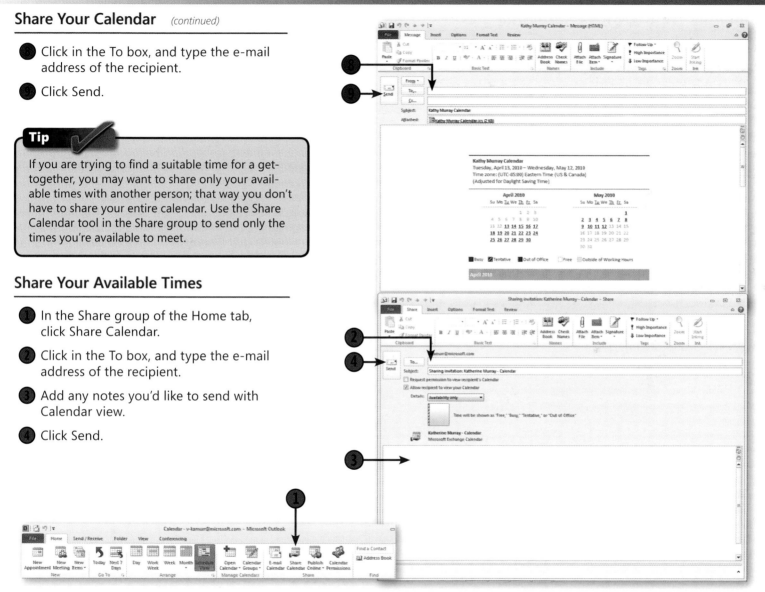

Viewing Your Group's Schedule

If you are using Exchange Server, Outlook lets you create a group of contacts and then view all of their schedules at the same time. You can create a number of groups to make it easier for you to see the information you need. After you create a group, you can quickly look at the calendars in it.

Create a New Group

1. While in the Calendar view, click Calendar Groups in the Manage Calendars group in the Home tab.

2. Click Create New Calendar Group.

3. Give the group a name.

4. Click OK.

5. In the Select Name: Contacts dialog box, click the names of people you want to add to the group.

6. Click Group Members.

7. Click OK.

> **Tip**
>
> You can easily add and remove people's calendars from a group calendar once you create it. Right-click the calendar name to display additional options for working with the group.

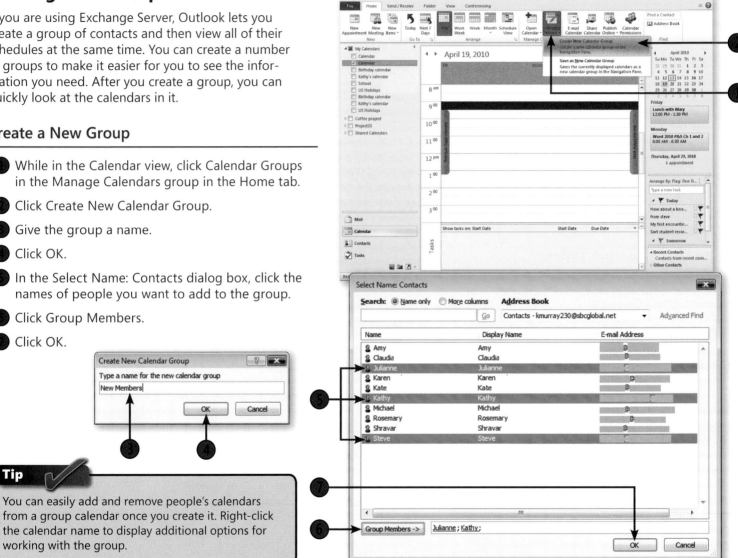

View and Manage a Group Schedule

1. While in the Calendar view, click the check box of the group calendar to see the calendars of all members in the group to clear.

2. To remove a calendar from the display, click its check box to clear it.

3. To add a new calendar to the group, right-click the group calendar name.

4. Choose Add Calendar, click From Address Book, and choose the person you want to add from the list of contacts.

Tip

Set your calendar permissions and control who has access to your information—and how much detail they can view—by clicking Calendar Permissions in the Share dialog box. On the Permissions tab of the Calendar Properties dialog box, you can add users and set the level of access you want each person to have.

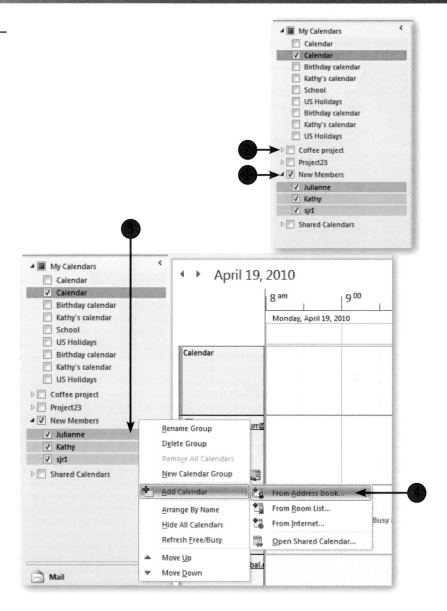

Scheduling a Meeting

A meeting is an activity that involves other people and sometimes requires you to reserve resources as well. A resource might be a conference room, VCR, slide projector, conference-call equipment, laptop computer, or other equipment. A meeting may involve you presenting to many others, or perhaps you will be having a one-to-one meeting with a colleague. Whether you plan to meet with one person or many, Outlook can help you set up the meeting by sending meeting invitations to participants, who can accept or reject the request or propose a new time to meet.

Create a Meeting in a Block of Time

1. Click Calendar in the Navigation Pane.

2. Highlight a block of time on the meeting day for the meeting.

3. Choose New Meeting in the New group on the Home tab.

4. Click To, and select attendees and resources from the Address Book, or type addresses manually.

5. Type a description of the meeting in the Subject box.

6. Type the location of the meeting in the Location box.

7. Add notes, directions, or comments for the meeting as needed.

8. Click Send.

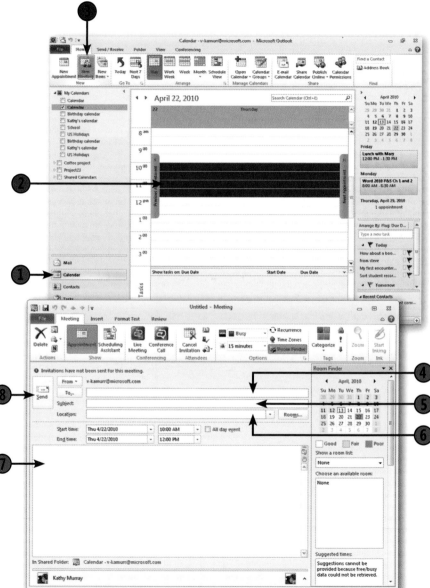

Tip

If a calendar group is selected when you click New Meeting, you will see two choices: New Meeting and New Meeting With All. If you want to send the meeting invitation to all people in your group calendar, choose New Meeting With All.

Specify a Meeting Date and Time Manually

1 Create a new meeting.

2 Add attendees, a subject, and a location for the meeting.

3 Click the arrow in the Start Time date field, and select the starting date.

4 Click the arrow in the Start Time hour field, and select the starting time of the meeting.

5 Click the arrow in the End Time date field, and choose the day the meeting will end.

6 Click the arrow in the End Time hour field, and select the ending time of the meeting.

7 Click Send.

Caution

Make sure that your attendee list includes correct e-mail addresses. If you attempt to send the meeting request to someone not in one of your address books, Outlook prompts you that the person cannot be validated.

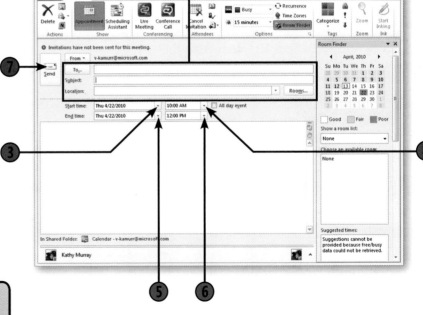

Managing Your Contacts

You can add contacts to Outlook's Contacts folder by creating a new contact in which you type information about someone or by grabbing the contact information directly from an e-mail message you receive. If you use the Outlook Social Connector,

Outlook 2010 also makes it easy for you to add contacts by gathering the information from friends and peers in your social networks and making it available to you in your Outlook Contacts view.

Use E-mail Message Information

1. In the Inbox, select the message with the contact information you want to save. If you don't have the Reading Pane displayed, open the message to access the From field.

2. Right-click the name or address of the person you want to add to your contacts list.

3. Choose Add To Outlook Contacts from the shortcut menu that appears. A new contact card opens, with some of the new contact's information already entered.

4. Type the pertinent information into the remaining fields.

5. Click Save & Close to save the contact information.

Tip ✓

Add To Quick Contacts may also appear on the list when you right-click the sender's name or address. If you're using Office Communicator, the Quick Contacts List appears in the lower right corner of your Outlook window and displays the online presence of your contacts, as well as information you can use to contact them by instant message, e-mail, or phone.

8

Try This!

Display the contact information of all your LinkedIn friends by clicking Contacts and then clicking the LinkedIn icon in the My Contacts area on the left side of the Contacts window.

Use the Contact Window

1. Click the Contacts icon on the Navigation Pane to display the Contacts folder.

2. Double-click the contact you want to open.

3. Type information about your contact information in the appropriate fields.

4. From the File As drop-down list, select one of the choices of how Outlook can display the contact's name, such as last name first, first name last, and so on.

5. Type any additional useful information in the Notes box in the lower right corner of the address card.

6. Click Save & Close to save your changes.

Caution

When typing a contact's e-mail address, be sure you type it correctly. An incorrect address will prevent your messages from being sent successfully. Take the time when typing a contact's e-mail address to double-check it for accuracy. You can, of course, change it later, but it's best to make sure it's correct the first time.

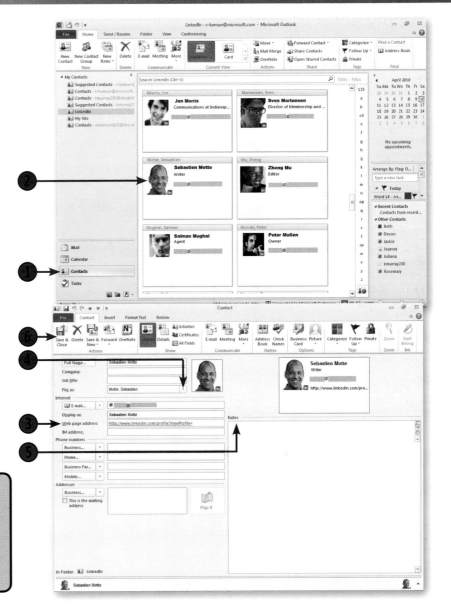

Keeping Track of Your Tasks

If you get more done when you keep a To-Do list, you'll love using tasks in Outlook 2010. You can add tasks easily by creating them yourself or by accepting a task that someone else assigns to you. If you create the task yourself, you can create it in several different ways: You can click in the To-Do Bar and type a new task; you can click Tasks in the Navigation Pane and display the Tasks window; or you can click New Items in the Home tab and choose Tasks from the list.

Outlook gives you a Tasks view you can use to manage both your tasks and the tasks that you assign to others. Outlook offers a number of tools for working with your tasks, including the Daily Task List that appears at the bottom of the Calendar, and the Tasks List in the To-Do Bar. The default view for the Tasks folder is the Simple List view, which shows whether the task is complete, the name (subject) of the task, and the due date.

Create a Task Quickly

① Click in the Task text box in the To-Do Bar.

② Type the new task.

③ Press Enter. The task is added to the bottom of the list.

Set the Task Name and Due Date

① Click the Tasks icon on the Navigation Pane to open the Tasks view.

② Click New Task in the New group of the Home tab to start a new task.

(continued on next page)

Tip

Creating a task in this way adds it quickly to the Task list but doesn't allow for any detail, such as due dates. You can enter more information about the task by double-clicking the task and entering your information in the Task window that appears.

Set the Task Name and Due Date *(continued)*

 Type a subject for the task.

④ Click the arrow to the right of Start Date, and choose the starting time for the task.

⑤ Click the arrow beside the Due Date field, and select a date from the calendar.

⑥ If you want Outlook to remind you as the deadline approaches, select the Reminder check box and set the date and time you want to be reminded.

⑦ Add notes, if necessary, about the task.

⑧ Click Save & Close.

Open the Task Item Window

① Click Tasks.

② Double-click a task to open the task's window.

③ Click Details in the Show group.

④ Click Save & Close to close the window.

Assigning Tasks

If you are part of the leadership of a group and use Outlook in your organization to send e-mail messages and make sure certain things get done, you may want to use Outlook to assign tasks to members of the group. Outlook sends the task assignment as an e-mail message, and the person then has the option of accepting or rejecting the task.

Assign a Task

1. Display the Task view, and click New Task in the New group of the Home tab.

2. Enter the Task subject.

3. Choose the Start and Due dates for the task.

4. Click Assign Task in the Manage Task group.

5. Type the person's name, or click To and select the person from your Contacts list.

6. Leave the Keep An Updated Copy Of This Task On My Task List check box selected if you want Outlook to keep track of the assigned task with a copy on your own task list that updates as the assignee works on the task.

7. Leave the Send Me A Status Report When This Task Is Complete check box selected to have Outlook send you a status report when the assignee completes the task.

8. Click Task to return to the task window.

9. Click Send.

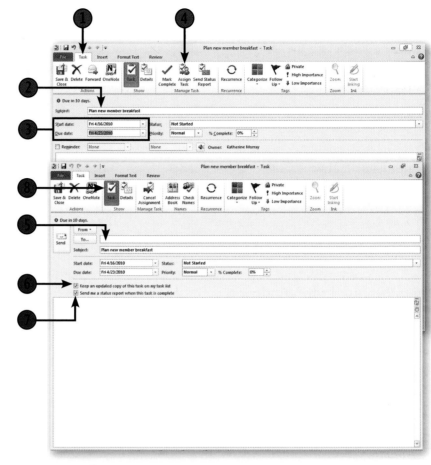

Tip

You can attach a file, insert pictures or diagrams, and enhance the format of the task by using the tools on the Insert and Format Text tabs. You can also use the tools on the Review tab to check the spelling of the task, translate the task into another language, or use other proofing tools on the task.

Tacking Up Notes

Outlook 2010 also includes a Notes feature that enables you to capture your thoughts, bits of conversation, items you want to discuss in your next meeting, and so on. You can create folders to store your notes and share the notes you create with others.

Outlook opens an empty window when you start a new note, ready for your text. You can easily edit a note to change its contents or add more text. Finally, when you don't need the note anymore you can simply delete it.

Add a Note

① Click the Notes icon at the bottom of the Navigation Pane to display the Notes view.

② Click New Note in the New group of the Home tab to start a new note.

③ Type text in the note window.

④ Click the Close button to save the changes and close the note window.

⑤ Outlook adds an icon to the Notes window for the new note.

Tip

To place a copy of a note on the Windows desktop, just drag it from the Notes window in Outlook and drop it on the desktop.

Tip

You can insert blank lines in a note simply by pressing Enter twice.

Creating and E-mailing Contact Business Cards

You can create customized business cards for people in your Contacts folder. You can share these business cards by sending them to others via e-mail.

Create a Contact Business Card

① In the Contacts folder, double-click on a contact to open it.

② Click on Business Card in the Options group of the Contact tab.

③ View a thumbnail preview of the business card.

④ In the Card Design area, you can add a picture and control how the picture appears.

⑤ Choose the information that is displayed on the business card.

⑥ You can change the text formatting for the currently selected field.

⑦ When you are done, click OK.

Try This!

You can add fields to a business card. Many people have more than one phone number or e-mail address. To add information to a business card during editing, under Fields, click Add. Choose a category from the menu and then choose the field to add.

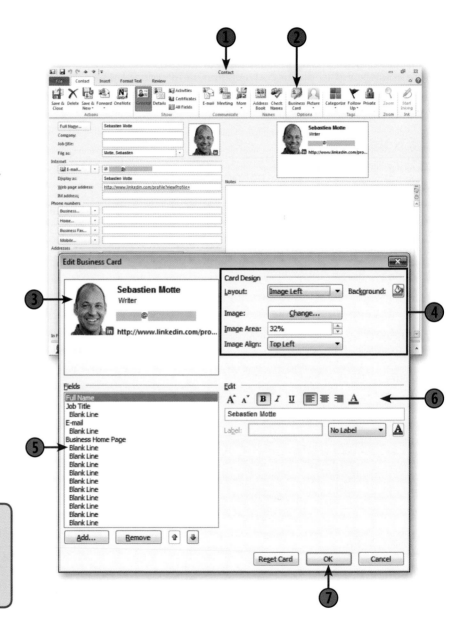

E-mail a Contact Business Card

① Click Mail in the Navigation Pane, and click New E-mail.

② Click Business Card in the Include group of the Insert tab.

③ Select a name if it is on the menu; otherwise, choose Other Business Cards.

④ Select the contact whose business card you want to send.

⑤ Click OK.

⑥ Enter a recipient's e-mail address.

⑦ Add a message.

⑧ Click Send.

Try This!

Send a business card from the Contacts folder. Open the Contacts folder, and locate the person whose business card you want to send. Right-click on the contact, and choose Send As Business Card. An e-mail message will open so that you can choose a recipient and add a message. When you are finished, click Send.

13

Creating a Publication in Publisher

Microsoft Publisher 2010 is one of the best-kept secrets of the Microsoft Office suite. Many people think of the program only as an Office afterthought—something you use when you need to create a brochure, a garage sale sign, or a banner for the friend who just had a baby. But Publisher actually offers a great collection of designs, tools, and features that make it easy for you to design and publish publications ranging from simple to sophisticated. In this section, you learn how to use Publisher to design, compose, and publish the materials—marketing or otherwise—you want to create.

Exploring the New Look of Publisher 2010

The biggest news for Publisher 2010 in this version of Office is that it now looks like part of the family, thanks to the addition of the ribbon interface in the Publisher window. When you start Publisher, you quickly recognize the familiar ribbon stretched across the top of the page. The tabs are organized according to the task you're likely to want to complete; you'll recognize the similarity with other programs you've already used, like Microsoft Word 2010 and Microsoft PowerPoint 2010.

Rulers

Page navigation

Ribbon

Picture

Work area

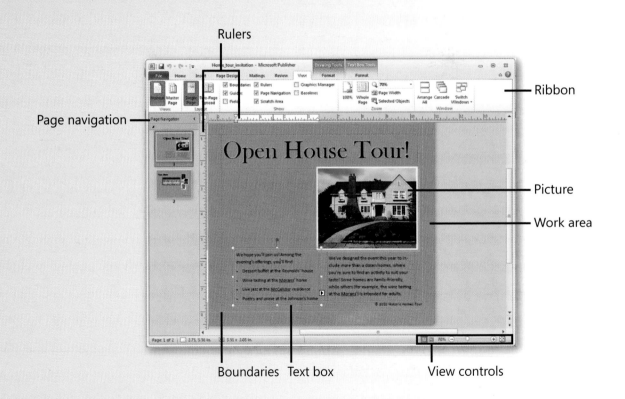

Boundaries　Text box

View controls

Understanding Publisher Objects

Creating a publication in Publisher is different than creating a document in Word, because when you add text and pictures to a page in Word, you simply place the content on the page and it all flows together as you specify. When you add text and pictures—including headings, quotes, body text, logos, and illustrations—to your pages in Publisher, the program adds them to the page as their own objects. This enables you to move text blocks around easily, position headings wherever you want them, and even layer elements and customize the content flow by arranging the objects as you like on the page.

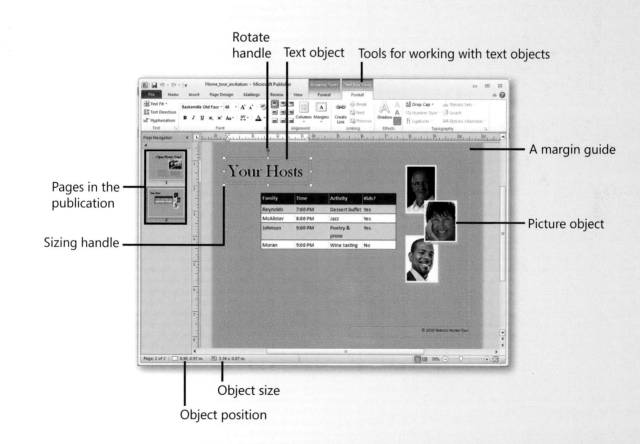

Rotate handle

Text object

Tools for working with text objects

A margin guide

Pages in the publication

Picture object

Sizing handle

Object size

Object position

Starting with a Template

Publisher 2010 comes with dozens of templates you can use to begin your own publications. Whether you are creating something simple, like an invitation to an Open House, or working on a complex newsletter with multiple columns, Publisher has a design you can use to get started. The whole process involves opening a template, saving it as your own publication, and then replacing the information in the text and picture boxes with your own content.

Use a Template

1 Start Publisher, or if it's already running, click the File tab and click New.

2 Select a publication category.

(continued on next page)

Click to see your saved templates.

Use a Template *(continued)*

 Click the design you want to use.

 Click Create or Download, whichever button appears.

 In the publication that appears, replace the placeholder text and pictures with your own content, and then name and save the publication.

Search the computer, and look online for additional designs.

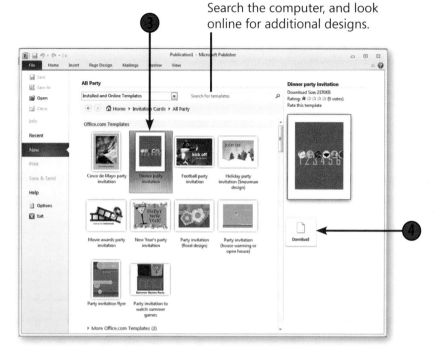

Tip ✓

If you start creating a publication but decide you don't like the design, click the Change Template tool in the Templates group of the Page Design tab, and select a different template. If you want to change the paper size, click the Size tool in the Page Setup group, also on the Page Design tab, and specify the page dimensions.

Tip ✓

If you plan to use a printer other than your default printer, click the File tab and click Print; then click the Printer arrow to display a list of choices. Select your printer so that only the features that are supported by the printer will be available as you create your publication.

Creating a Publication from Scratch

If none of the designs Publisher provides (or any design you've saved as templates) meets your needs for the publication you want to create, you can start with a blank publication, add the elements you want, and arrange them to look just the way you want them to.

Start the Publication

1. Click the File tab, and click New.

2. Click More Blank Page Sizes.

3. In the Standard area, click the page size you want for the document you will create.

4. Choose a different color scheme and font scheme if you want.

5. Click Create to open your publication.

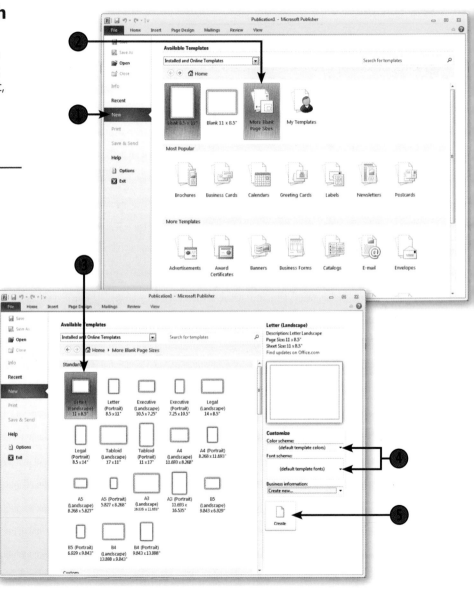

> **Tip**
>
> If you choose either Blank 8.5 x 11" or Blank 11 x 8.5" when you create a new publication, the document is opened immediately and you don't have the option of changing the color and font schemes.

> **Tip**
>
> You can create and add common business information—such as your company name and logo, address, and Web address—by clicking the Business Information arrow and clicking Create New.

Set Up the Look of the Publication

 Click the Page Design tab.

Click the More button in the Schemes gallery to see a beautiful collection of color schemes you can choose. Click the one you want to use.

Click Background if you want to add a background to the page.

Click Change Template if you want to apply an existing template to this page.

Click Size if you want to change the dimensions of the page.

Click Guides to choose the way horizontal and vertical guides appear to help you align the objects you add.

Click the Save tool in the Quick Access toolbar to save your publication.

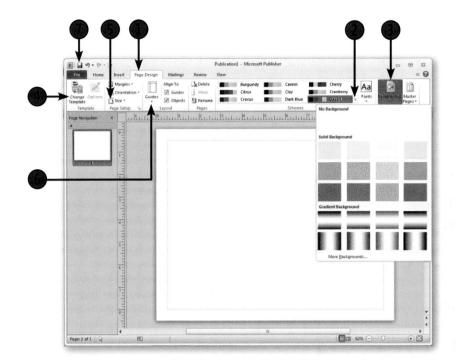

Tip

Once you finish setting up the look of your publication, you can save it as a template if you'd like to use this look for other Publisher files as well. Click the File tab and click Save As. In the Save As dialog box, enter a name for the file, and click the Save As Type arrow. Choose Publisher Template, and click Save. You will be able to start a new Publisher file based on the template by clicking New, clicking My Templates, selecting your new template, and clicking Create.

Adding Text

All the text in a Publisher publication is contained in text boxes, called a *text object*. To add text to your publication, you first insert a text box and then put your text inside the text box. If there's too much text to fit into the text box, you can make the text box bigger, reduce the size of the text, or have the text continue in another text box on the same page or on another page in your publication.

Add Text

1. Open your publication, and click the Zoom In or Zoom Out button so that you can see the text area clearly.

2. Click the Draw Text Box tool in the Objects group of the Home tab.

(continued on next page)

Add Text *(continued)*

 Drag to create a text box on the page.

 Click in the text box to activate it.

 Type or paste your text.

 Resize the text box to fit the text if necessary.

 Use any of the tools on the Text Box Tools Format tab to format the text the way you want it. You might, for example, want to choose a new font or size for the text.

 Move the text box by dragging the border to the location you want.

See Also

Read "Flowing Text Among Text Boxes" on pages 314–315 to learn how to flow text from one text box to another, and "Tweaking Your Text" on pages 316–317 to learn more about formats you can apply to text in your publications.

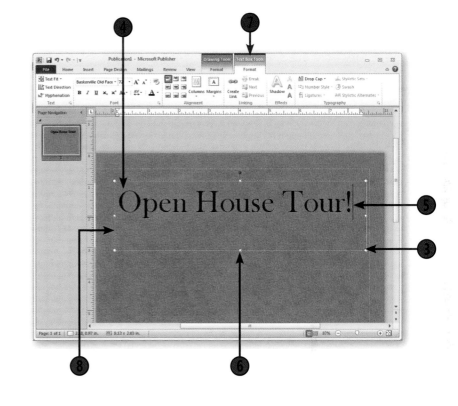

Flowing Text Among Text Boxes

Even though you put text in text boxes so that you can arrange them on the page as you like, you can easily flow long text into two or more connected boxes. This enables you to continue a story from one side of a page to the other, from one sidebar to the next, or from one page to another. Publisher makes this process easy for you by providing buttons you can click to flow text into other text boxes.

Flow the Text

1. Copy the text (press Ctrl+C) from its source— a Word document, for example.

2. With your publication open in Publisher, create the text boxes you'll need.

3. Click in the first text box, and paste your text (by pressing Ctrl+V).

4. Click the Text In Overflow button.

(continued on next page)

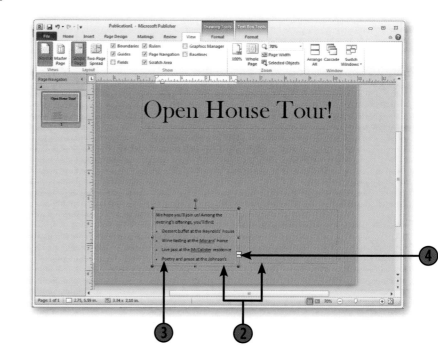

Flow the Text *(continued)*

5 The pointer changes to a pitcher, which lets you know that the text is ready to "pour" into the next frame.

6 Click in the next frame and the text flows automatically. If the Text In Overflow button appears again, continue clicking and "pouring" until all the text has been placed.

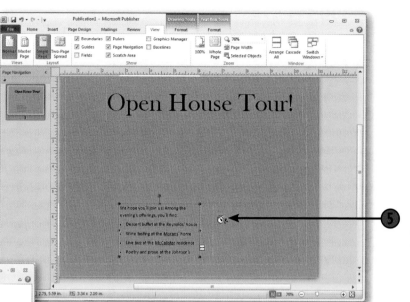

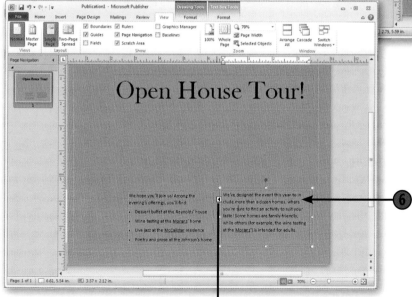

The link to the previous text box

Tip ✓

You can connect text boxes before you add any text. Then, when you add your text, it will automatically flow from one text box to the next.

Tip ✓

Use the Previous and Next tools in the Linking group of the Text Box Tools Format tab to review the entire set of connected text boxes in your publication. Use the Break tool if you want to remove the link from one text box to the next.

Tweaking Your Text

Even if your publication will include many pictures, it's important that the text you add looks as good as it can. Start by choosing a clear, easy-to-read font. Then you can improve the overall look of your text by tweaking some subtle but important details: namely, the *scaling, tracking,* and *kerning* of the characters. Now in Publisher 2010, you can also incorporate high-end typography features like ligatures and stylistic sets, which enable you to fine-tune the look of OpenType fonts. Sometimes small details make a big difference.

Improve the Look of the Text

1. Select the text you want to improve.

2. On the Text Box Tools Format tab, click the Character Spacing tool in the Font group.

3. Select More Spacing.

4. Select a type of tracking, or enter a percentage, to adjust the distance between all the characters of the selected text.

5. Select a type of kerning, and the amount of kerning, to fine-tune the space between two selected characters without changing the dimensions of the characters themselves.

6. Select the Kern Text At check box, and set the minimum point size for character pairs that tend to look "gappy" because of their shapes (for example, VA, WA, To, Te) so that they'll always be automatically kerned.

7. Click OK.

Add Text Effects

1. Select the text or click in the word you want to change.

2. Click the Text Box Tools Format tab.

3. Choose one of the following tools in the Effects group:
   - Shadow, adds a drop shadow to the text
   - Outline, turns the selected text into outlined characters
   - Engrave, makes the text look as though it is set into the publication
   - Emboss, makes the text appear to stand out from the publication

Choose a Ligature Style and a Stylistic Set

1. Select the text you want to change.

2. On the Text Box Tools Format tab, click Ligatures in the Typography group.

3. Choose Standard Only.

4. Click Stylistic Sets.

5. Select the style that fits the look you want for your text.

Tip

Ligatures and stylistic sets are available for only a select number of fonts included with Office 2010. You can use Gabriola as an example to demonstrate the various typography features.

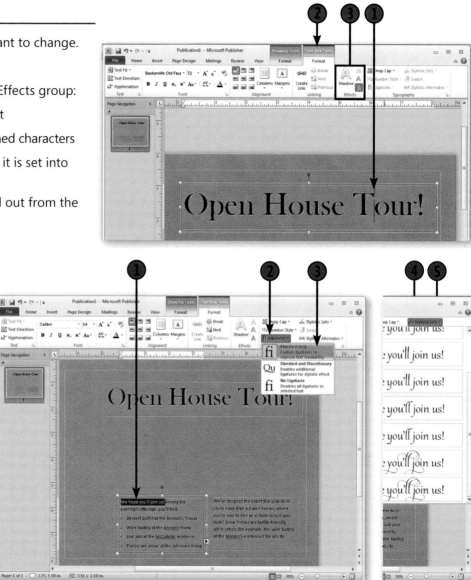

Inserting and Modifying a Picture

Publisher 2010 includes some great picture-editing tools that make it simple for you to make your photos and drawings really shine. The picture-editing features enable you to adjust brightness and contrast, apply various artistic effects, rotate an image, and even crop an image in your publication.

Insert a Picture

1. Display the page on which you want to add the picture.

2. Click the Insert tab.

3. Click Picture.

4. In the Insert Picture dialog box, navigate to the folder you want, click the picture, and click Insert.

5. Adjust the picture on the page by resizing it and dragging it to the location where you want it to appear.

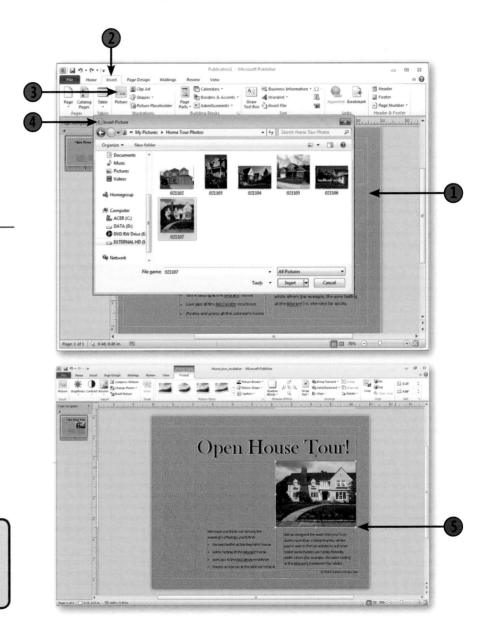

Tip

Resize a picture easily by positioning the mouse pointer on the edge of the picture until you see a double arrow; then drag the side or corner in the direction you want to resize the image.

Modify the Picture

1 With the picture selected, click the Picture Tools Format tab.

2 Add a picture style by clicking the example you like in the style gallery.

3 Adjust the brightness of the image.

4 Change the contrast to clarify the picture.

5 Apply a color wash by clicking your choice in the Recolor gallery.

6 Click the rotate handle, and drag the picture in the direction you want to rotate it.

7 Click Crop to display the cropping handles on the image, and drag the handles until the image shows only the portion you want to keep. Press Enter to complete the crop.

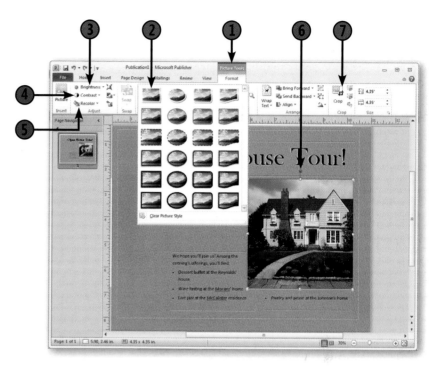

Tip

If you don't like the changes you've made, you can click Undo in the Quick Access toolbar at any point to remove your most recent edits. Additionally, you can click Reset Picture in the Adjust group of the Picture Tools Format tab to return the picture to its original state.

Adding a Table

You may want to use a table to organize and present your information with the greatest possible clarity in a publication. Publisher comes with a series of design formats that help you create exactly the type of table you need for your specific purpose.

Insert the Table

1. With your publication open in Publisher, click the Insert tab and click Table in the Objects group.

2. On the grid that appears, drag to select the number of columns and rows you want to add to the table.

3. Add your content to the table.

4. Click the Table Tools Design tab, and choose a table format you want to apply.

(continued on next page)

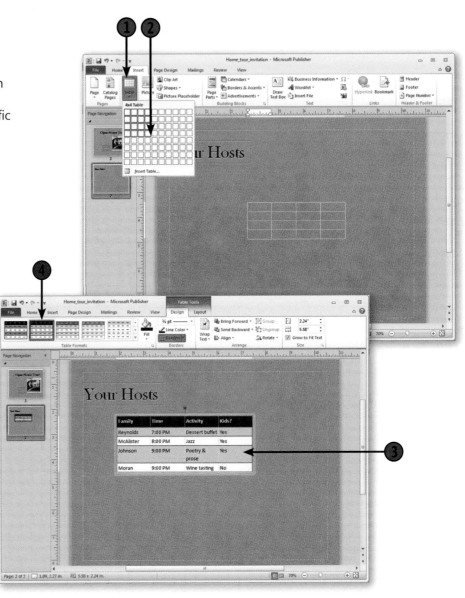

Insert the Table *(continued)*

5 Add columns and rows by using the tools in the Rows & Columns group of the Table Tools Layout tab.

6 Align content in the table cells by using tools in the Alignment group.

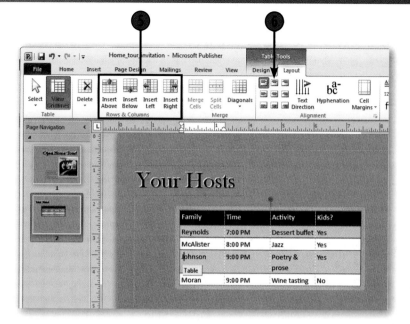

Tip

Another way to create a table is to click the Insert tab and click Table. Then select Insert Table at the bottom of the list. This displays the Create Table dialog box, where you can enter the number of rows and columns you want to create and then click OK to create the table.

Try This!

Move your new table to a new position on your page by clicking the outline of the table and dragging it to the appropriate spot.

Tip

You can easily change the size of a table by positioning the mouse on one of the edges or corners of the table, and when the mouse turns to a double arrow, click and drag the table in the direction you want to resize it.

Repeating Objects on Every Page

If you want certain design objects to repeat on every page of your publication—for example, a picture, a logo, a background pattern, and so on—you can place the object on a *master page*. Then, whenever you create a new page, the material on the master page will appear on the new page.

Add the Repeating Objects

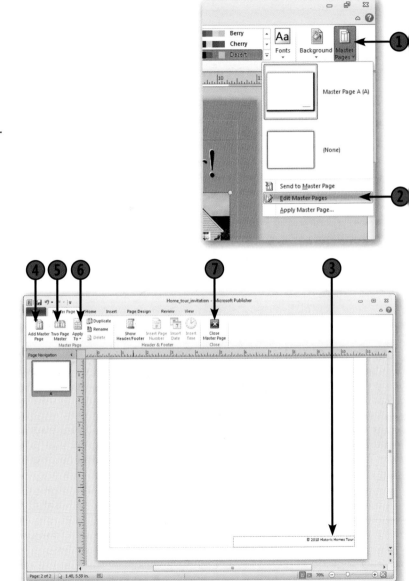

1. With your publication open in Publisher, click the Page Design tab and click Master Pages in the Page Background group.

2. Click Edit Master Pages.

3. Add the object or objects that you want to be repeated on every page.

4. Click the Add Master Page button if you want an additional master page so that you can create a different layout in part of the publication, and place on that second master page the objects you want to be repeated.

5. Click Two Page Master if you want to add elements to the master pages for right and left pages in your document.

6. Click Apply To, and choose whether you want to apply the master page elements to all pages in the document, to the current page, or to pages you select.

7. Click the Close Master Page button to return to your publication's Normal view.

Tip

A master page contains more than repeating objects; it controls the margins, the layout grid, the background color, and any headers and footers that you're using.

Adding Building Blocks

Sometimes the best ideas you have for your publication spring from something someone else suggested. You can use Building Blocks in Publisher 2010 to boost your inspiration. You'll find a collection of ready-to-use elements in the Building Blocks group on the Insert tab.

Insert a Building Block

1. Click the Insert tab.

2. Choose Page Parts to display a gallery of headings, pull quotes, sidebars, and stories; click one to add it to your page.

3. Click Calendars to display a gallery of calendars you can add to your page.

4. Click Borders & Accents to view a variety of graphics images you can use as borders on your page.

5. Choose Advertisements to see a gallery of fun ads and coupons you can add to your page and customize with your own content.

6. Edit the part after it's in your document by using the tools on the Drawing Tools Format and Text Box Tools Format tabs.

See Also

Read "Stacking and Grouping Objects" on pages 326–327 for information about grouping and ungrouping objects.

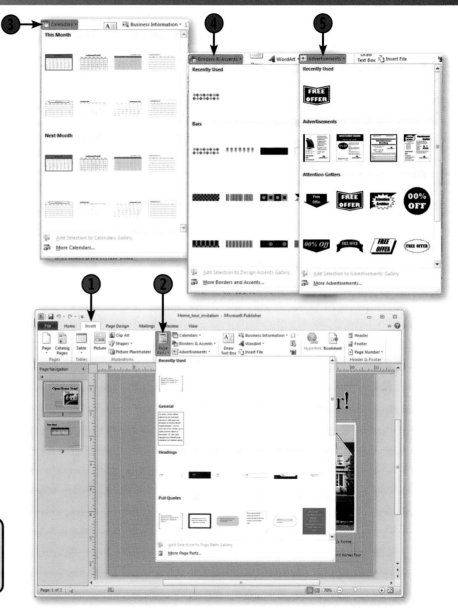

Arranging Objects on the Page

Publisher 2010 includes a number of tools that help you make sure the objects on your page are lined up nicely together. You can begin by displaying the boundaries of all your objects so that you know where one ends and another begins. Then use margin guides to specify the amount of space between your content and the edge of the page; use grid guides to line up objects either horizontally or vertically; use baseline guides so that the lines of text align horizontally across the page even if they're in different text boxes; and use the ruler guides to align each object to a specific measurement.

Set Up Your Guides

1. Show the boundaries of the objects on your page by clicking the View tab and clicking Boundaries in the Show group.

2. Click Guides to display the margin guides as well as the vertical and horizontal guides when you drag an object on the page.

(continued on next page)

Tip

You can change the settings for the way margin, layout, and baselines guides appear by clicking the Page Design tab and clicking Guides in the Layout group. Click Grid and Baseline Guides to display the Layout Guides dialog box, where you can enter your changes and click OK.

Set Up Your Guides *(continued)*

❸ Click Baselines to display lines at the base of all your lines of text. This helps you align the content of your publication across multiple columns.

❹ As you drag or resize an object in your document, notice how it aligns with the grid guidelines.

Position an Object at an Exact Location

❶ Click in the horizontal ruler, and drag a horizontal guide to the location you want on the page.

❷ Click in the vertical ruler, and drag a vertical ruler guide to the location you want on the page.

❸ Click the Page Design tab, and make sure that Align To Guides is selected in the Layout group.

❹ Move or resize the object so that its boundaries align with a horizontal or vertical ruler guide, or to the intersection of a horizontal and vertical guide.

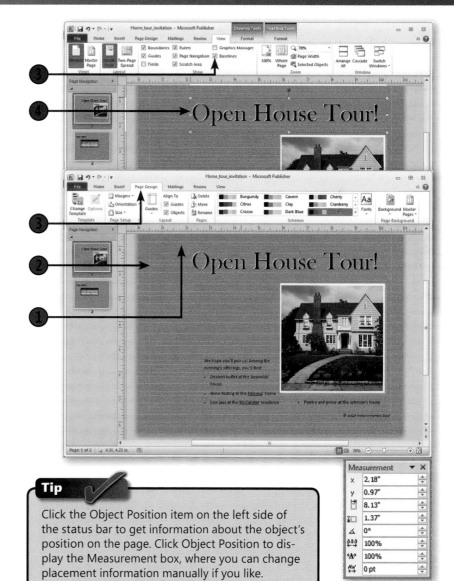

Tip

You can drag as many vertical and horizontal guides from the rulers as you need. For example, you might want to add guides above and below where you want to position an object, or position guides to the right and left of an item you add.

Tip

Click the Object Position item on the left side of the status bar to get information about the object's position on the page. Click Object Position to display the Measurement box, where you can change placement information manually if you like.

Stacking and Grouping Objects

One great feature in Publisher is the ability it gives you to *stack*, or *layer*, several objects and to adjust the order in which they're stacked. After you've assembled the objects you've chosen into the arrangement you like, you can group them so that they function as a single unit that you can then easily move around or resize.

Arrange and Group the Objects

- With your publication open on the screen, click an object you want to layer.

- Drag one object on top of another object.

- With the first object still selected, click Send Backward in the Arrange group of the Home tab.

(continued on next page)

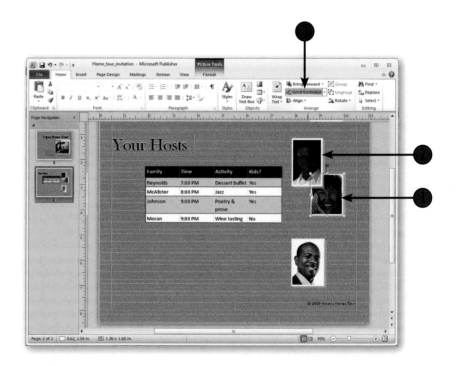

Arrange and Group the Objects *(continued)*

● Drag another object to layer with the first two.

● Click the bottommost object, and click Bring Forward in the Arrange group.

● Press Shift, and click each object in the stack so that all three are selected.

Click Group in the Arrange group. The objects are combined into one object, and you can move and resize them as a single item.

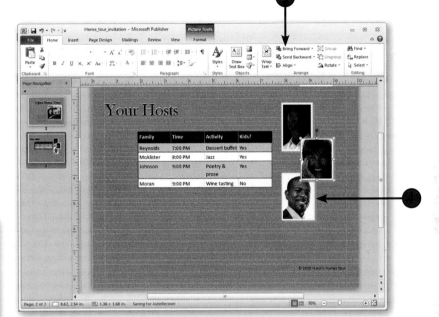

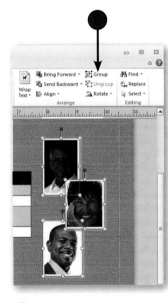

Tip ✓
You can easily return a group of items to individual objects by clicking the group and clicking Ungroup in the Arrange group.

Tip ✓
When you're working with several stacked objects that you want to group, it can be difficult to select an object that's stacked underneath other objects by clicking it. To select all the objects, use the mouse to drag a selection rectangle around all the objects, and then group them.

Flowing Text Around an Object

You can add style and sophistication to your publication by flowing the text of your story around an object—a picture or shape, for example. You do this by setting the text wrapping for the object that the text wraps around.

Set the Text Wrapping

In a publication that contains a text box and the object you want the text to wrap around, right-click the object, and choose Format from the list. (The name of the dialog box varies depending on the type of object selected—for example, if you select a shape, the command name is Format AutoShape.)

(continued on next page)

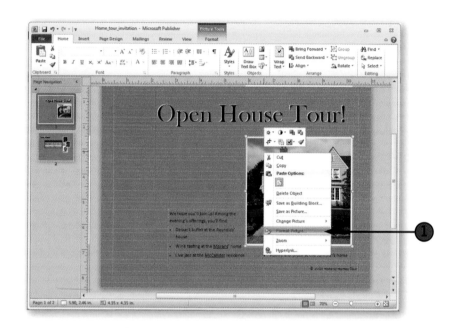

Set the Text Wrapping *(continued)*

2 On the Layout tab, select the text-wrapping style you want.

3 Specify how you want the text to wrap around the object.

4 If you selected the Square wrapping style and would rather not use the automatic setting, clear the Automatic check box, and set the values for how closely the text will wrap around the object.

5 Click OK.

6 Drag the object into a text box that contains text, and adjust the position of the object so that the text wraps around the object in exactly the way you want.

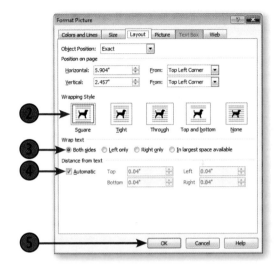

Try This!

Set the text wrapping to Tight for an object, and drag the object into a text box that contains text. Point to Wrap Text on the Home tab, and choose Edit Wrap Points from the list. Drag a square black wrapping point into a new location to change the way the text wraps around the object. Continue moving wrapping points until you get the wrapping effect you want. Click outside the object when you've finished.

Reusing Content

When you're creating a long publication or you plan to create several publications that are related to your current one, you might want to duplicate certain items—a picture, a design, a logo, or a slogan, for example—and use them in different projects. Instead of returning to the first use of the item and copying and pasting it where you need it, you can save your content as a page part and then insert it wherever you want it with just a couple of clicks.

Create Your Own Page Part

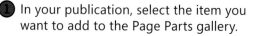

1 In your publication, select the item you want to add to the Page Parts gallery.

2 Click the Insert tab, and choose Page Parts in the Building Blocks group.

3 Click Add Selection To Page Parts Gallery.

(continued on next page)

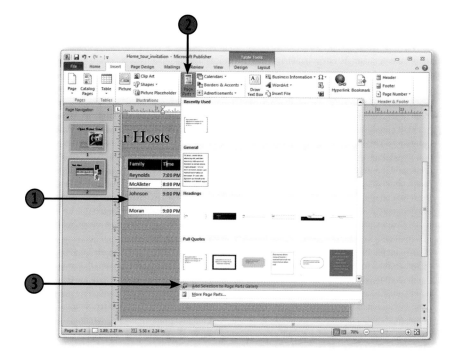

Create Your Own Page Part (continued)

④ In the Create New Building Block dialog box that appears, type a title and a descriptive name for the item.

⑤ Choose a category for the content.

⑥ Enter keywords related to the content.

⑦ Click OK.

⑧ Click Page Parts, and find your new part at the top of the gallery.

Inserting Your Contact Information

Publisher 2010 can store the contact information for your organization or business and insert it at the appropriate point in publications so that you don't need to type the material each time. You can easily add, change, or remove business information at any point you're working with a publication.

Add Your Business Information

1. With your publication open on the screen, click the Insert tab and click Business Information in the Text group.

2. Click Edit Business Information.

3. Enter your name and title.

4. Type your organization name, and provide the address.

5. Type phone and e-mail information.

6. Add a motto or tagline.

7. Add a logo if desired.

8. Type a name for the saved information.

9. Click Save.

> **Tip**
>
> The information you enter will be available to you when you click Business Information in the Text group of the Insert tab. To add the information to a publication, simply select the item you want from the displayed gallery.

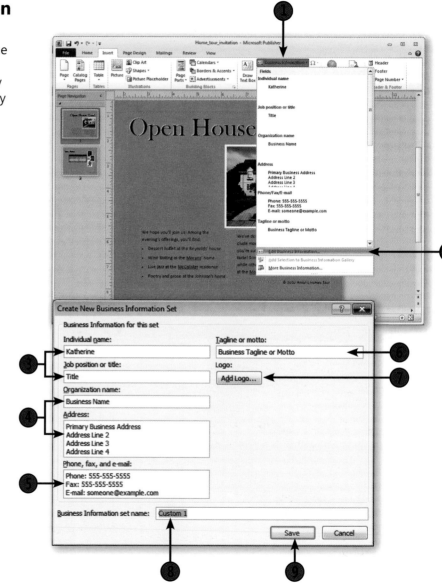

Checking Your Publication

Especially when you're finding your way through creating a publication yourself for the first time, it's nice to have someone look over your shoulder and give you some good feedback about it before you share it with others. Publisher 2010 does this by offering the Design Checker. You can use this tool to get feedback on your publication and fine-tune things before you release it to the waiting world.

Check the Design

① Complete and save your publication.

② Click File, and in the Info tab, click Run Design Checker.

③ Point to a problem that Design Checker has identified, click the down arrow button, and choose one of the following:

- Go To This Item, to jump to the problem item and adjust the problem manually

- Fix, to automatically fix the problem, bearing in mind that not every problem can be fixed automatically

- Never Run This Check Again, to discontinue using the specific check that reported the problem

- Explain, to display Publisher Help, read why this is a problem, and learn about any automatic or manual fixes

④ Repeat step 3 for any other identified problems.

⑤ Click Close Design Checker when you've finished.

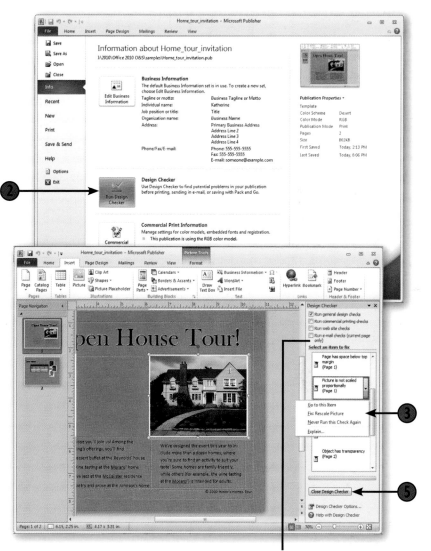

Select or clear check boxes to change which items Publisher checks in your publication.

Sending a Publication as E-mail

Want to send an inviting, high-energy e-mail from a publication you created in Publisher? The program makes it easy for you to send the current page or your entire document with just a few clicks of the mouse. You can also choose from several formats so that you can be sure you're sending in a format others can use.

E-mail Your Publication

1 Create and save your publication. Click the File tab, and choose Save & Send.

2 Click Send Using E-mail.

3 Choose one of the following options:

- Send Current Page, to send the current page as an HTML page.

- Send All Pages, to include all pages in a single HTML page in the e-mail message.

- Send As Attachment, to attach the Publisher file to the e-mail message. (Recipients will need to have Publisher installed to view the file.)

- Send As PDF, to send the publication as a PDF file.

- Send As XPS, to send the document as an XPS file.

(continued on next page)

E-mail Your Publication *(continued)*

④ Address the message, and add a subject.

⑤ If Publisher detected any errors, click the Design Checker button and fix the error or errors using the Design Checker task pane.

⑥ Click Send.

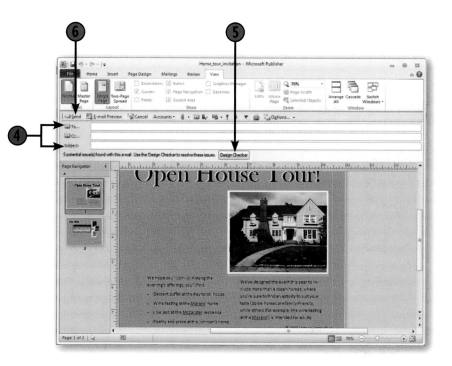

Tip

You can see how the publication will look to your recipients by clicking E-mail Preview in the center panel of the Save & Send tab.

Printing Your Publication

Although you can use Publisher to send your publications as e-mail messages, chances are that you will often print what you produce. You'll find that Publisher gives you exceptionally fine control of the printing process so that you can designate exactly what's printed and how it's printed.

The Final Step: Print It!

1. Click the File tab, and click Print.

2. Select the printer you want to use.

3. Choose which pages you want to print.

(continued on next page)

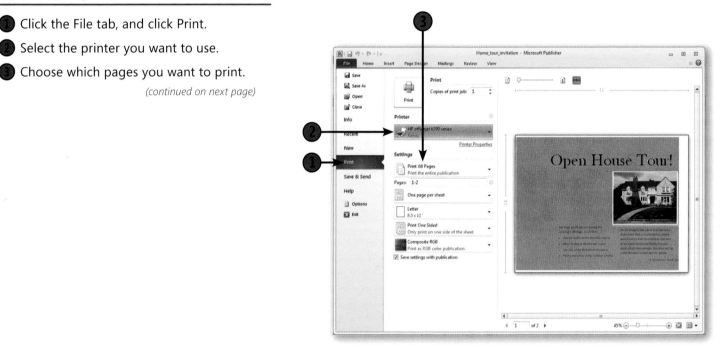

The Final Step: Print It! *(continued)*

④ Click to choose the number of pages you want printed on each page.

⑤ Choose One Sided or 2 Sided printing.

⑥ Preview your publication as it will appear in print.

⑦ Click to preview multiple pages at once.

⑧ View the various pages in your publication.

⑨ Click Print.

Increase transparency

Decrease transparency

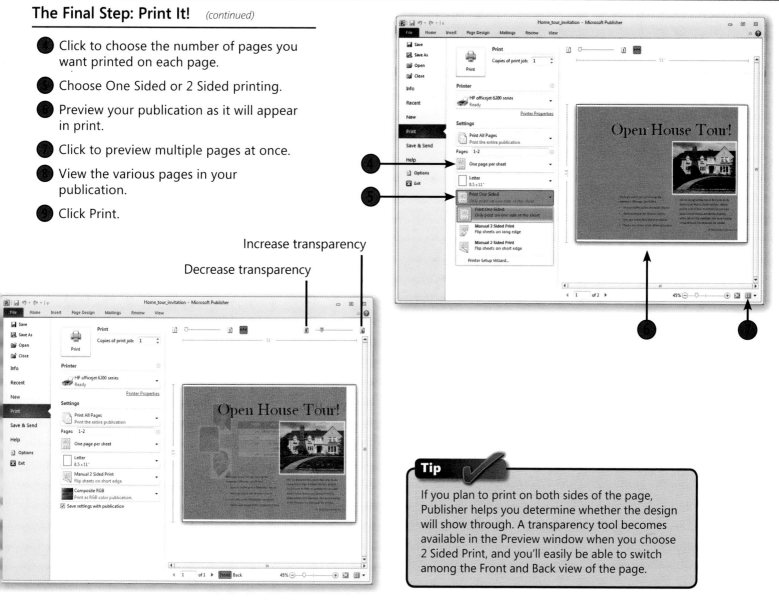

Tip

If you plan to print on both sides of the page, Publisher helps you determine whether the design will show through. A transparency tool becomes available in the Preview window when you choose 2 Sided Print, and you'll easily be able to switch among the Front and Back view of the page.

14

Organize and Share Information in OneNote 2010

Microsoft OneNote 2010 is one of the best kept secrets of the Office 2010 suite. Designed to collect notes in whatever way you like to record them, OneNote enables you to create flexible workbooks that record your typed ideas, pictures, Web snippets, audio recordings, drawings, pictures, and more. The blank page and easy-to-navigate tabbed notebook sections make it simple for you to add, organize, and share the information you collect. What's more, you can easily create notebooks that you share with your team so that all the people working on a project with you can collect ideas in the same place.

OneNote is just a click away in Microsoft Word 2010, PowerPoint 2010, and Microsoft Outlook 2010, as well. You can use the Linked Notes feature in Word and PowerPoint to display notebooks and grab some of the information you've recorded (which can help you make your Word documents and Power-Point presentations even better). You can also send an Outlook task directly to OneNote for inclusion among other notes you share with others. And when you're browsing the Web, Internet Explorer includes a Send To OneNote feature that makes it easy for you to grab Web clippings and save them in the notebook of your choice.

What's Where in OneNote?

Your first task in OneNote involves starting the program and learning about the various features in the OneNote window. Start OneNote 2010 by clicking Start, clicking All Programs, and choosing Microsoft OneNote 2010 in the Microsoft Office folder. As you can see, the OneNote window is different from any other program window you've seen. The open area is perfect for capturing notes on the fly, and the various tools in the ribbon and in the navigation pane make it simple to find your way around the program.

Exploring the OneNote Window

- Available notebooks are listed along the left side of the window.

- Tabs show different notebook sections.

- Pages are listed along the right side of the window.

- Tabs offer tools related to various note tasks.

- The status bar indicates the progress of any ongoing processes.

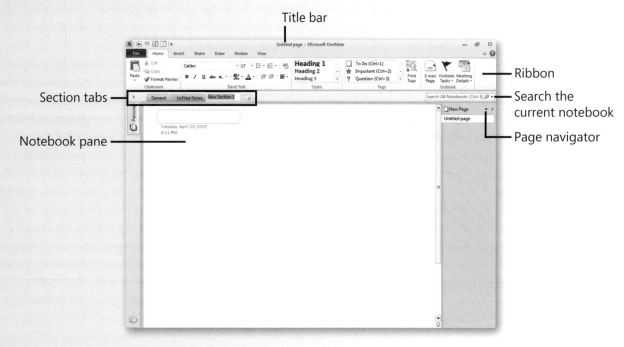

OneNote Basics: Gathering Your Thoughts

The best thing about OneNote is that it works the way you do. If you want to grab content from the Web, OneNote makes it easy. If you want to print your notes directly to your OneNote notebook, the easy integration with Word makes that possible.

You can record voice notes, scribble and draw diagrams to your heart's content, and even drag and drop video clips and pictures directly onto your OneNote pages.

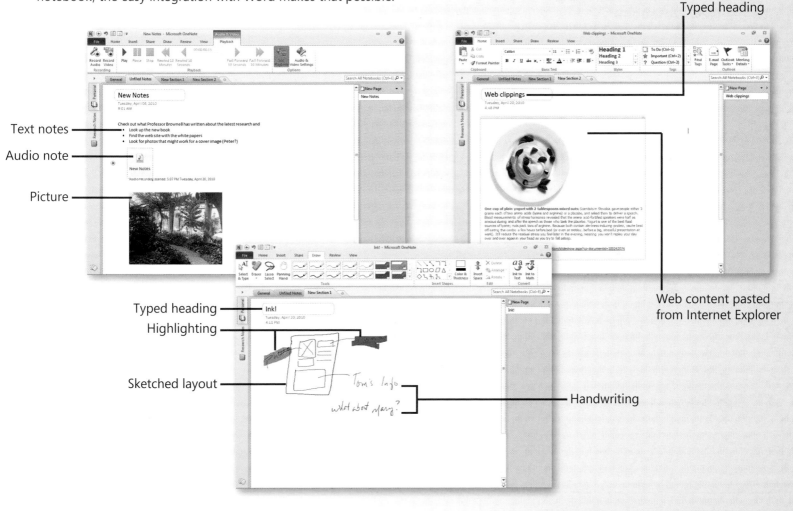

Typed heading

Text notes

Audio note

Picture

Typed heading

Web content pasted from Internet Explorer

Typed heading

Highlighting

Sketched layout

Handwriting

Creating a OneNote Notebook

When you start OneNote 2010 for the first time, a notebook named Personal opens for you to use. You can keep this notebook as is and delete the Microsoft content that is designed to show you the basics of the program. You can also create your own notebook—or many notebooks—by following the steps given here.

Create a New Notebook

1 Start OneNote 2010, and click File to display Backstage view.

2 Click New.

3 Click My Computer.

4 Type a name for your notebook.

5 Change the folder location if necessary.

6 Click Create Notebook.

Tip

You can also create shared notebooks that you and your coworkers can add notes to on the fly. For more about creating and working with a notebook you share, see page 352.

Adding and Working with Sections

Adding sections to your OneNote notebook is as simple as pointing and clicking. OneNote enables you to create and name new sections on the fly, put together section groups (to help you organize similar information), and even choose different colors for your sections to make the different content pieces stand out so that you can find them easily.

Start a New Section

1 Click the notebook you want to use.

2 Click the tab farthest to the right in the section tab row.

3 Type a name for the new section.

4 Add content on the new page as you see fit. Simple!

Tip

You can create as many sections as you like in your OneNote notebook. The only rule of thumb should be for you to keep the organization simple enough that you can find everything you need.

Create a Section Group

1 Right-click a section tab.

2 Click New Section Group.

3 Click to add sections to the group.

4 Add content to the pages.

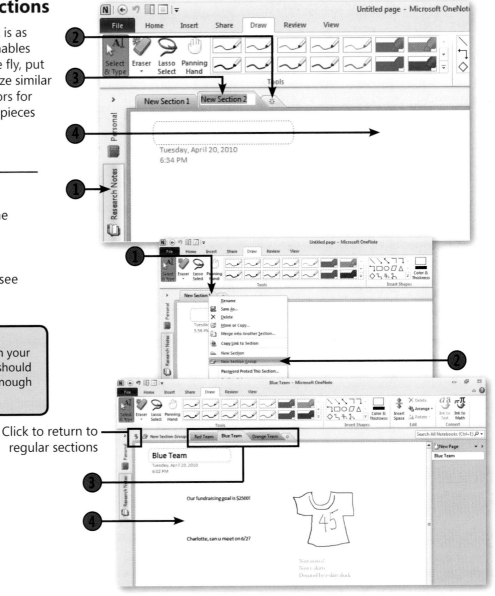

Click to return to regular sections

Inserting and Working with Notes Pages

When you're ready to add pages to your OneNote section, you can start with a blank page or create a new page using one of the many templates OneNote provides. Using a template enables you to put your information into a specific format that may help you find it easily again later.

Create a Page Based on a Template

1. Click the notebook you want to use.
2. Click the section where you want to add the page.
3. Click the down arrow to the right of New Page.
4. Choose Page Templates.
5. Click to extend the different template categories.
6. Select the template you want to use.

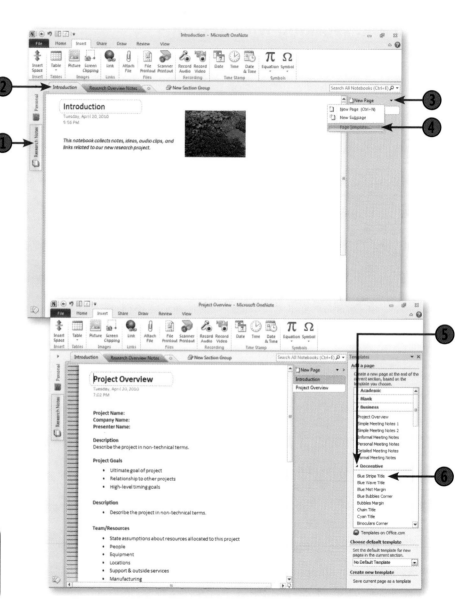

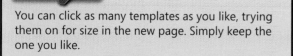

Tip

You can click as many templates as you like, trying them on for size in the new page. Simply keep the one you like.

Set a Default Template

① With the notebook open on the page, click the New Page arrow.

② Choose Page Templates.

③ At the bottom of the task pane, click Templates On Office.com to find additional templates online.

④ Click the Choose Default Template arrow, and select the template you want to use from the list that appears.

⑤ Create a new template by customizing the page in the current OneNote view and clicking Save Current Page As A Template.

Create a Blank Page

① Click the section in which you want to add the page, and click the New Page arrow.

② Click New Page (or press Ctrl+N) to create a page that is equal to the selected page.

③ Click New Subpage to create a page that is a subpage of the current page.

④ You can also point to a page and when the New Page icon appears where you want to add the page, click the mouse and the new page is added.

Tip

Create a subpage when you want to connect new information with an existing page. This way, when you move the primary page, the subpages will move with it.

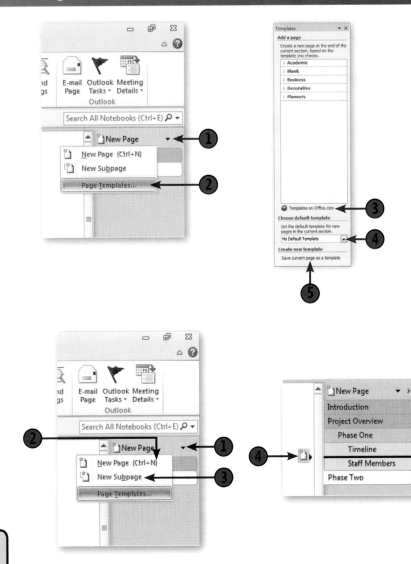

Inking in OneNote

One of the great things about OneNote is the freedom it gives you to capture notes in whichever way you work best. If you want to draw a quick sketch on a page, OneNote makes it easy for you. The inking capabilities in OneNote 2010 have been expanded to include a wider variety of brush tips, as well as highlighting, shapes, and more.

Using Ink and Draw Tool

1 Click the page where you want to draw.

2 Click the Draw tab.

3 Click the pen tool you want to use.

4 Draw on the page using your mouse pointer or stylus.

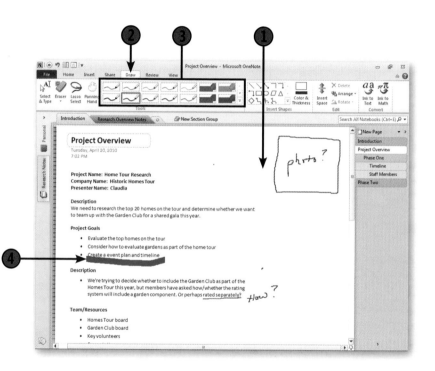

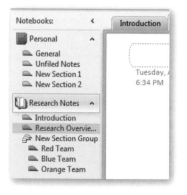

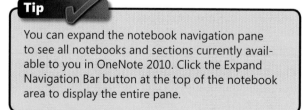

Tip

You can expand the notebook navigation pane to see all notebooks and sections currently available to you in OneNote 2010. Click the Expand Navigation Bar button at the top of the notebook area to display the entire pane.

Adding a Shape

1 In the Insert Shapes gallery, click the shape you want to draw.

2 Click Color & Thickness.

3 Choose the line thickness you want.

4 Click the color you want to use.

5 Click OK.

6 Click and drag to draw the shape on the page.

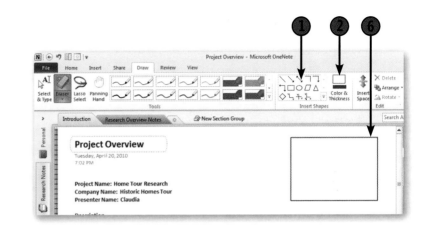

Tip

You can control the way shapes align by using the Lock Drawing Mode and Snap To Grid tools, available in the Insert Shape gallery. Click the More button to display the option list, and click each of the tools. The shapes you draw will align with the underlying grid, making it easy for you to arrange the shapes and notes on a page.

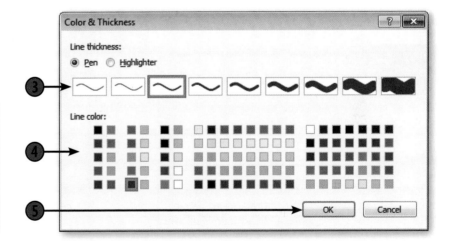

Adding Audio Notes

Do you think better on your feet, perhaps dictating into a digital recorder or your computer headset? If you'd like to add audio notes to your pages, you can easily record your thoughts, the audio from a meeting, a jingle for your new Web site, or any other note you'd like to add.

Record Audio

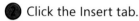 Display the page on which you want to add an audio note.

Click the Insert tab.

Click Record Audio.

Record your audio note.

Click Stop.

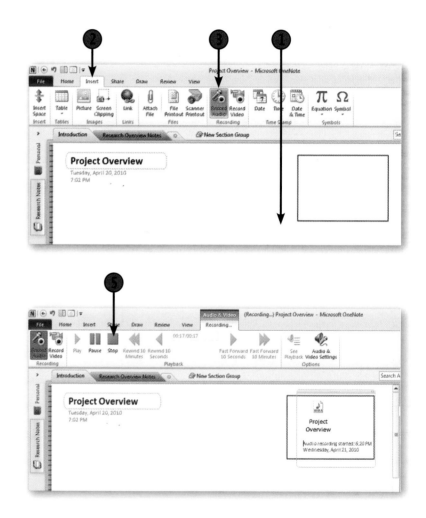

Tip ✔

OneNote doesn't display any visual queue to let you know that the audio is in fact recording, so just start speaking as soon as you click Record Audio.

Tip ✔

Another high-end feature OneNote supports is the Ink To Math feature, available in the Convert group on the Draw tab. This tool takes an equation you've drawn on the page and converts it into a real equation you can use in notes or other documents. In addition to the Ink To Math feature, OneNote includes the Equation tool on the Insert tab, which enables you to add professional equations to your notebook pages.

Playing Your Audio Note

1 Click the audio note icon on the page.

2 Click Play.

3 Click a Rewind control to return to previous content.

4 Click a Fast Forward control to move ahead in the recording.

5 Click Pause to pause playback.

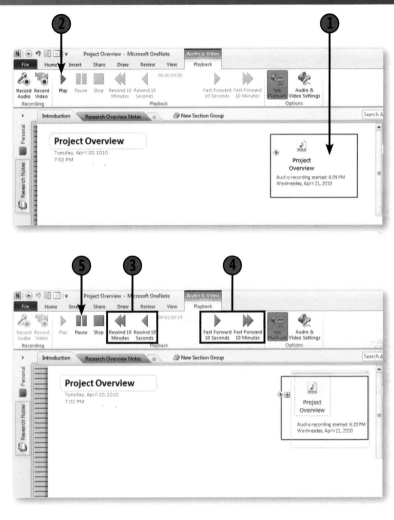

Tip

Once your notes are in OneNote, they will be super easy to find. The improved Fast Search feature now searches for words, phrases, sections, and titles the instant you begin typing a character in the search box. You can also search for information by author, content type, or date entered.

Tip

You can also add video clips to OneNote 2010. You simply need a connected Web camera, and OneNote will capture the live video feed in real time and post it on your page.

Grabbing Web Clippings

If you're like many of us, you see lots of things you like online. When you're researching possible fundraisers for your non-profit organization, you may find a number of ideas online that can help you plan for your next special event. You can click the content you like and paste it directly into your OneNote notebook—in the section and on the page you choose—by following these steps.

Clip Web Content

1. In Internet Explorer, display the page with the content you want to save.

2. Click Tools.

3. Click Send To OneNote.

(continued on next page)

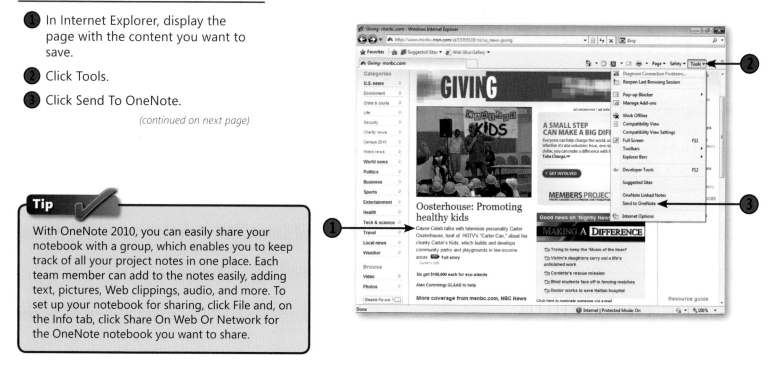

Tip ✓

With OneNote 2010, you can easily share your notebook with a group, which enables you to keep track of all your project notes in one place. Each team member can add to the notes easily, adding text, pictures, Web clippings, audio, and more. To set up your notebook for sharing, click File and, on the Info tab, click Share On Web Or Network for the OneNote notebook you want to share.

Clip Web Content *(continued)*

4 Click the notebook you want to use.

5 Click the section in which you want to paste the information.

6 Click OK.

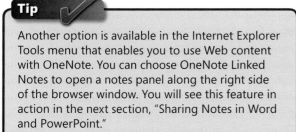

Tip

Another option is available in the Internet Explorer Tools menu that enables you to use Web content with OneNote. You can choose OneNote Linked Notes to open a notes panel along the right side of the browser window. You will see this feature in action in the next section, "Sharing Notes in Word and PowerPoint."

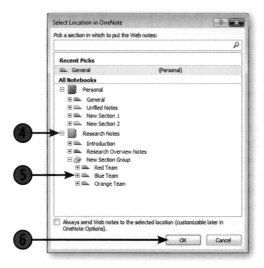

Sharing Notes in Word and PowerPoint

OneNote enables you to gather, organize, and access your notes no matter which program you are using. If you are creating a document in Word, you can easily access your OneNote notes using the Linked Notes feature. Likewise, in PowerPoint, you can use Linked Notes to review and include captured notes in your presentations.

When you create Linked Notes, OneNote includes a link to the linked document or presentation so that you can easily find the text or slide content again at a later time. The link is maintained in the notebook whether you include content from Word documents, PowerPoint presentations, Web pages, or even other OneNote notes pages.

Use Linked Notes in Word

① In Microsoft Word, open the document you want to use with your OneNote notes and select the text you want to include.

② Click the Review tab.

③ Click Linked Notes.

④ Choose the notebook and section you want to link to in OneNote.

⑤ Click OK.

(continued on next page)

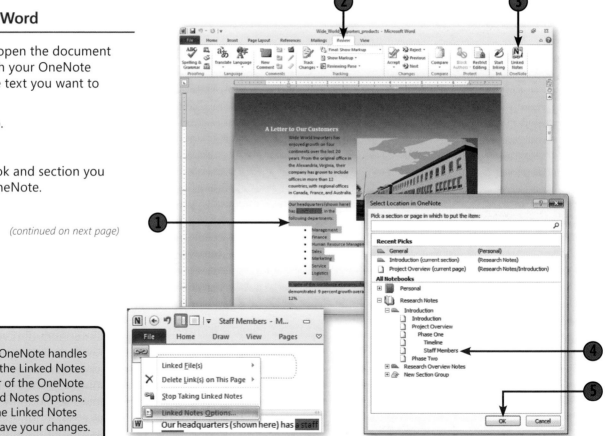

Tip

You can change the way OneNote handles Linked Notes by clicking the Linked Notes tool in the top left corner of the OneNote page and choosing Linked Notes Options. Change any settings in the Linked Notes settings and click OK to save your changes.

Use Linked Notes in Word *(continued)*

6 Drag the Word content to the OneNote page.

> **Tip** ✓
>
> You can also print a Word document directly to your OneNote notebook if you want to preserve your document along with the notes you are gathering. Simply click File and click Print. Then in the Printer area, click Send To OneNote 2010 and click Print.

Work with Linked Notes in PowerPoint

1 In Microsoft PowerPoint, display the slide with the information you want to save to your OneNote notebook.

2 Click the Review tab.

3 Click Linked Notes.

4 Click the notebook, section, and page you want to link to in OneNote.

5 Click OK.

6 Copy and paste or drag the PowerPoint content to the OneNote page.

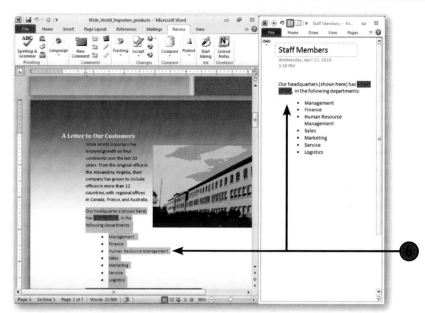

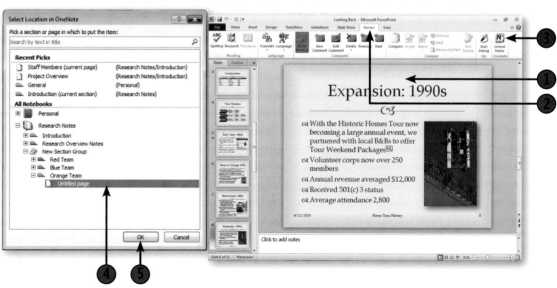

Saving Outlook Data to OneNote

OneNote is also naturally connected to Outlook 2010 so that you can capture information from all different aspects of the program. You can save e-mail messages you receive and send; you can capture tasks, appointments, or even contacts. Depending on the view you're using, Outlook 2010 includes the OneNote tool in either the Move or Actions group on the Home tab, and you can use the tool to insert the information you want to save into the notebook, section, and page you choose.

Share a Message with OneNote

① In Outlook, select the message you want to share with OneNote.

② Click the Home tab.

③ Click OneNote.

(continued on next page)

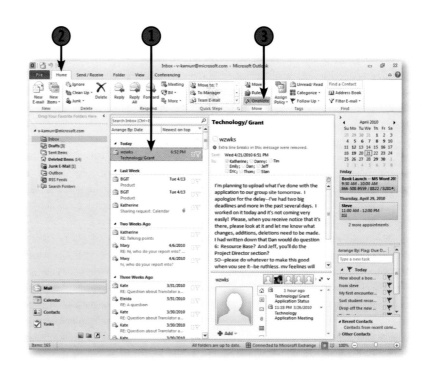

Share a Message with OneNote _(continued)_

4 Choose the notebook, section, and page where the message should appear.

5 Click OK.

6 Make any changes as needed to the message information in OneNote.

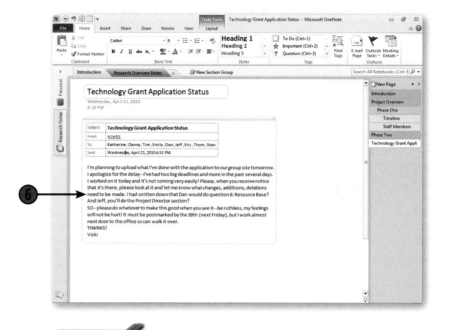

Tip ✓

For both tasks and contacts, you can send selected information to OneNote by clicking the item and clicking OneNote in the Actions group on the Home tab.

Tip ✓

If you need to access your notes from a variety of locations, you can save your OneNote notebook to the OneNote Web App and access it anywhere you can get online. Perhaps you want to look something up in your notes when you're visiting the director of the garden club, or you want to show a potential vendor what you're planning for the next Home Tour logo design. If you have a Windows Live ID or access to a Microsoft SharePoint site, you can store your notebooks online and view, edit, copy, and share your content easily.

Tip ✓

To copy an appointment from Outlook to OneNote, click Calendar and select the appointment you want to use. Click OneNote in the Actions group of the Calendar Tools Meeting tab.

Working with Side Notes and Unfiled Notes

OneNote 2010 also includes a variety of ways for you to view the notes you collect in your notebooks. Click the View tab to see the range of choices. New Side Note, available in the Window group of the View tab, opens a note box you can use to add special content, ideas you aren't sure where to file, or reminders for things you want to follow up on later. When you close a Side Note, it is added to your Unfiled Notes page, which stores the unfiled content until you are ready to assign the note to a specific page, section, or notebook.

Create a Side Note

① Open the notebook in which you want to add the side note.

② Click the View tab.

③ Click New Side Note in the Window group.

④ Type the text for the new note.

⑤ Click Close.

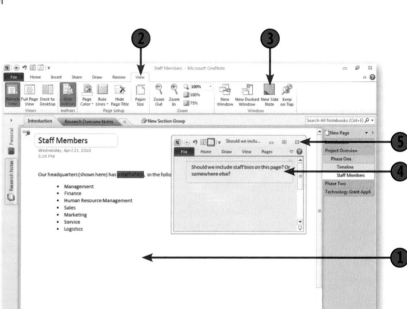

Tip

A message lets you know that the new side note is filed automatically in your Unfiled Notes. You learn how to view Unfiled Notes in the next section.

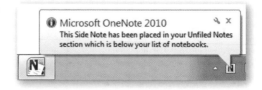

Microsoft OneNote 2010

This Side Note has been placed in your Unfiled Notes section which is below your list of notebooks.

View and Merge Unfiled Notes

① Click the Unfiled Notes icon.

② Review the notes.

③ Right-click the note tab.

④ Click Merge Into Another Section.

⑤ Choose the section in which you want to store the new notes.

⑥ Click Merge.

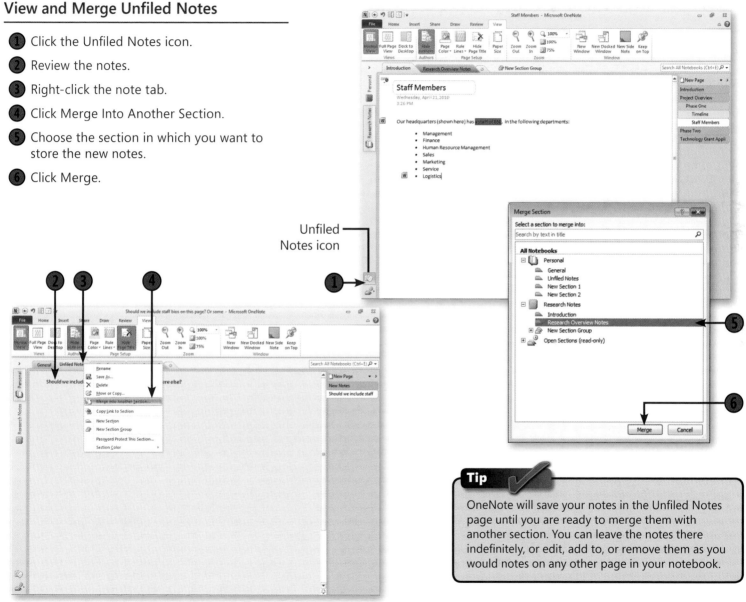

Unfiled Notes icon

Tip

OneNote will save your notes in the Unfiled Notes page until you are ready to merge them with another section. You can leave the notes there indefinitely, or edit, add to, or remove them as you would notes on any other page in your notebook.

15

Working in Access

Microsoft Access 2010 is the database program in the Office 2010 suite. If you are using either Office Professional 2010 or Office Professional Plus 2010, you'll find that Access 2010 is available in your version of the software. The word *database* may sound super technical—understandable only to people with an affinity for programming—but in reality, a database is simply a way to store your data. Like your recipe card holder. Or your DVD rack. Every item that helps us store, sort, or organize ideas or information could be considered a kind of database.

Access 2010 includes improvements that make the program easier to use than ever for those of us who *aren't* programmers by including ready-to-use templates, Quick Start fields, simple data formatting, and application parts that can plug right in and give you the tools you need to sort, arrange, and report on the data you collect.

What's Where in Access?

The first step in getting to know Access 2010 involves surveying the lay of the land. This section shows you three views of Access you are likely to see. The first is the Access window; the second shows you how the window looks when you're working with a table in Datasheet View; and the third shows Report View.

Exploring the Access Window

- The title bar displays the name of the database and the window control buttons.

- The tabs on the ribbon give you access to different tools based on the category you select.

- The Navigation pane displays database objects you've created in the current database.

- The object window displays any open database objects.

- The status bar indicates the progress of any ongoing processes.

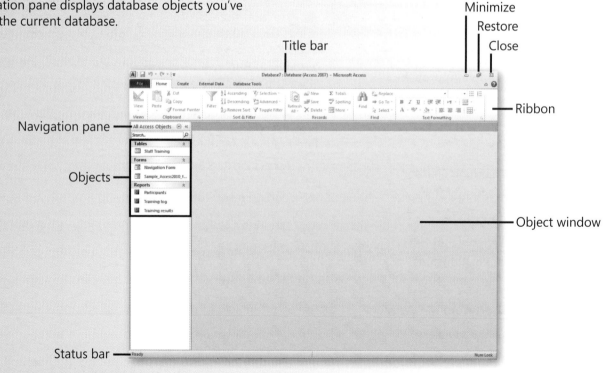

Minimize
Restore
Close
Title bar
Ribbon
Navigation pane
Objects
Object window
Status bar

Taking a Look at Datasheet View

- The object tabs display the names of all open database objects.

- Each row is one data record, containing multiple fields of information.

- Each column is one field in a data record. (For example, Firstname contains the first name of the customer whose data is stored in the record.)

- The Close button enables you to close the active database object with a single mouse click.

- Opening a database object in Design View displays contextual tabs that contain design and formatting tools.

- The horizontal scroll bar enables you to move side to side within your object.

- The vertical scroll bar enables you to move up and down within your object.

- Right-clicking a control on the body of a database object while you display the object in Design View displays a contextual menu that enables you to edit the selected control.

Reviewing Report View

- Double-clicking a report opens it in the object window.

- You can scroll through the report to view data.

- You can sort or filter the data in the report according to settings you enter.

- Click Layout View in the lower right corner to display the Report Layout Tools you can use to apply themes and format the look of the report.

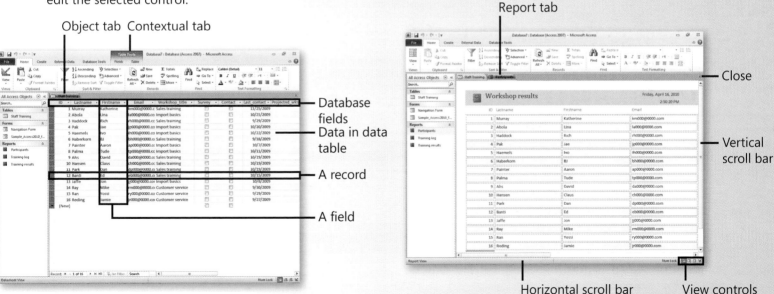

Object tab   Contextual tab

Report tab

Database fields

Data in data table

A record

A field

Close

Vertical scroll bar

Horizontal scroll bar   View controls

Databases: A Simple Approach

Even if you haven't had a reason to create a database before, Access 2010 offers a pleasant surprise—the process of creating data tables to store, sort, and display your data really isn't difficult. And taking it a few steps further—so that you can create a report of, say, all the garden club members who attended the Historic Homes Tour this year—is just a matter of knowing where to click.

But just in case the idea of databases intimidates you (and you're not alone in that), let's consider a practical example of a way in which a database can help you store information and actually makes things more convenient for you (as opposed to burdening you with more details you need to remember).

Ways to Store Data

Suppose that you want to create a membership list of all the people who have donated to your small community organization, the Historic Homes Tour. You have only one big event a year and publish a couple of newsletters (when you find the time), but other than that you're happy with about 15 volunteers and an annual attendance for your Historic Homes Tour of about 400.

But this year some of your board members have been talking about branching out a bit. Perhaps a partnership with the local garden club would bring even more attendees. And

Attendee names

Attendee e-mail addresses

Attendee location

maybe you could co-sponsor a booth at the Designer's Home Show in the fall?

This all requires a more intentional way to manage your data—so that you know who your members are, who your volunteers are, who is already donating to your cause, and who might be a good potential donor in the future. Right now, you've got copies of bank deposit slips with donor names, but not much else. The box on your shelf full of slips may provide backup for your totals if you need them—you can always go back and add everything again, right? But if you want to use your data to do the following things, sorting slips isn't going to be too effective:

- Find all the people who have donated to your organization in the last three years

- Determine where in town your donations are coming from

- Find out who has returned from year to year

- Learn who gave the most, who gave the least, and who gave most often

- Gather the addresses and e-mail addresses of all your attendees

You get the idea. The slips of paper are a form of database, but they aren't the most useful way to store data. In Access 2010, you can store this data and easily sort it, arrange it, filter it, and spruce it up to look good in a report that you can share with your board members—as well as the members of the garden club.

Basic Database Concepts

The data tables you create in Access organize your data in columns and rows. Each row is a record, and each column is a field. Each record contains multiple fields. For example, in a client database, each row contains information for

one client, and each field contains different data items for the individual record. In the following image, the highlighted row is one record, and each column (Lastname, Firstname, Email, Location) is a field.

Access 2010 and Relational Tables

Storing all that information in an Access database saves you time and trouble when you need to sort your data in specific ways. But there's another great point to consider: relationship. A relational database like Access is able to link the data tables you create and create relationships among your data. So you might store information about the businesses that provided goods and services for your home tour in one data table, and have a list of your purchase orders in another table, and when the data for one of the vendors changes—for example, the vendor gives you a new address—the change is reflected in both tables.

This is just the tip of the iceberg for what you can do with data in Access 2010. When you see how easy it is to get your data under control, you'll enjoy exploring the various features in Access 2010 that make it all possible.

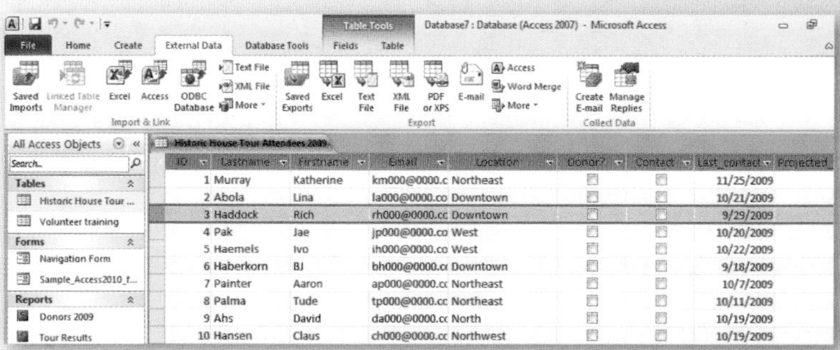

Creating a Database from a Template

Access 2010 makes creating a database easier than ever, thanks to the addition of new pre-built templates you can use to jump-start your own database. You can choose a template from a number of categories and—if that's not enough—once you create the database, you can use application parts to add ready-made tables for your own data.

Create a Database from a Template

1. Start Access 2010, and when the program opens, Backstage view is displayed. New is already selected.

2. Select a template category.

3. Click the desired template.

4. Type a name for your database.

5. Click the folder icon.

(continued on next page)

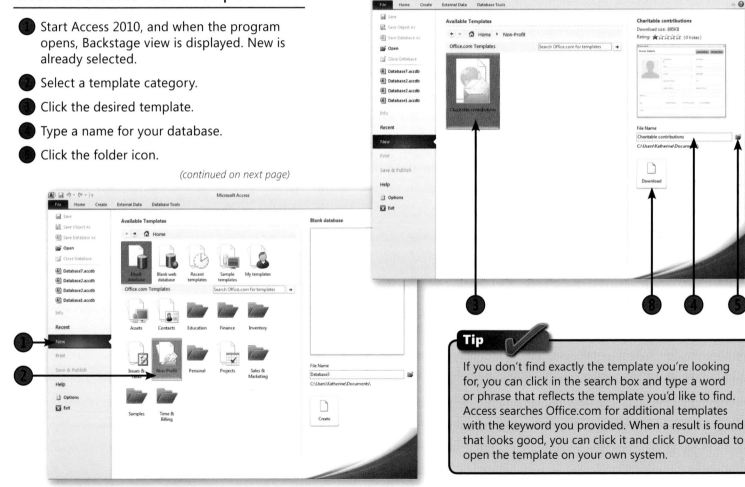

(continued on next page)

> **Tip**
>
> If you don't find exactly the template you're looking for, you can click in the search box and type a word or phrase that reflects the template you'd like to find. Access searches Office.com for additional templates with the keyword you provided. When a result is found that looks good, you can click it and click Download to open the template on your own system.

Create a Database from a
Template   *(continued)*

6 Navigate to the folder where you want to store your database.

7 Click OK.

8 Click Download.

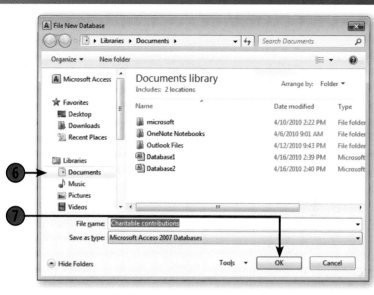

Working with a Template

1 After you click Download, the new template opens in Access.

2 The template may be a fully developed database with a dashboard, tables, queries, reports, and forms already designed.

The only thing you need to do to begin using the template is open a table and enter your data. Double-click the table you want to use, and it opens in the object window.

Double-click a table to open it and begin entering your own data

Dashboard

Tables

Queries

Forms

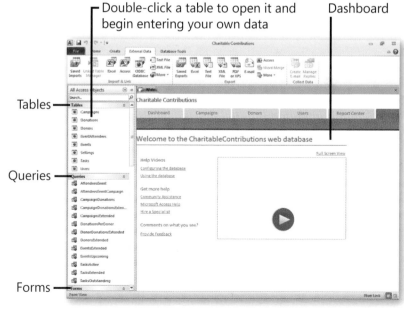

Using an Existing Database

You can easily open an existing database in Access 2010 and begin working with that data using all the new program features. When you start Access, Backstage view appears automatically. If you've used a database in Access 2010 previously, you can click Recent to open a recently used database. If you want to open a database file you haven't yet used with Access 2010, you'll use Open, found in the list of commands at the top of Backstage view.

Open a Recently Used Database File

1 Start Access 2010.

2 In Backstage view, click Recent.

3 If you want to keep the file at the top of the Recent list so that you can find it easily, click the push pin.

4 Click the database file you want to open.

> **Tip**
>
> You can change the number in the Quickly Access This Number Of Recent Databases field to increase (or decrease) the number of databases available to you in Backstage view.

Open an Existing Database File

① Click the File tab to display Backstage view.

② Click Open.

③ Navigate to the database you want to use.

④ Click Open.

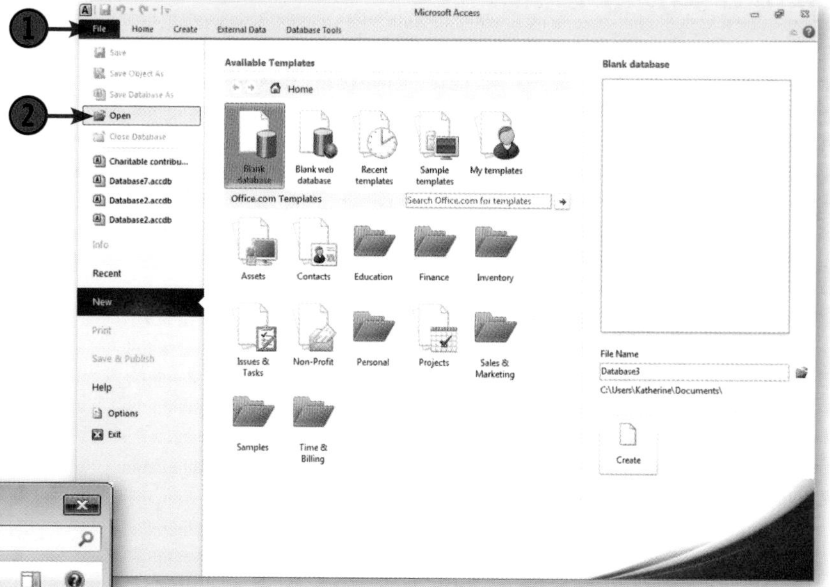

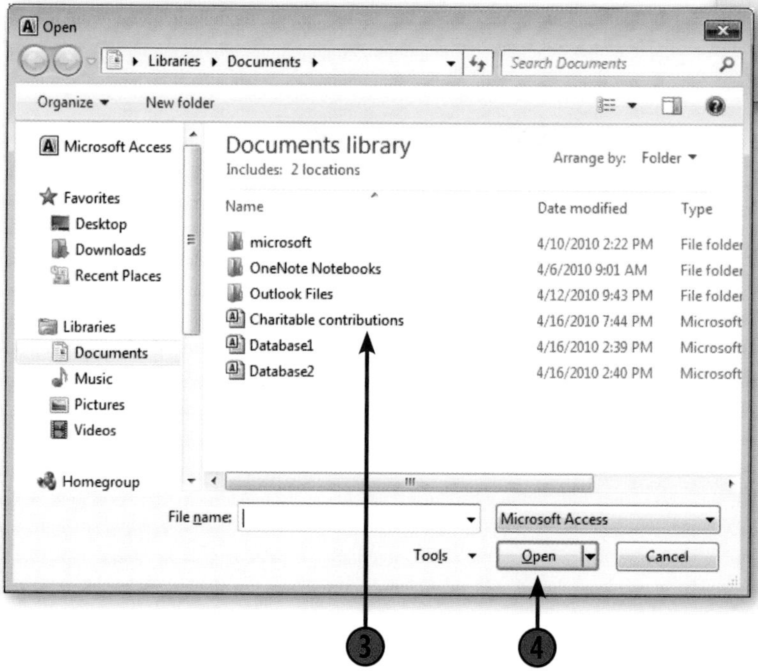

Tip

Access opens much more than other Access files. You can open MDE files; ADE files; ACCDE files; files created in SharePoint Foundation, dBASE 5, dBASE IV, and dBASE III; Excel files; Exchange files; Outlook files; and text files. You can also open ODBC databases in Access 2010.

Adding a Data Table

Adding your data to the new database is simple. Just click and type, pressing Tab to move from one column to the next. Of course, before you begin entering data, you need to think about what kind of information you want to collect—and where it should go.

When you type data into a blank table, Access assigns generic names to the fields, such as Field1, Field2, and so on. After the data's in the table, you can open the table in Design View and name the fields, define data types, and so on.

Create a New Table

1 Click the Create tab.

2 In the Tables group, click Table.

(continued on next page)

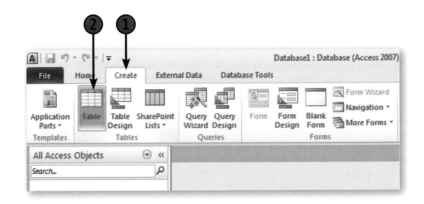

Tip

When you create a field by typing, Access defines the table's first field as a sequentially numbered field named ID, which serves as the table's primary key field. You should leave the ID field in the table, but you may want to rename it to something more descriptive so that you can identify it if you use it as a foreign key. If the table's name is Tour, for example, you could name the field TourID.

Create a New Table   *(continued)*

3 Type the data for the first new field, and press Tab.

4 Repeat step 3 until you have typed all the data for one record, and then press Enter twice to return to the first field.

5 Click Save.

6 Type a name for your table.

7 Click OK.

8 Click the Close box for the table.

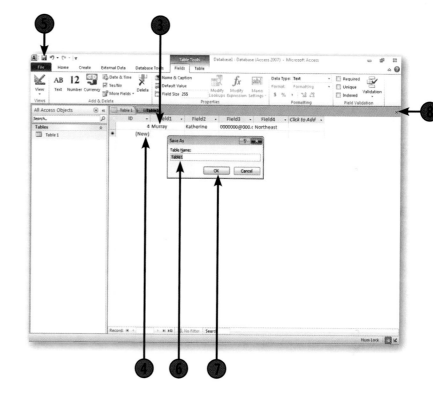

Tip

Now Access 2010 includes a set of Quick Start fields you can add with a click of the mouse. Quick Start fields are fields commonly used in databases—for example, Address, Category, Name, Payment Type, Phone, Priority, Start and End Dates, Status, and Tag are all Quick Start fields. You'll find these fields by clicking the data table, clicking the Table Tools Fields tab, and clicking More Fields. Scroll down to the bottom of the list to find Quick Start fields, and click the field you want to add.

Adding and Changing Fields and Records

It's easy to create tables in Access, but you're not stuck with the first version of a table. After you create a table, you can modify it by adding, deleting, and reordering fields. You can also rename the fields that were added by default and assign the data type you want to use. Although the order of your fields doesn't affect how your table functions within the

database, changing their order can make it easier for you and your colleagues to understand your table's structure. Data types are important because they help Access know how to read, sort, and display the data you entered. (For example, is a number to be shown used in a calculation, used as a street address, or used as a date?)

Rename Fields

1. Right-click the field name you want to change.

2. Click Rename Field.

3. Type the new name for the field.

Set the Data Type and Format

1. Click the field you want to change.

2. Click the Table Tools Fields tab.

3. Click the Data Type arrow and choose the data type.

4. Choose the format for the data.

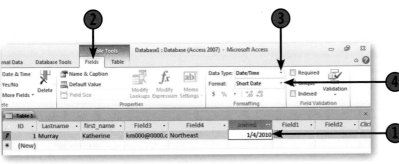

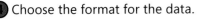

Tip

Access 2010 also enables you to easily add calculated fields to your data table. Click to position the mouse where you want the field to appear, and click the Table Tools Fields tab, click More Fields, and scroll down to Calculated Field in the Yes/No Fields category. Click Calculated Field and then choose the type of field you want to create.

Add and Remove Fields and Records

① Right-click the field (column) to the left of where you want to add a field, and click Insert Field.

② Or click the Click To Add link at the top of the next blank column.

③ Click the field type in the displayed list.

④ Type a name for the new field.

⑤ Right-click a column and click New Record.

⑥ Right-click in the record and click Delete Record.

⑦ To delete a field, right-click the label of the column you want to remove and click Delete Field.

⑧ To reorder fields or records in your table, drag the column or row to the new location and release the mouse button.

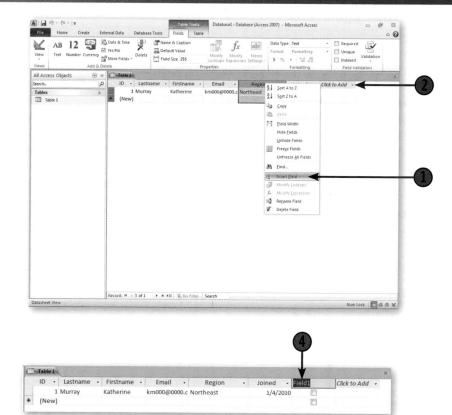

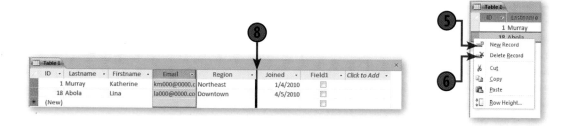

Adding Data to a Table

After you open a table, you can edit the existing data, add new data, or copy data from one cell and paste it into another. You can edit text using the same techniques you use in other Office 2010 programs. When you cut or copy table data, the Office Clipboard keeps track of the last 24 items you cut or copy. If you want Access to undo the last change you made, you can do so by pressing Ctrl+Z or by clicking the Undo button on the Quick Access toolbar.

Select Data

1. Move the mouse pointer over a cell until the pointer turns into a white cross, and then click in the cell.

2. Double-click a word to select it.

3. Drag the mouse pointer over text to select it.

Delete Data

Undo

1. Click to the right of the text to be deleted, and press Backspace to delete it one character at a time.

2. Select the text, and press Delete.

Undoing Operations

- To undo an operation, click the Undo button in the Quick Access toolbar.

Copy and Paste Data

 Select the data you want to copy.

Right-click your selection, and click Copy.

Select the range of cells where you want the data to be pasted.

Right-click the selection, and click Paste.

Caution

If you are copying and pasting a field or record, be sure that there is no data in the cells in which the copied information will be pasted; otherwise, the data in the existing cells will be replaced with the pasted information.

Importing Data

If you've already got data in a database somewhere, you can easily import it into Access 2010 so that you don't have to retype it. (This saves both busywork and the possibility that you might add some typing errors.) You can easily add tables to your database using the External Data tab. Of course, copying tables from another database enables you to use the data as it exists at the time you make the copy, so any updates you make to the original table after you copy it are not reflected in the copy, and vice versa.

Copy a Table from Another Database

1 Click the External Data tab.

2 Click Access.

3 Click Browse.

(continued on next page)

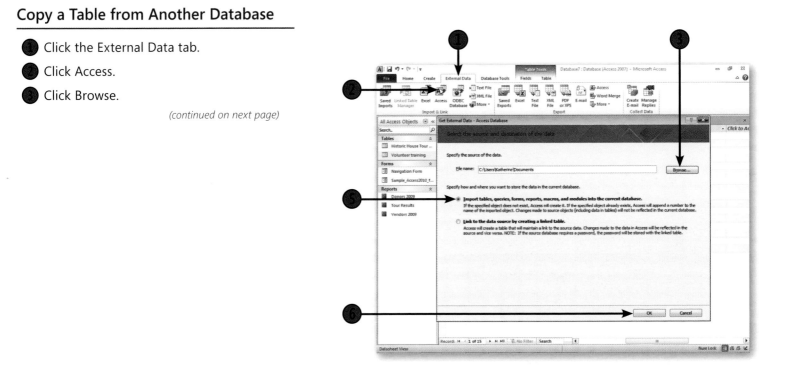

Copy a Table from Another
Database   *(continued)*

④ Double-click the database from which you want to import the table. Select the Import Tables, Queries, Forms, Reports, Macros, And Modules Into The Current Database option.

⑤ Click OK.

⑥ Click the table or tables you want to import.

⑦ Click OK.

Tip ✓

You can import data from other types of database objects by clicking the object type (for example, Queries) in the Import Objects dialog box and then clicking the object from which you want to get your data.

Tip ✓

If you clicked a table to include it in the list of tables to be imported but have changed your mind, you can click the table again to deselect it.

Exporting Data

In addition to storing, organizing, and working with the information in your database, you may want to export your data so that you can share it with others or use it in different ways. Access gives you a number of choices for the formats in which you choose to export your data. The process is similar no matter which format you choose. You can easily export Access data using tools in the External Data tab or by right-clicking the table you want to use.

Export Table Data

1 Right-click the table that contains the data you want to export.

2 Click Export.

3 Click the format for the data you are exporting.

(continued on next page)

You can also choose the tool you want in the External Data tab to export table data.

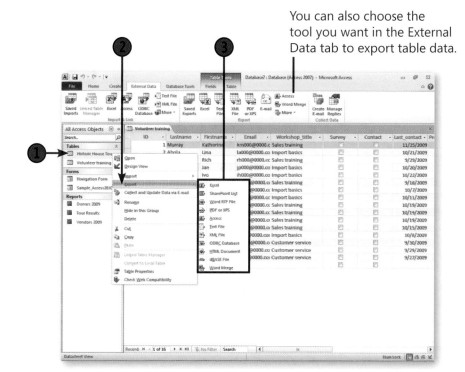

Export Table Data *(continued)*

4 Type the file name or click Browse, and choose a destination file.

5 Choose settings related to the specific format you selected.

6 Click OK.

7 If you want Access to save the export steps you've selected, select the Save Export Steps check box.

8 Click Close.

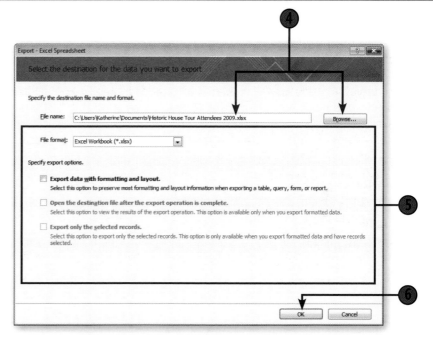

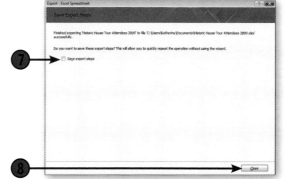

Tip

If you select the Save Export Steps check box, Access will display a form you can use to record the export so that you can recall it later. To recall the export, on the External Data tab, in the Export group, click Saved Exports, click the export you want to replay, and then click Run.

Defining Table Relationships

In some cases, you may want to create a relationship among two tables so that you can expand the way you can sort and report on the data you're collecting. This ability to link two (or more) tables is one reason why relational databases are so powerful—you make your data easier to read by creating simple tables and then use your computer's processing power to combine tables of data into useful information you can use in different ways. When you create a relationship between two tables, you match fields in the tables that often have the same name or similar names. For example, you might link the ID field in the Historic Home Tour Attendees table with the MemberID field in the Volunteer Training table. In the first table, the ID field is known as the *primary key field*, and in the second table, the linked field is known as the *foreign key field*.

Define a Relationship

1. Click the Database Tools tab.
2. Click Relationships.

(continued on next page)

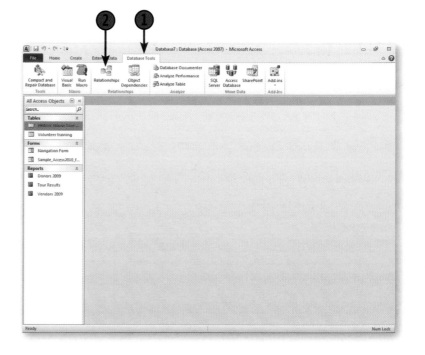

Define a Relationship   *(continued)*

3 If one or more of the tables you want to relate don't appear in the Relationships window, click the Show Table button.

4 Click the first table to add to the Relationships window.

5 Click Add.

6 Repeat steps 4 and 5 as necessary.

7 When you finish adding tables, click Close.

8 Drag the primary key field from the first table to the corresponding foreign key field in the second table.

9 Click Create.

10 Click Close.

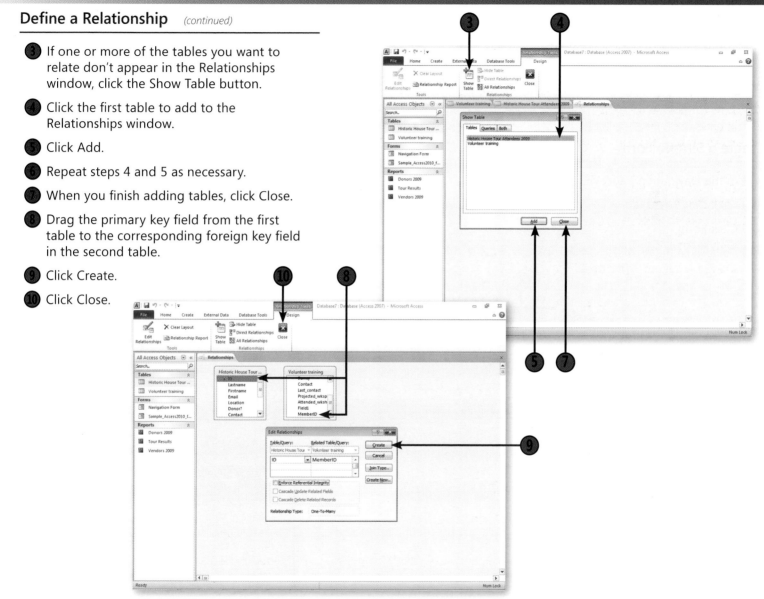

Creating a Form

Access makes it possible for you to create powerful and complex forms, but there will be plenty of occasions when a simple form that contains all the fields from a table will meet your needs. Creating a simple form is a straightforward process. Select the table from which you want to create your form, and then tell Access you want to create a simple form based on that table and you're done. Access 2010 also includes the new Navigation Form, which enables you to create a kind of dashboard experience for the people who will be filling out the forms you create.

Create a Simple Form

1. In the Navigation pane, click a table.
2. Click the Create tab.
3. Click Form.
4. Customize the form using the tools in the Form Layout Tools tabs.

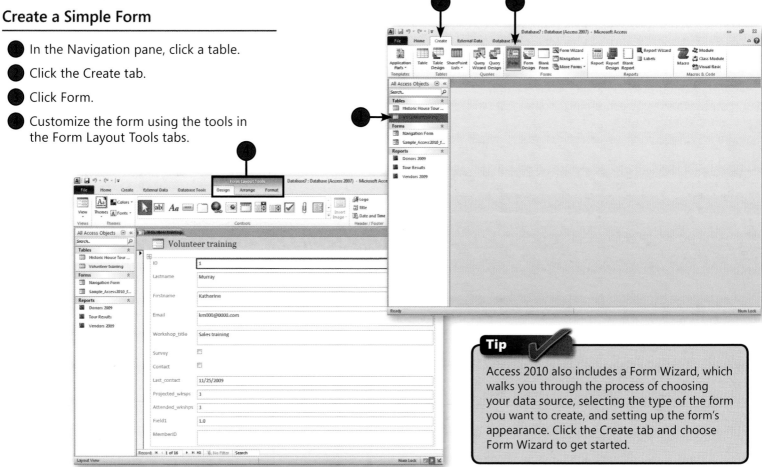

Tip

Access 2010 also includes a Form Wizard, which walks you through the process of choosing your data source, selecting the type of the form you want to create, and setting up the form's appearance. Click the Create tab and choose Form Wizard to get started.

Create a Navigation Form

1. Click the table you want to use as the basis for the form.

2. Click the Create tab.

3. Click Navigation in the Forms group, and choose the layout style you like.

4. Click Show All Tables in the Fields List area.

5. Click to display table fields.

6. Drag the fields you want to use onto the navigation form.

7. Save and close the form.

Creating a Report from the Data

Although you can generate reports from the data in a single table or query, you may want to combine data from more than one table or query into a single report. For example, you might have attendee data in one table and volunteer data in another table, and then want to create a report in which you can see who among your volunteers attended the most recent homes tour. You can do that by creating a report using the Report Wizard.

Step Through the Report Wizard

1. Click the Create tab.

2. Click Report Wizard in the Reports group.

3. Click the Tables/Queries down arrow, and then choose the first table or query from which you want to draw values for the report.

4. Click a field in the Available Fields box, and then click either of the following buttons:
   - > to add the selected field.
   - >> to add all fields to the report.

5. Click Next.

(continued on next page)

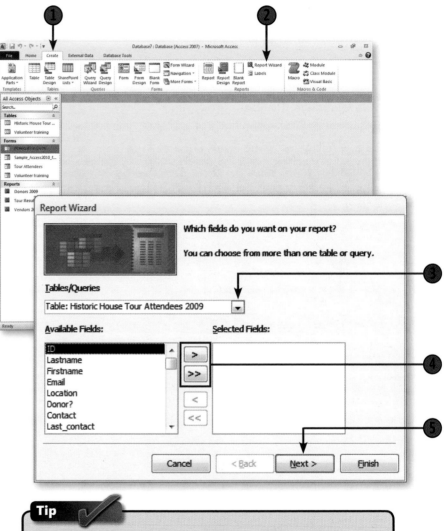

Tip

You can remove fields from the Selected Fields pane of the Report Wizard by clicking the field name and then clicking either Remove, to remove the selected field, or Remove All, to remove all fields.

Tip

To add all of a table's fields to your query, click the Add All (>>) button. You can also remove a field by clicking the Remove (<) button or remove all fields by clicking the Remove All (<<) button.

Step Through the Report Wizard   *(continued)*

6 If you created a report based on a query that uses primary key values from more than one table, a wizard page appears asking you to select preliminary grouping criteria for the report's records. Click the name of the field by which you want to group the fields.

7 If necessary, click the first field by which you want to group the report's contents and then click Add. Repeat to add grouping levels.

8 Click Next.

9 Click the first field's down arrow, and click the first field by which you want to sort the report's contents.

10 If necessary, click the sort options to toggle between Ascending and Descending.

11 Click Next.

12 Use the controls on the remaining wizard pages to select a layout, page orientation, style, and name for the report. When you're done, click Finish.

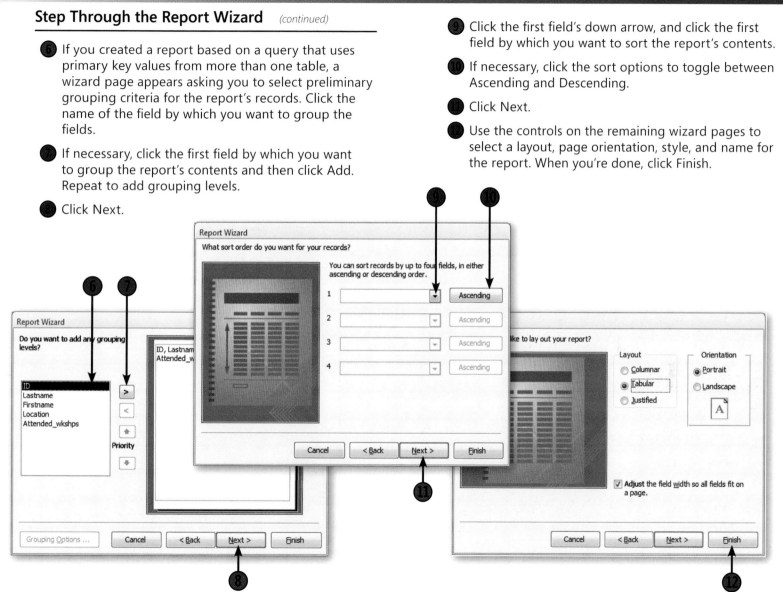

Formatting Reports

Access 2010 now includes the same themes you'll find in other Office 2010 applications, which enables you to give the same look to your data that you give to your documents, worksheets, and e-mail messages. What's more, you can use the conditional formatting features in Access 2010 to call attention to specific data items in your reports to ensure that those viewing the file see what's most important about the data you're presenting.

Format a Report Using Themes

1 Open the report you want to format.

2 Click the Report Layout Tools Design tab.

3 Click Themes.

4 Click the theme you want to apply to the report.

Tip ✓

Now in Access 2010 you can choose the same themes for your reports that are available in other Office 2010 programs. This means that you can choose a theme for your Microsoft PowerPoint 2010 presentation that is also reflected in your Access data tables. Nice.

Add Conditional Formatting to a Report

1. Create a report for the table you want to use.

2. Select the field to which you want to add conditional formatting.

3. Click the Report Layout Tools Format tab.

4. Click Conditional Formatting.

5. Click the New Rule button.

6. Click Compare To Other Records.

7. Click OK.

8. Click OK again.

Conditional Formatting Rules Manager

Show formatting rules for: Attended_wkshps

New Rule | Edit Rule | X Delete Rule

Rule (applied in order shown) | Format

OK | Cancel | Apply

New Formatting Rule

Select a rule type:

Check values in the current record or use an expression
Compare to other records

Edit the rule description:

Data Bar format settings:

Show Bar only

	Shortest Bar	Longest bar
Type:	Lowest value	Highest value
Value:	(Lowest value)	(Highest value)

Bar color [   ] Preview: [   ]

OK | Cancel

Tip

The first option in Select A Rule Type (in the New Formatting Rule dialog box) enables you to display specific formatting based on the data in your table meeting a specific criterion. The second option, Compare To Other Records, enables you to compare data in all records in a specific field.

Querying Information from Your Data Tables

A query is a sort procedure that produces a result of the specific data you want from your table. You can save queries to use repeatedly—for example, you might create a query that shows all new members in your Northeast region and that you can run monthly to see how your membership is growing in that area. Access 2010's Query Wizard walks you through the process, making it easy to identify the tables and fields you want to appear in your query. What's more, you can choose whether to have Access display detailed results (that is, the individual query rows) or summarize the query's contents for you.

Create a Detailed Query

1. Click the table you want to use.
2. Click the Create tab, and click Query Wizard.
3. Click Simple Query Wizard.
4. Click OK.

(continued on next page)

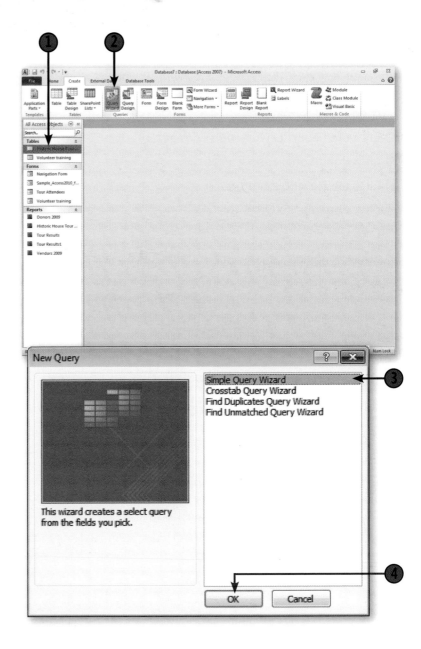

Create a Detailed Query   *(continued)*

⑤ Click the Tables/Queries down arrow, and then click the table or query with the fields you want to use in your query.

⑥ Click the first field to include in the query's results.

⑦ Click Add.

⑧ Repeat steps 6 and 7 to add more fields (and step 5 to change the table or query from which you draw fields).

⑨ Click Next.

⑩ Type a name for your query.

⑪ Click Finish.

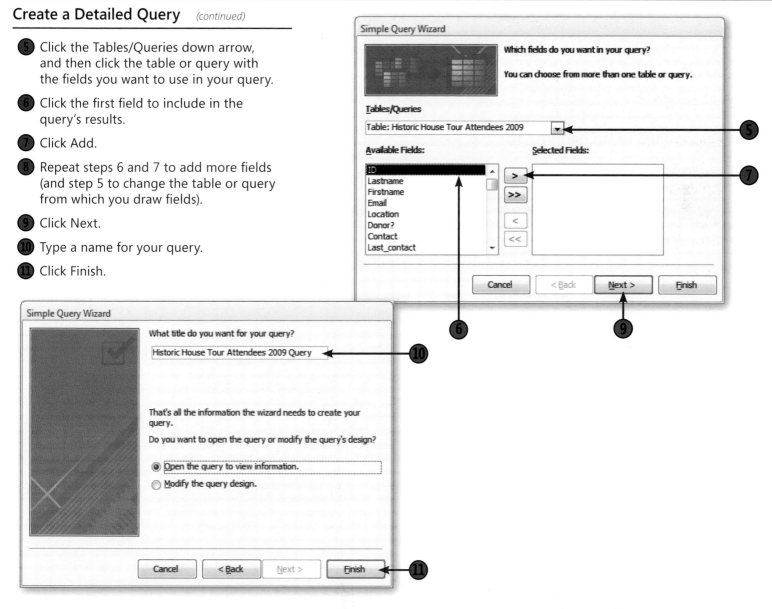

Analyzing Data with a PivotChart

Just as you can create tables that you can reorganize on the fly to emphasize different aspects of your table and query data, you can also create dynamic charts, called PivotCharts, to show your data in different ways. By changing the grouping order of the fields used to create your PivotChart, or by limiting which values are presented in the PivotChart, you answer specific questions posed by you and your colleagues. In addition to changing how your data appears in the chart, you can even change the type of chart you use to display your data!

Step Through the PivotChart Wizard

1. Open the data table you want to use.

2. Click the Table Tools Fields tab.

3. Click View, and click PivotChart View.

(continued on next page)

Step Through the PivotChart Wizard *(continued)*

④ Drag fields in which you want to provide values for the PivotChart's category axis rows from the Chart Field List box to the Drop Category Fields Here area.

⑤ Drag fields in which you want to provide values for the PivotChart's data series from the Chart Field List box to the Drop Filter Fields Here area.

⑥ Drag the fields in which you want to provide values for the body of the PivotChart from the Chart Field List box to the Drop Data Fields Here area.

⑦ Click Services Area to choose the location for the selected field if you don't want to drag and drop it on the chart.

⑧ Click Save.

Change a PivotChart Chart Type

① Display the table that contains the PivotChart.

② If necessary, click the Design tab.

③ Click the Change Chart Type button.

④ Click the Type tab.

⑤ Click the new chart type.

⑥ Click the subtype of the chart you want to create.

⑦ Click the Close box.

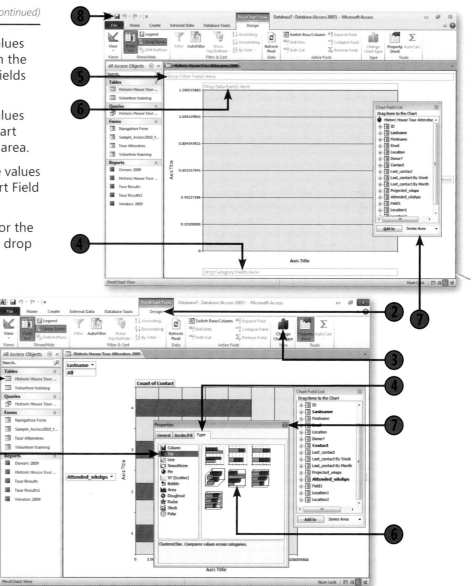

16

Customizing and Securing Office

Office 2010 is more customizable than ever, because in addition to all the things you could already change about the various programs—colors, fonts, the Quick Access toolbar, and more—now you can change the very heart of the navigation: the Office 2010 ribbon. Now you can create new tabs and tab groups and add your own tools—even macros you create yourself—to your own custom tabs. And that's just the beginning of the ways you can tailor Office 2010 to work the way you do: You can load up the Quick Access toolbar with items you use frequently; customize the program windows to have each file open in its own window, or use only one window to switch among files; show or hide items on the status bar; and change the overall color scheme for the program window.

If people who use earlier versions of Office need access to your files, you can save those files in a compatible format and you can use the new Accessibility Checker to ensure that all people can read the files you create. Office 2010 also includes some new security features. Find out how to work with Protected View, protect your files with a password, and set various levels of protection that dictate the type of access you'll allow. You'll find information in this section about using *digital IDs and digital certificates,* as well as ways to protect your system from malicious macros and other evils.

Customizing the Ribbon

One of the exciting new features in Office 2010 is the ability to customize the ribbon. You can create your own tabs and add the groups and tools you need to work with the files you create. This customization enables you to put your favorite tools within easy reach so that your Office programs work just the way you want them to.

Create and Rename a New Tab

1. In any Office 2010 program, click the File tab.
2. Click Options.
3. Click Customize Ribbon.
4. Click New Tab.
5. Click the new tab.
6. Click Rename.
7. Type a new name for the tab, and click OK.

> **Tip** ✓
>
> By default, a new group is created when you add a new tab. You can add more groups to the tab by clicking New Group at the bottom of the Customize The Ribbon list.

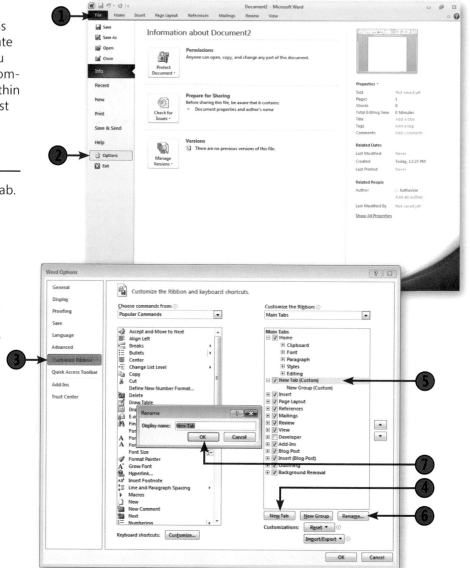

Rename and Add Tools to the Group

1 Click the new group that was created automatically.

2 Click Rename.

3 Type a name for the group, and click OK.

4 In the Choose Commands From list, click the tool you want to add to the group.

5 Click Add.

6 Repeat Steps 4 and 5 as needed until you have added all the tools you want.

7 Click OK.

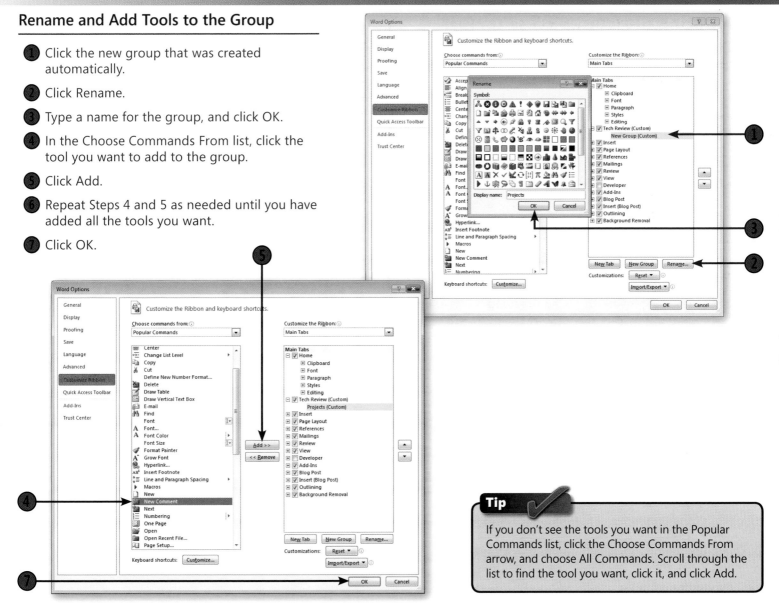

Tip

If you don't see the tools you want in the Popular Commands list, click the Choose Commands From arrow, and choose All Commands. Scroll through the list to find the tool you want, click it, and click Add.

Customizing the Quick Access Toolbar

The Quick Access toolbar is the place to keep the tools you use often and want to use regularly. Positioned in the top left corner of all your Office 2010 programs, the Quick Access toolbar can be customized to include all your favorite tools and galleries. You can also change the location of the Quick Access toolbar so that it appears either above or below the ribbon.

Add or Remove Items Common to the Quick Access Toolbar

① Click the down arrow at the right of the Quick Access toolbar.

② On the Customize Quick Access Toolbar menu, click to select any unselected items that you want to add to the toolbar.

③ Click any selected items that you want to remove from the toolbar.

④ Right-click any item anywhere on the ribbon that you want to add to the toolbar, and choose Add To Quick Access Toolbar from the shortcut menu.

⑤ If the toolbar becomes too large to fit on the title bar or if you want easier access to it, click the down arrow at the right of the toolbar, and click Show Below The Ribbon on the menu.

See Also

Read "Using the Ribbon" on pages 12–13 for information about minimizing the ribbon when you don't need it.

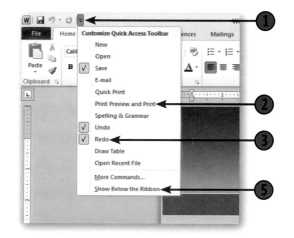

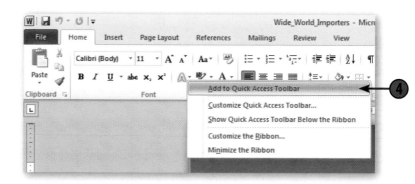

Control the Customization

1 Click the down arrow at the right of the Quick Access toolbar, and on the Customize Quick Access Toolbar menu, click More Commands to display the program's Options dialog box with the Customize category selected in the left pane.

2 Choose whether you want the changes to affect only the current document or all documents.

3 Specify the category of commands you want to select from.

4 Click a command that you want to add to the toolbar.

5 Click Add.

6 To remove a command you don't use, select it and click Remove.

7 To change the order in which commands will appear on the toolbar, click a command and use the up or down arrow to move the command.

8 Repeat steps 3 through 7 to make any further customizations to the Quick Access toolbar. Click OK when you've finished.

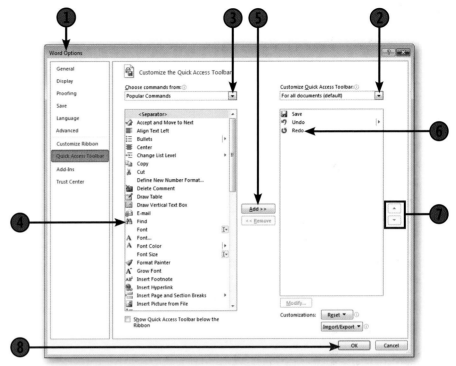

Tip ✓

You're not limited to standard commands on the Quick Access toolbar. You can include styles, fonts, macros, and many items that aren't available from the ribbon.

Tip ✓

When you add or delete items using the Customize Quick Access Toolbar menu or the shortcut menu on the ribbon, you'll see that version of the toolbar in all your documents. If you want to see that version of the toolbar in the current document only, use the program's Options dialog box to specify that you want to save these changes in the current document only.

Customizing the Work Area

The work area, or program window, is where you do your work in the various Office 2010 programs, so you'll probably want to customize it to fit your own personal style. In Microsoft Word 2010, Microsoft Excel 2010, Microsoft PowerPoint 2010, Microsoft Access 2010, and Microsoft Outlook 2010, you can show or hide items on the status bar, set the ribbon to appear only when you need to use it, change the overall color scheme for the window, and so on.

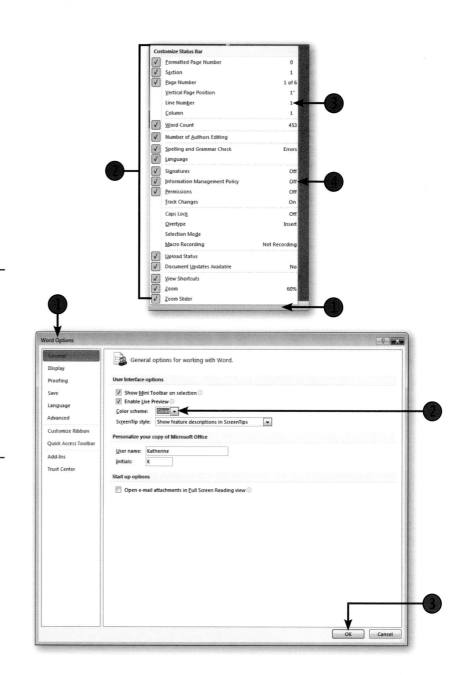

Show or Hide Items on the Status Bar

1. Right-click anywhere on the status bar.

2. Review the choices in the Customize Status Bar list.

3. To show an item that isn't currently displayed on the status bar, click the item.

4. To hide an item that's currently displayed, click the item.

Change the Window's Color Scheme

1. Click the File tab, click Options, and then select the General category in the left pane.

2. Specify the color scheme you want.

3. Click OK.

Change What's Shown

1 Click the Advanced category in the left pane.

2 In the Display category, select the number of files you used recently that are displayed on the Office menu.

3 In Word and Excel, select the units of measurement if you want to use units different from the default units for your country or region.

4 Select this check box if you want each open file in this program to have its own window and its own button on the Windows taskbar; clear the check box if you want only one window for the program so that you can switch among open files.

5 Make any other display settings that are specific to your program.

6 In Word, click the Display category, and select the formatting marks you want to be displayed. In Word, select any other items you want to be displayed.

7 Click OK.

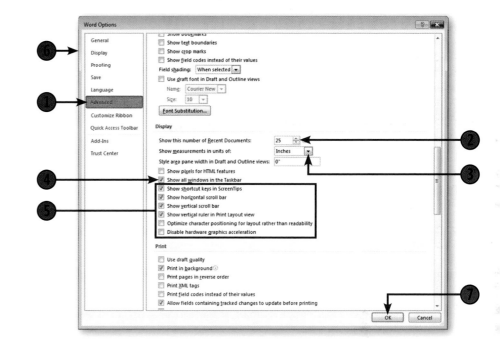

Tip

Each program has different settings in its Display section because each program displays different types of information in its own way. Explore the different areas of the Advanced category to see the extent to which you can customize each program.

Customizing Your Editing

Your Office programs are set up to use the most common editing settings that, in most cases, make your work easy and produce fine results. However, if some settings aren't exactly right for your working style, or if you need to adjust settings to comply with a design or some other specification, you can easily modify the editing settings. Each Office program has its own type of settings, but some universal settings apply to all or most of the programs.

Adjust Program Options

1 Click the File tab, click Options, and click Advanced.

2 In Word, PowerPoint, and Microsoft Publisher 2010, select this check box to select whole words when only a part of a word is selected but the selection extends outside of a word. Clear the check box to select portions of adjacent words.

3 In Word, Excel, PowerPoint, and Publisher, select this check box to allow dragging content to a new location. In Excel, select the Enable Fill Handle And Cell Drag-And-Drop check box.

4 Choose the default settings you want to use for Paste with Live Preview.

5 Click OK to save your changes.

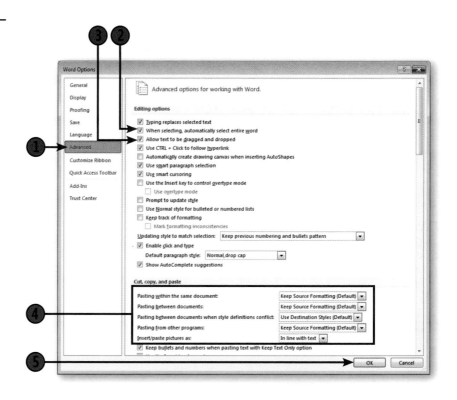

Changing Your User Information

Office programs routinely insert certain information into your files, using data that you've supplied. For example, when you're reviewing a file, your name, your initials, or both are used to identify your comments. However, all that automation is useless if the information you supplied is incorrect or if it's nonexistent. Fortunately, you can easily correct or add the information.

Change Your Name and Address

1. Click the File tab, click Options, and in the Options dialog box, click General if necessary.

2. If your name is incorrect, select it and type your correct name.

3. To change or correct your initials in any program except Excel, select the initials and then type the initials you want to use.

4. In Word, click the Advanced category.

5. In the General section, enter, correct, or replace your mailing address.

6. Click OK.

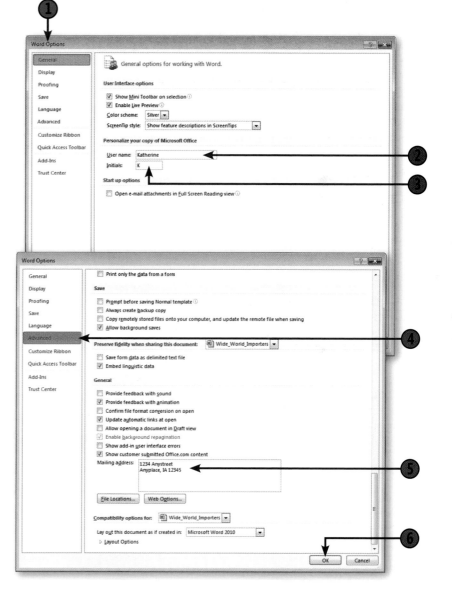

Customizing the Spelling and Grammar Checkers

Depending on the type of file you're creating, you might need to tailor the levels of spelling and grammar checking to make them appropriate for that type of file. You can customize the types of checking the program does, and you can even designate certain text not to be checked at all. Now in Office 2010 you can also choose specific language dictionaries to assist you when you are translating content in your document.

Specify What's to Be Checked

1. Click the File tab, click Options, and then click Proofing.

2. Select this check box to tell the program to check the spelling of each word as you type it.

3. In Word and PowerPoint, select this check box to instruct the program to check spelling based on the context in which a word is used (for example, to detect whether "form" should be used instead of "from").

4. Select the options to be included in the spelling check.

5. Select these check boxes to have each phrase and sentence checked for proper grammar as it's completed and to have your grammar checked whenever the program checks your spelling. Specify whether you want the program to check grammar alone or grammar together with writing style. Click Settings to define the grammar rules you want Word to use to check your document.

6. Specify if and when you want spelling errors not to be displayed; and, in Word or in the Outlook Editor, if and when you want grammar errors not to be displayed.

7. Click OK to use your new settings.

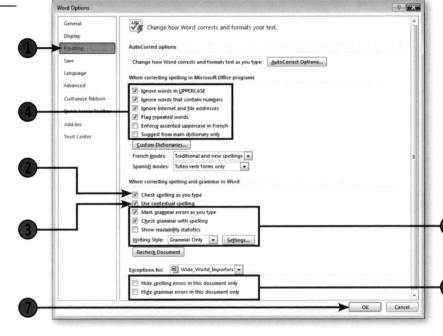

Tip

Click the Recheck Document button if you previously told Word to ignore misspellings or grammatical errors in this document but you now want any errors to be marked.

Customizing Your Spelling Dictionaries

The Office programs use one or more dictionaries to check your spelling. When there's a word in your file that's correct but that isn't recognized—an unfamiliar technical or scientific term, for example—you can tell your program to add that word to your custom dictionary. If you already have a custom dictionary that includes those words or terms, you can add that dictionary to the list of dictionaries you're using. Also, if you discover any incorrectly spelled words in your dictionary, replace them with the correct spelling; otherwise, your program will consider the incorrect spelling to be correct.

Add a Dictionary

1. Click the File tab, click Options, and click the Proofing category. Click the Custom Dictionaries button to display the Custom Dictionaries dialog box.

2. If there's an existing dictionary you want to use, click Add, and in the Add Custom Dictionary dialog box that appears, locate the dictionary file. Click Open.

3. Select the language for an added dictionary if you want it to be used only for that specific language.

4. To create a dictionary by adding entries, click New, use the Create Custom Dictionary dialog box to name the dictionary file, and click Save.

5. To add or delete words in a dictionary, select the dictionary and click Edit Word List.

6. Do either of the following:

   • Type a word you want to add, and click Add.

   • Select a word you want to remove, and click Delete.

7. Click OK.

8. Verify that the dictionaries you want to use are selected and that those you don't want to use aren't selected.

9. Click OK.

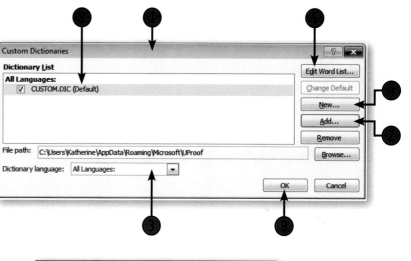

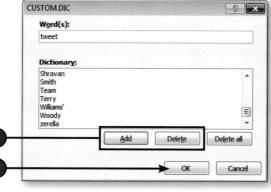

Changing the Location and Type of Saved Files

If you don't like the locations where Word, Excel, PowerPoint, or Access store your files by default, you can change the destination folders as you like. This becomes very important if you're working with other people who require access to your files on a particular shared drive or folder. What's more, if others are using a different version of Office, you can set the default format so that your files are in a format that's compatible with earlier versions. If you consistently save your Word files in a format that was available prior to Word 2007, you may want to modify the Compatibility settings on the Advanced tab of the Word Options dialog box so that your documents have the correct layout for the format in which you save them.

Change the File Locations and Formats

1. Click the File tab, and click Options. In Word, Excel, and PowerPoint, click Save. In Access, click General.

2. For each file location you want to change, enter the new location; or click the Browse button (if there is one), locate the destination folder, and click OK.

3. Select the default format in which you want to save your files.

4. In Word, to change the location of other types of files, click Advanced and scroll to the General section. Click the File Locations button to display the File Locations dialog box.

(continued on next page)

Change the File Locations and Formats   *(continued)*

5 Click the item whose location you want to change, click Modify, and in the Modify Location dialog box, locate and select the folder that you're designating as the new location; click OK.

6 Specify the location for any other file types, and click OK when you've finished.

7 Click OK to close the program's Options dialog box.

Understanding Security in Office 2010

Today viruses are all over the Internet. Every computer user needs some sort of anti-virus program that scans incoming files for potential threats and keeps their computer safe from attack. Office 2010 includes improved security features that evaluate files before you open them and then prompt you if something unrecognized is found.

The developers of Office 2010 found that one area vulnerable to attack was the process of opening a file from a previous version of Office. For this reason, they developed a new security approach that goes on behind the scenes when you open a new document. The file must pass a series of checks—called a file validation process—before it is considered a safe file. If the software finds anything suspicious, the document is displayed in Protected View.

Office 2010 shows you that a file is in Protected View by displaying a message bar across the top of the work area. If you know the sender of the file or are certain the file is safe, you can click Enable Editing to remove the protection and edit the file normally. You can change which files Office 2010 flags for protection by changing the settings in the Trust Center.

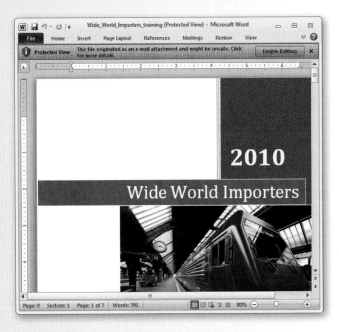

Working with the Trust Center

You use the Office 2010 Trust Center to set up your preferences for the way your files are opened, shared, and protected. You can create lists of trusted publishers, documents, and locations that don't have to be authenticated each time you receive a document from them.

You'll find the Trust Center by clicking the File tab and clicking Options. At the bottom of the category list, click Trust Center and then click Trust Center Settings. This table lists each of the categories in the Trust Center and explains how you can use those options to safeguard your files.

Office 2010 Trust Center

Category	Description
Trusted Publishers	Enables you to create a list of publishers you trust so that any content you receive from the publisher is opened freely without restriction.
Trusted Locations	Gives you the ability to create a list of trustworthy locations—for example, shared folders and SharePoint workspaces.
Trusted Documents	Creates a list of documents you have specified as trusted. After a document is marked as trusted, macros and all content is enabled automatically.
Add-Ins	Enables you to specify whether any application add-ins must be signed by a trusted publisher.
Active X Settings	Lets you choose whether ActiveX controls will be allowed to play in regular more or in safe mode. You also set the level of restriction for the running of the controls.
Macro Settings	Sets whether macros are automatically disabled or enabled.
Protected View	Enables you to choose the situations in which Protected View is used.
Message Bar	Lets you show or hide the Message Bar.
File Block Settings	Gives you the ability to choose whether specific file types are blocked from being open or saved.
Privacy Options	Lets you set privacy options for the current file, run the Document Inspector, and set translation and research options.

Changing File Validation

You can tell Office 2010 which file types you want to validate before opening the files. This controls when Protected View is used to safeguard files that you are opening. You can choose that files be checked when you open a file, save a file, or both.

Set File Types

1. Click the File tab.

2. Click Options.

3. Click Trust Center.

4. Click the Trust Center Settings button.

(continued on next page)

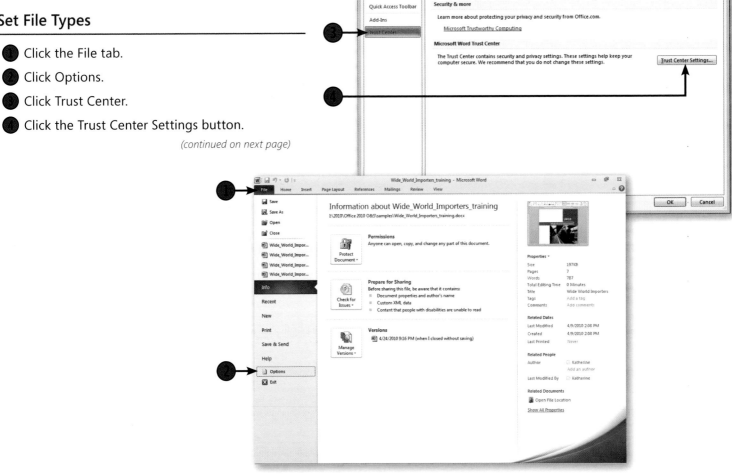

Set File Types   *(continued)*

5 Click the File Block Settings category.

6 Click to clear the check mark in any file type you don't want to select. Click to add a check mark in the Open and Save columns for file types you do want to check.

7 Click OK.

File Block Behaviors

Setting	Description
Do Not Open Selected File Types	The selected files are blocked and will not be opened.
Open Selected File Types In Protected View	Opens the selected file in a safe mode that is protected from other files and processes.
Open Selected File Types In Protected View And Allow Editing	Opens the selected file type in safe mode but allows the user to edit as normal.

Choosing What's Displayed in Protected View

The Protected View message bar appears when you have tried to open a file that has either been blocked or determined to be in a file format flagged for blocking. If you want to see the contents of the file or you know the person or company who sent it, you can open the file in Protected View. Protected View is a safe mode that enables you to view the file without it potentially impacting your other files. When you know the file is okay, you can click Enable Editing to open the file normally.

Office 2010 enables you to choose when Protected View is used for your files. You'll find the settings for Protected View in the Protected View category in the Trust Center.

Set Protected View Settings

1. Click the File tab.

2. Click Options.

3. Click Trust Center, and click Trust Center Settings.

4. Select Protected View.

5. Click to remove the check mark of any setting you do not want to keep.

6. Click OK.

Tip

You can modify the settings at any time. If you later want to restore a protection you removed, simply display the Protected View category again and click the check box to reinstate the check mark for that option.

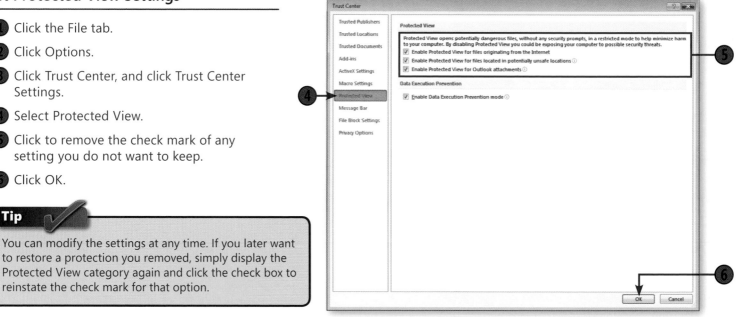

Password Protecting a File

Office 2010, like its predecessors, makes it easy for you add passwords to your Word, Excel, and Power-Point files. Now in Office 2010, you can add encryption to your password to ensure that your file is as secure as possible.

Add a Password

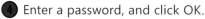

1. Click the File tab, and then click Info.

2. On the Info tab, click Protect Document in the Permissions area.

3. Click Encrypt With Password.

4. Enter a password, and click OK.

Caution

Note that when you set an encrypted password for your Word, Excel, or PowerPoint file, the password cannot be recovered if you forget the password later. For this reason, you should keep a copy of your passwords in a safe place you can access easily.

Tip

You can also set the password during the Save As process by clicking (in the Save As dialog box) the Tools arrow, choosing General Options, and entering the password required to open the file. If you plan to share the file with others, you can enter a separate password that you share with co-authors to enable modification and file sharing.

Limiting File Changes

Not only do you need to make sure that the files you open are safe, but you need to be able to protect the files you create so that people can change only what you want them to change in the file. You can set protection levels on individual files that make it possible for you to limit editing in a document, for example, or protect sections or the structure of a worksheet so that others' ability to change the content of the file is limited.

Set File Permissions

1 Click the File tab.

2 On the Info tab, click Protect Workbook (or Protect Document).

3 Click one of the following:

- Protect Current Sheet in Excel lets you set access permissions for the current file.

- Protect Workbook Structure in Excel lets you preserve the structure of the workbook so that it can't be changed.

- Restrict Editing in Word enables you to control the types of editing that can be done in the file.

(continued on next page)

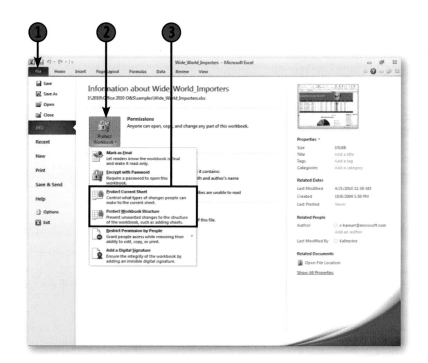

Tip ✓

Formatting restrictions limit users to changing styles used in the document, and editing restrictions enable you to specify whether you want users to view the file as read-only or you will allow them to enter tracked changes, comments, or complete forms.

Tip ✓

PowerPoint enables you to restrict others' ability to copy, edit, or print content in your PowerPoint presentation. You can also mark a file as final so that others can view—but not modify—the file.

Set File Permissions *(continued)*

④ In Excel, select the items you want to set and click OK.

⑤ In Word, select the Allow Only This Type Of Editing In The Document check box.

⑥ Select the type of change you want to allow.

⑦ Indicate who these change apply to.

⑧ Click Yes, Start Enforcing Protection.

Tip ✓

Word, Excel, and PowerPoint all give you the option of adding a digital signature to your document to verify a document's integrity. The digital signature feature in each of these applications requires a signature service from a third-party vendor. You can begin the process by selecting the Add A Digital Signature option in the Protect selection of the Info tab, and a prompt will offer you the option of finding a signature service on Office Marketplace.

Tip ✓

You can also limit the access others have to your files by restricting the permissions they have based on their role. The Restrict Permission By People option in the Protect settings on the Info tab (in Backstage view) of Word, Excel, and PowerPoint enable you to choose the group of people who you want to give access to your document.

Recovering Unsaved Versions of a File

One of the great safety-net features in Office 2010 is that the various programs actually save your files for you in case you forget. Because the programs store your unsaved files automatically, you can return to a previous version if you need to find information you accidentally deleted or items you revised in error.

Recover Unsaved Files

1 Click the File tab.

2 Click Manage Versions.

3 Click Recover Unsaved Documents.

4 Select the file you want, and click Open.

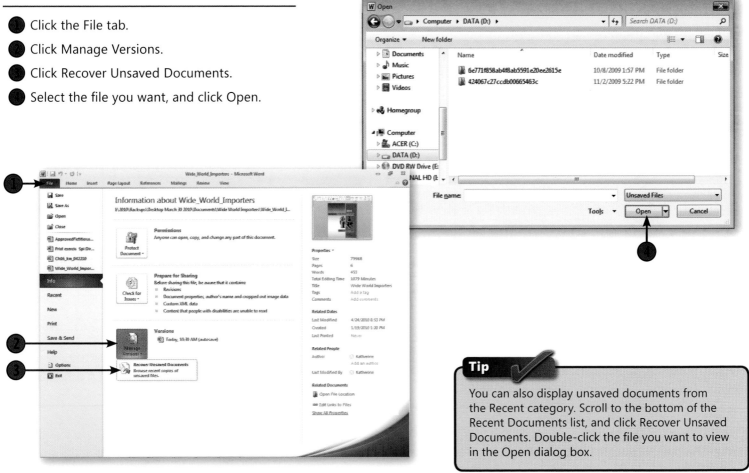

> **Tip**
>
> You can also display unsaved documents from the Recent category. Scroll to the bottom of the Recent Documents list, and click Recover Unsaved Documents. Double-click the file you want to view in the Open dialog box.

Setting AutoRecover Options

At one time or another, you've probably lost some work on your computer. Whether you forgot to save a file or were the victim of a power outage, it's a frustrating and depressing experience that you vow will never happen again. You can safeguard your work and prevent most losses by using the AutoRecover feature, which remembers to save files even when you don't.

Choose AutoRecover Options

1. In Word, Excel, and PowerPoint, click the File tab, click Options, and click the Save category.

2. Select this check box if it isn't already selected.

3. Set a short interval to specify how often you want the AutoRecover information to be saved.

4. Change the default file location for AutoRecover files if you like.

5. Click OK.

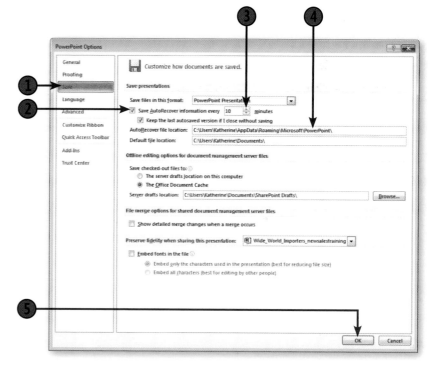

Tip

In Word, you can further safeguard your files by automatically creating a backup copy of your document each time you save it. You can also create a local copy of a document that you've opened from a network location. Make these settings in the Save section of the Advanced category in the Word Options dialog box.

Signing a Document or Workbook with a Digital Signature

In the world of business and commerce, certain documents need to be signed and, often, witnessed. When a document is transmitted electronically, not only does it need to be signed, but the signature must be verifiable. Word and Excel take care of this in two ways. Each provides an easy way to set up an electronic document for a signature by either typing the signature or using a scanned image of the signature inserted as a picture. Additionally, both Word and Excel attach a *digital certificate* that has been issued to the signer from a reliable source. The digital certificate verifies the identity of the signer. With the digital certificate attached, the document or workbook is considered digitally signed. To prevent any alterations to the file after it has been signed, the digital signature is invalidated if any changes are made.

Set Up the Signature

1. Click in the document where you want to add the signature line, and click the Insert tab. Click Signature Line in the Text group.

2. In the Signature Setup dialog box, enter the name and, optionally, the title and e-mail address of the suggested signer.

3. Modify the instructions to the signer if you want.

4. Specify whether you want to allow the signer to add comments when signing the file.

5. Specify whether you want to include the date on which the file was signed.

6. Click OK. Save and close the document or workbook. If the file is intended for someone else's signature, send it to that person.

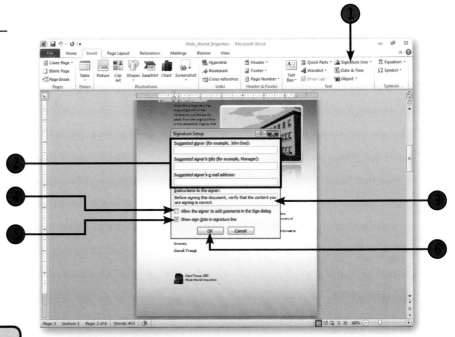

Tip

You need a digital certificate (also called a digital ID or a digital signature) to be able to digitally sign a document. If you try to sign a document without one, you'll be prompted either to purchase one from a third party or create your own. If you create your own certificate, it will be available to validate your signature on your computer only.

Tip

The typed or scanned image of a signature is used only to visually indicate who signed the document. It's the digital certificate that accompanies the document that provides the proof that the document is digitally signed.

Sign the Document

1. Open the file that has been prepared for your signature, and double-click the signature line.

2. In the Sign dialog box that appears, do either of the following:

   - Type your name in the box.

   - Click Select Image, and use the Select Signature Image dialog box to locate the picture file that contains your signature. Click Open in the dialog box to insert the signature image.

3. If the text box that states the purpose of signing is shown, click in the box and enter any information you want.

4. Verify that this digital signature name is the name of the digital certificate you want to use to verify your identity. If it isn't, click Change, and in the Select Certificate dialog box, select the digital certificate you want. Click OK.

5. Click Sign, and save the file.

6. Send the digitally signed file to whoever required you to sign it. The digital certificate will accompany the file, and the recipient will be able to examine the certificate to verify that you signed it and that the file hasn't been altered since you signed the certificate.

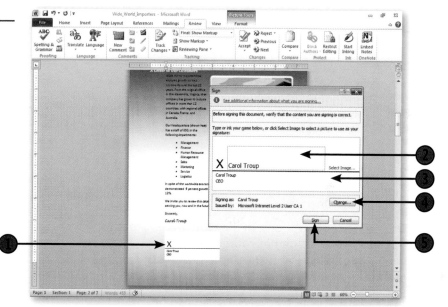

Caution

A digital signature might or might not be recognized as a legal signature, depending on the type of document and your local laws.

See Also

Read "Signing a Document or Workbook with a Digital Signature" on page 414 for information about verifying that the digital signature is valid in a digitally signed document you've received.

Tip

There are various providers of digital signing certificates and other methods of digitally signing documents that might be legally recognized in many instances. To investigate these, click the down arrow at the right of the Signature Line button and choose Add Signature Services from the menu.

Setting Macros, Add-Ins, and ActiveX Controls

Macros are programs you use to automate actions in other programs—repeating a series of commands, for example. *Add-ins* are programs or other items—more smart tags, for example—that you can add to your program to extend its capabilities. *ActiveX controls* are items that provide extra functionality—displaying special dialog boxes or toolbars, for example. Unfortunately, sometimes these items either are so poorly written that they cause operational problems or are written maliciously with the explicit intention of causing harm. To combat these risks, Word provides very strong protections against malfunctioning and malicious macros, add-ins, and ActiveX controls. However, these protections sometimes prevent good and effective tools from being used, so you might need to adjust your security settings to balance security and functionality.

Modify the Settings

① In Word, Excel, PowerPoint, and Access, click the File tab and click Options. In the Options dialog box, click the Trust Center category in the left pane, and click the Trust Center Settings button to display the Trust Center dialog box. Then click the Add-ins category.

② Select this check box if you want to require that all add-ins come from a trusted source. Each time an add-in from another source tries to be used, you'll be asked whether you want to use it.

③ In Word, Excel, and PowerPoint, click the ActiveX Settings category, and select the level of security you want for ActiveX controls.

④ Select this check box if it isn't already selected.

⑤ Click the Macro Settings category, and select the level of security you want for macros.

⑥ Click any categories that are specific to the program, and make the changes you want.

⑦ Click OK.

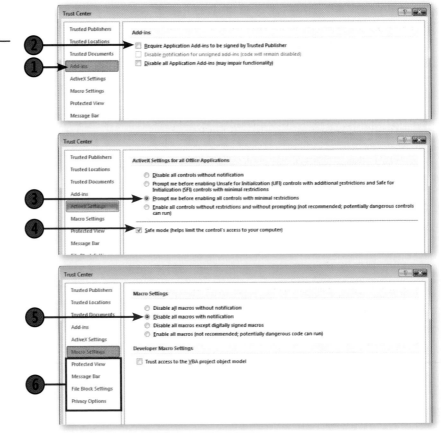

Checking File Compatibility

Although Word, Excel, and PowerPoint 2010 are fully compatible with the 2007 versions of the program, the file formats and some of their features aren't fully compatible with earlier versions. Although people running earlier versions will be able to open these Office 2010 files using a converter (provided they've installed it, of course), some features and/or content might be changed or lost. To see which features aren't fully compatible and will be changed or lost, run the Compatibility Checker before you distribute the document, workbook, or presentation.

Run the Check

1. With your document, workbook, or presentation completed and saved, click the File tab, and in the Info category, click Check For Issues.

2. Choose Check Compatibility.

3. Click and choose the version you want to be compatible with.

4. Scroll through the list of items that will be changed or lost.

5. Click Find to locate the issue in the worksheet.

6. Click Help to get more information about the issue.

7. Click to copy results to a new worksheet.

8. Click to always check compatibility when saving the worksheet.

9. Click OK.

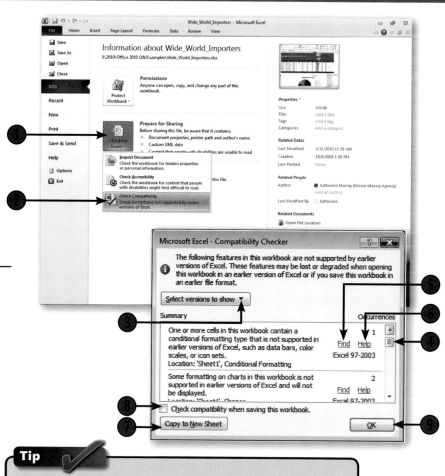

Tip

If you're not sure whether the changes are acceptable, point to Save As on the Office menu, and click the program's 97–2003 format in the gallery that appears. In the Save As dialog box, enter a different name for the file and click Save. Scroll through your file and examine the changes to see whether they're acceptable. If they are, distribute your original file; if they aren't, edit the file to eliminate the incompatibilities.

Index

Symbols

* (asterisk)
 in calculations, 180, 182
 file names and, 26
\ (backslash), 26
^ (caret), 182
= (equal sign), 180
/ (forward slash)
 in calculations, 180, 182
 in file names, 26
> (greater than), 26
< (less than), 26
– (minus sign), 182
( ) (parentheses), 182
% (percent sign), 182
+ (plus sign), 26, 182
| (vertical bar), 26

A

absolute cell references, 180, 188
Access. *See also* databases
 Access window, 360–361
 analyzing data, 388–389
 compatibility issues, 30
 database basics, 362–363
 Datasheet view, 361
 exporting data, 376–377
 fields and records, 363, 368–372
 Form Wizard, 380
 forms, 380–382
 importing data, 374–375
 Navigation Form, 380, 381–382
 other file formats and, 367
 overview, 5, 359–362

PivotCharts, 388–389
 queries, 386–387
 Query Wizard, 386–387
 Quick Start fields, 369
 Report view, 361–362
 Report Wizard, 382
 reports, 382–385
 storing data, 362–363
 table relationships, 363, 378–380
 tables, 368–369
 templates, 364–366
 using existing databases, 366–367
 views in, 360–362
actions
 action items in Word, 125
 Actions buttons in PowerPoint, 229
 Actions group in Outlook, 346–355
 additional actions in Word, 125
 assigning to slides, 229
 keyboard shortcuts for, 19
 order of, 182
 redoing, 19
 shortcut menus and, 16
 undoing, 19
Actions group in Outlook, 346–355
ActiveX controls, 416–417
add-ins, 416–417
addition, 182
address books, 264, 285
addressing
 e-mail messages, 264, 295, 297
 envelopes, 136–137
aligning objects, 311
 in Publisher, 324–326
aligning text
 in Excel cells, 162
 keyboard shortcut for, 19
 in PowerPoint slides, 215

in Publisher, 321, 324
 in Word
 converting text to tables for, 100
 hyphenation and, 103
 Linked Styles and, 82
 setting alignment, 88
 tables, 102
alphabetical sorting
 in Excel, 192
 in Word lists, 119
 in Word tables, 118
animation
 in charts, 227
 customizing, 228
 running in presentations, 250
 saving files and, 255
 setting effects, 226–227
 of slide elements, 226–227
 triggering, 208–227
Animation Painter feature, 227
Animation Trigger feature, 227
annotating presentation slides, 251
appointments
 adding detail to, 286–287
 recurring appointments, 287
 reminders for, 287
 setting up, 286
arithmetic operators
 defined, 182
 for formulas, 180
 order of precedence for, 182
Artistic Effects feature, 36
asterisk (*)
 in calculations, 180, 182
 file names and, 26
attendees, for meetings, 294–295
audio
 assigning actions and, 229

audio, *continued*
   audio notes in OneNote, 348–349
   presentation narration, 240–241
   in presentations, 232–233
   in slide transitions, 228, 234
   in slides, 232–233
AutoCorrect feature (Word), 71–72
automatic hyphenation (Word), 103
AutoRecover options, 413
averaging a series of calculations, 185

B

backgrounds
   in Excel charts, 203
   formatting in slides, 212–213
   in publications, 311, 322
   removing in pictures, 39
   styles for slides, 211
backing up files, 413
backslash (\), 26
Backstage view
   file and program information, 22
   layout and features, 22
   overview, 5
   printing files from, 23
baselines, in Publisher, 324–325
bold formatting, 19
bound documents, 107
boundaries, object, 324–325
broadcasting presentations, 258–259
browsing for help, 24
Building Blocks feature, 323
bulleted lists (Word)
   creating, 96
   formatting, 97
   styles for, 82
business cards (Outlook)
   adding fields to, 302
   creating, 302
   customizing look of, 285

e-mailing, 302–303
business information (Publisher), 310, 332

C

calculations. *See also* formulas; functions
   cell values, 182–183
   order of precedence in, 182
   series of, 188
   summing data, 181, 184–185
Calendar view, 288
calendars (Outlook)
   adding appointment detail, 286–287
   controlling access to, 293
   overview, 285
   publishing to Web, 290
   setting up appointments, 286–287
   sharing, 290–292
   sharing available times, 291
caret (^), 182
case, changing, 19
cell addresses. *See* cell references
cell references
   absolute, 180, 188
   in arguments, 187
   in calculating values, 183
   copying cell content and, 177
   defined, 147
   determining, 177
   in formulas, 180
   names instead of, 177
   old style of, 177
   in printing, 180. *See also* print areas
   R1C1 reference style, 177
   in ranges, 177
   relative, 180, 188
cell values, 147
cells
   conditional formatting, 174–176
   defined, 147
   deleting content, 159

   formatting, 154–155, 162–164
   naming ranges of cells, 147
   selecting, 154
centered text (Word), 88
changing user information, 399
character styles, 82
   in Publisher, 316–317
   in Word, 82, 84
charts (Access)
   animation in, 227
   PivotCharts, 388–389
charts (Excel)
   backgrounds in, 203
   combining, 206
   creating, 202
   customizing, 206
   data series charts, 206
   formatting, 204–205
   layouts, 203
   line types in, 203
   overview, 147, 201–202
   PivotCharts, 197
   styles, 204
   themes, 204–205
   3-D effects in, 176–203
   types of, 201
citations of sources, 132–133
citing references in Word, 130–131
citing sources in Word, 132–133
clip art
   clip art audio, in slides, 232–233
   finding and inserting, 40
Clipboard, 20–21, 372
co-authoring
   contacting co-authors, 77
   editing conflicts and, 76
   SharePoint Server and, 6
   SharePoint Workspace and, 76
   Windows Live and, 76
   Word documents, 76
     instant messaging and, 77
     file changes and, 77

X

About the Author

Katherine Murray has been writing about Microsoft Office since the earliest version was available, way back in the dark ages of DOS. She's excited by many of the new features and enhancements in Office 2010 and loves the collaboration features, translation tools, artistic effects, and "access anywhere" approach that enables users to continue working on Office 2010 files from any point they have Web access. Katherine has published a blog called *BlogOffice* for many years that offers tips and techniques on various Office versions. She is also the author of *Microsoft Word 2010 Plain & Simple*, *First Look Microsoft Office 2010*, and *Microsoft Word 2010 Inside Out*, all from Microsoft Press.

What do you think of this book?

We want to hear from you!

To participate in a brief online survey, please visit:

microsoft.com/learning/booksurvey

Tell us how well this book meets your needs—what works effectively, and what we can do better. Your feedback will help us continually improve our books and learning resources for you.

Thank you in advance for your input!

Stay in touch!

To subscribe to the *Microsoft Press® Book Connection Newsletter*—for news on upcoming books, events, and special offers—please visit:

microsoft.com/learning/books/newsletter